INSIDE THE DEMOCRATIC PARTY

INSIDE THE DEMOCRATIC PARTY

JACK REDDING

with a Foreword by J. HOWARD McGRATH

THE BOBBS-MERRILL COMPANY, INC.
PUBLISHERS

INDIANAPOLIS   NEW YORK

First Edition

FOREWORD

BY J. HOWARD MCGRATH
FORMER CHAIRMAN OF THE DEMOCRATIC NATIONAL COMMITTEE

THE YEAR 1948 will long be remembered as the year
in which the Democratic regime that had come into
being in 1932 was supposed to end. All the political prognosti-
cators had foretold the pending doom of Harry S Truman and
his party. Historians will recall that national election because
it upset in no uncertain terms the predictions of the wise and informed. Students of American political history will study the
events that preceded this campaign with searching interest to
find the cause of its unforeseen and very dramatic result.

To that end, this book, *Inside the Democratic Party*, should
be invaluable. Jack Redding has chronicled the events that preceded this election with great fidelity. Although the book carries
the reader on up to the present, both Redding and I had our
finest hour in 1948. I shall therefore confine my remarks mainly
to that year. Historians should be grateful to him for the minute
notes that he kept on the ever changing facets of the American
political scene in the years 1947 and 1948.

I first knew Jack Redding intimately when I was chosen to be

5

the Chairman of the Democratic National Committee and he was serving as Director of Public Relations for that committee. To me he was a very unusual personality. In political life, I had not been accustomed to dealing with a man of such forthright convictions and direct approach. I think my first impression of Jack Redding was to be afraid of his daring proposals, but I soon realized that in this man I had an ally who thoroughly understood politics and, even more important, appreciated human reactions to political issues and problems.

At the time that I was serving as Chairman of the Democratic National Committee, I was United States Senator from the state of Rhode Island. In that office I was not lacking in problems to keep me busy during all the working hours of the day. I necessarily depended heavily upon the advice of my trusted colleagues serving on the committee, particularly Gael Sullivan and Jack Redding.

Gael Sullivan was my friend from childhood. We had been educated in the same schools and each of us was following an ambition to rise in the political field. Gael was dynamic and imaginative and he made a mighty contribution to the Democratic Party during the years he served as assistant to Bob Hannegan, my predecessor.

Many of the events that Redding tells about in this book I had long since forgotten. It is gratifying to know that in those busy and most often discouraging days someone was keeping a chronology of events. I do not recall that a more thorough record of a political campaign with its intimate details of personalities and circumstances has ever been written before.

This work is not a biography or an autobiography, but a blow-by-blow description of what went into making the victory of November 1948, a victory so sweet to Democrats all over the nation. It should be of great interest to political students who seek the answer to the question of what makes for ultimate victory in a political campaign. It should likewise be a reminder that the seeds of political success are sown far in advance of any election day, and that it is the sum total of the little things that happen which leads to eventual victory at the polls.

As I look at the election of 1948 it appears to have been divided into two distinct phases. First was the period beginning with the 1946 congressional elections and ending with the national conventions of 1948 which nominated Thomas E. Dewey and Harry S Truman respectively. In this period the Democratic National Committee's effort was wholly one of organization and building the party to operational efficiency at all levels in spite of the tremendous diversions and divisions which beset it. This included publicizing the record of the Republican Eightieth Congress and keeping the voters mindful of how this record compared with what they had enjoyed under long years of the New Deal and the Fair Deal. In my opinion the Democratic National Committee performed its greatest function and its principal role in this first period. Adhering strictly to the functions of a national committee as an organizing branch of the party, it effectively set the stage for a hard-hitting campaign which President Truman was destined to carry to the people.

The second period of this fateful and historic election ran from the time of the national conventions up to Election Day. President Truman now capitalized on the organization work that had been done; he took the fight, as no man in history has ever done before, directly to the people. President Truman won his own election almost single-handed, you might say. It was he who, from the time of his nomination in Philadelphia to the counting of the ballots on Election Day, had faith in himself and in the party, and he kept the spark of faith alive in many wavering members of his own party.

No purpose would be served in this foreword by elaborating on the parts played by different people. The Democratic Party, by historic tradition, is the party of the many. It takes all hands to combat successfully the entrenched powers that in every national election are at the command of the Republican Party.

As National Chairman of the campaign I am grateful to all. I am grateful, too, that I was destined to be the Chairman under such a fighting believer in Jeffersonian Democracy as our then Commander in Chief, Harry S Truman. And I am happy to count as one of my blessings the fact that I had by my side a faithful and fearless practitioner of political truths as he saw them—the author of this book, Jack Redding.

INSIDE THE
DEMOCRATIC
PARTY

CHAPTER 1

THE ROOM was dim and misty in the dying day. Lights had not yet been turned on. Chairman J. Howard McGrath's place at a large round table was fitted with three telephones and an easy chair. Thirty more chairs were set around the table for expected party chieftains.

We had been telling Democratic Party workers, "Remember in November." Now it WAS November—November 2, 1948, Election Day—and these were the headquarters of the Democratic National Committee in the Biltmore Hotel in New York.

Outside McGrath's private quarters was a larger room and beyond that was the newsroom with the teletypewriters banked row on row. McGrath would get reports via telephone from party leaders in the states while the newsprinters would supply the returns coming from regular sources.

But now headquarters was deserted, or nearly so. In the gloom I saw a young *Herald Tribune* reporter whom I knew only vaguely. He was about third string—thus were Democratic chances of winning rated by the assignment editor at the *Trib*. The newsman came forward to intercept me, somewhat embarrassed, for his assignment was to get an advance story of defeat.

"Nobody here." He made it a statement.

"Not yet."

"Do you think this is the way it'll be?"

It was a naïve question, overeager. I answered, "No. It won't be this way. It's early yet. The polls are still open here in the East. Everyone's still working."

"Then you think you have a chance?"

"Look, friend—" the questions irritated me—"you're here to cover what your boss thinks is a losing cause. If he's right you'll get your story as it develops. And that story will be much better than any you can get from me. If your boss is wrong, and I think he is, you've got the top assignment of the day. What more can you ask? Now let me be."

He wandered off. Then I saw Fritz Pasley. A successful author, Fritz had worked on the Chicago *Tribune* with me years before. Now he was a feature writer for the New York *Daily News*. "The place," he said, swinging his arm to indicate the darkening room, "is swimming in atmosphere."

"Too dark."

"That's what I mean. Don't turn on the lights. The place seems perfect just as it is. Maybe no one should even show up. It would be fitting."

He thought about that for a minute. "But of course your people will show up. Any preparations for a celebration?"

"There won't be a party here. If people want a drink they'll buy it themselves. The committee isn't buying any liquor. This is a working headquarters."

"No plans for a celebration? Well!" He made notes. "You know," he said, "I seem to get all the stories of final rites. A few years ago it was my job to bury Roosevelt. Now I'm writing the story of the burial of Roosevelt's party."

I turned away, but couldn't resist saying, "Fritz, don't write your piece too early! You might have to do a skinback."

He laughed. I went on out of the room, into the elevator and up to Howard McGrath's suite. He was looking at a news digest which we had prepared for him.

"You saw these?" he waved the sheaf of papers at me.

"Didn't read them."

12

"Required reading," he said. "It's a sure cure for overconfidence. Here's Boston . . . the *Herald's* poll: Truman, 46.6 per cent; Dewey, 48.2 per cent. They don't rate Wallace, but he must be getting some according to their own figures. They say Dewey will win the state by 65,000." He snorted. "New York *Daily News* poll, statewide: Truman, 44.1 per cent; Dewey, 49.2 per cent; Wallace, 6.7 per cent. Maybe we shouldn't have spent that last money if these figures are right. Here's Iowa: Truman, 41 per cent; Dewey, 54 per cent; Wallace, 2 per cent. Those figures make Jake More look bad. He thinks we'll win the state by 40,000."

I nodded.

McGrath went on: "The Chicago *Tribune*, on Illinois, they say Truman, 43.6 per cent; Dewey, 54.4 per cent; Wallace, 2 per cent. And the Chicago *Sun-Times*—they've been supporting us?"

"They've been supporting us. You know, 'Poor Harry. He can't win. But we'll go down with the ship.' What do they say?"

"Truman, 45.89 per cent; Dewey, 52.86 per cent. They don't rate Wallace. Here's the Philadelphia paper, the *Inquirer*: Truman, 39.3 per cent; Dewey, 57.9 per cent; Wallace, 2 per cent." He shuffled the papers a moment. "Here's one you'll like: Ft. Lauderdale, Florida: Truman, 23.15 per cent; Dewey, 62.96 per cent; Thurmond, 12.96 per cent. Hell!" He threw the papers on the floor. "If I believed what I read in the papers I'd go home."

Then something caught his eye and he stooped to pick up the digest again. "That death's head, Gould Lincoln." He read, " 'An end of a strange political alliance. Dewey certain to win. . . .' " McGrath let the papers fall once more to the floor. "Gould's jumping the gun on the funeral. He'll sing another song tomorrow. Let's go!"

Downstairs headquarters was beginning to come alive. The lights were on. Staff people were at their working posts. Those without specific tasks were clustered, awaiting returns. The room was quiet except for sporadic clicking from the newsprint-

13

ers. I went into the printer room as Howard went to his desk. Returns from Block Island, Rhode Island, were just coming across. They were six to one for Dewey. It shook me. I tore the sheet from the machine and took it to McGrath.

Howard glanced at the returns indifferently. "They'll be ahead up there on the early returns. All those little island districts are Republican. We'll take the state easily."

Dorothy Vredenburgh, the party secretary, turned from her phone. "I've got Arvey." Howard picked up the receiver. "How are you, Jack? . . . Tired? . . . You'll be more tired before the night's out. How does it look to you?" He motioned me to pick up the extension.

Arvey was talking: ". . . Close, Howard, very close. By 25,000 either way. I think it'll go our way . . . I'm betting $75,000 I got from Ned Brown on a loan. . . ." He laughed at a question of McGrath's. "No . . . not a real bet. It's money I'm putting into getting out the vote. If the edge is that close, the margin can come from the city wards here in Cook County."

McGrath nodded. "Good man. How's that other thing? Can they steal those votes downstate?"

Arvey talked quickly. "No, Otto Kerner [the United States District Attorney in Chicago] has deputized, along with the other District Attorneys in Illinois, enough men to cover every downstate county. Each man has a subpoena for the ballot boxes and the officials, to go *duces tecum* to the United States District Court, in case they refuse to count the votes tonight and try to take the ballots home with them. We'll have a count tonight and an honest one."

"Good." McGrath nodded. "I'm glad you told me about that, Jack. This may mean the election." He hung up, then said to Mrs. Vredenburgh, "Get Roosevelt in California!"

He turned to me. "You know about that downstate Illinois gimmick?"

I nodded. It was an old game that has been played in many places by both parties for half a century or more. In downstate

14

counties it was customary to count the ballots at the close of the polls but to make no returns. The excuse would be that it was too late. The Republican judge of election would put a penciled total on an envelope, stuff the ballots in his pockets and take the whole shebang home. The Democrats, shut out, had to guess what he did in the morning. They claimed he erased the penciled totals and, knowing how many votes were needed, doctored the results to provide the necessary margin. Then the returns would be made officially. To get back into the ballots to check the penciled returns would then take court action and in a national election this was a practical impossibility. Arvey's action was designed to prevent holding the returns, and to force immediate reports. It was shrewd politics.

Roosevelt was on the line now. Howard asked about the volume of voting. Then he told Jim, "I think you've got the decisive point. We need California. Keep your people working to get out the vote, no matter what you hear from back here by radio or newspaper. This will be close. California may well be the key. Push your people to get out the vote!"

I asked if he wanted to talk to Pennsylvania leaders. He shook his head. "I think Pennsylvania's gone. So's Jersey. But it might be close. Let's not bother them now."

Jim Sauter, a New York radio producer who worked with the committee during the campaign, was keeping a tally. He picked up the new returns, still scattered but coming in now with greater frequency. "Harry's ahead," he murmured, "but it's spotty."

"It's early yet," said McGrath. "May shift a lot for a while."

Outside, the newsprinters were now going in a steady clamor. The crowd still was not large. A few party men were standing around talking. The newsmen—photographers, newsreel men and reporters—were few, mostly second-string men. Sam Brightman nodded toward them. "The big shots are over at the Roosevelt. They'll be over here later."

New York returns were coming in. The tension began to mount. Truman was ahead in the country. He was ahead in New

15

York. Jim Farley made his appearance. A few more newsmen showed up. The story at Truman headquarters was getting better. No one thought Harry could win but the fight was going to be closer than anticipated.

At the Roosevelt, where Governor Dewey waited to accept the victory, all was complacency. The great hall was gaily bannered. A balcony, flag-draped, was ready for Tom Dewey to make his acceptance speech. Champagne corks were already popping. There was a little annoyance that Dewey had not yet taken the lead, but the general attitude was that it was just a matter of time.

Over the radio Kaltenborn and Dick Harkness were starting the refrain that would become famous: "Mr. Truman is still ahead but these are returns from a few cities. When the returns come in from the country the result will show Dewey winning overwhelmingly."

Neither Kaltenborn nor Harkness deigned to visit Democratic headquarters, preferring to sweat out their ordeal in more comfort. The broadcasters assigned to the Biltmore were roughing it. Ken Fry, the committee's radio publicity director, had brought in matched lines so that tone quality was good. But we had been unable to supply studio facilities and the radio men went on the air man-in-the-street fashion with milling spectators stumbling over the telephone cables which littered the floor.

Television—in its infancy—had one not very sequestered corner, one camera, one bright light, and for background scenery a simple hotel wall. As the night wore on, guests appearing on TV began to sit on the floor for interviews, thus sparing aching feet.

It seemed as if there was a radio show on the air every other five minutes. Sam Brightman came to me with Walter Fitzmaurice of *Newsweek*, who was doing a broadcast for the American Broadcasting Company. "Walter needs someone to talk for the Democrats on his eight o'clock show," said Sam. "Who can we get?"

I took a fast look around the room. "He wants McGrath," added Sam. "I told him it was too early yet."

16

"Much too early. How about Jim Farley?"

Fitzmaurice nodded. "Farley would be fine. Will you get him? I've only got a few minutes now before I'm on the air."

Jim Farley was only too glad to go on. "What do you want me to say?"

"Jim, you're a political analyst in your own right. Say what you think. But don't say anything that might slow the people going to the polls in the West. They're still voting on the Coast. Don't pick up that line about Dewey trailing now but going to win when returns come in from other than the cities."

I went over to a radio tuned to Fitzmaurice's broadcast. In a few minutes Farley was on the air being interviewed. He talked about Truman's lead in the popular voting, spoke of his lead in New York, then said, "But this is only an early lead. He cannot win, for when the reports come in from the country—the Dewey strongholds—his early lead will fold up."

I was horrified. First I was going to jump Farley, but I decided to keep still. A scene would only create more stories. I went back into McGrath's office and listened as he talked to party leaders in Connecticut where the Truman forces were clinging to a minor lead. He nodded and hung up. Looking at me, he shrugged. "We lose Connecticut. We've still got a lead but the districts to be heard from are almost all Republican. Dewey's got Connecticut." He picked up another telephone.

Sauter turned to me from his pile of newsprinter copy. "We got Rhode Island."

Howard was smiling, "That's fine. That's fine!" Hanging up the telephone he said, "We'll sweep Massachusetts. I knew it. I knew it. We were bound to win with that vote."

He was referring to the referendum on the Massachusetts ballot as to whether state health authorities should be allowed to give out birth-control information. The Catholic Church in Massachusetts had waged a holy war to have its members at the polls to vote against the question. The vast outpouring of Catholic voters, largely Democratic, meant we had every right to

17

expect the Democrats, out to vote on the birth-control referendum, to stay and vote in the presidential and gubernatorial elections. Our hopes had proved right. Massachusetts was ours.

Pennsylvania was gone. We hadn't carried Philadelphia by enough votes to counteract the rural returns. Pittsburgh was all right but again the Truman edge wasn't big enough.

Jersey was gone. The Wallace vote did it. Then the lead in New York began to dwindle. We had only a 45,000 edge with but a few hundred precincts to be heard from. Someone said the precincts that were still out were New York City districts. Maybe we could make it.

McGrath had Paul Fitzpatrick, New York state chairman, on the line. Then he shook his head. "Well," he said, "I didn't think we would take New York."

To my question he answered, "City districts still out in the main, but Republican territory. Paul's projection shows we're through. We've lost the state. It'll be close but . . ."

He examined the returns that Sauter handed him. "There it goes." Dewey had gone into the lead. He studied the figures a moment. "Wallace cost us the state."

Brightman came in. "The newsmen want a statement on New York. From the Chairman."

McGrath looked at me. "I'm not going to say anything about New York. Not going to say anything right now. Too early." Brightman nodded and left.

McGrath gave the summary sheets back to Sauter, saying, "This thing would be a breeze if Wallace and Thurmond weren't in it."

Virginia was safe. Our early lead in Maryland was slipping. South Carolina was gone, due to Thurmond. Truman's popular vote lead was holding up but the early rosy promise was diminishing. The New York loss after it seemed we had won the state was disheartening. The East was in and we were behind. Now it was the Midwest returns we were scanning.

Truman had an enormous lead in Illinois. But the returns

18

were from Chicago and Cook County. Downstate was not heard
from except in scattered returns. Ohio was looking pretty good.
But then there came a call from our Ohio leaders. Perhaps Wallace would cost us Ohio as he had lost Jersey and New York.

In an astute political maneuver the Republicans had managed
to have lists of electors on the presidential ballot. At the top of
each ballot were the names of the presidential and vice presidential candidates. Below these were listed the names of the presidential electors who would cast their ballots in the electoral
college. This arrangement was perfectly legal in Ohio. The
point was that it offered no problem to Republicans but confused
many Democrats into spoiling their ballots. They would place a
cross in the square before Truman's and Barkley's names. Then
many voters, apparently seeing an old familiar Democratic name
in the list of Wallace electors, placed a check in front of an individual Wallace elector's name.

This spoiled the ballot. Our Ohio headquarters told us,
"There are thousands of these spoiled ballots. And the spoiled
ones are all Democratic. I think we'll have to take court action
to get them validated."

"Legal action's no good." McGrath's face was grim as he
spoke. "How many all told do you guess?"

"Maybe a hundred thousand in the state."

"Work on it!" said McGrath. "Have your people fight for
every ballot. They're bound to save some." He sat still for a
minute after hanging up. "That could wreck us in Ohio. It
means California and Illinois. We've got to have those two!"

Jack More, Iowa state chairman, came on the phone to say
we'd take the state for Truman. Suddenly out of Wisconsin
came a cheering word. We had better than an even chance to take
the state. All of us were amazed and delighted. Meantime
Maryland finally went sour—by only 9,000 votes. That was
a blow.

And the Illinois lead was dropping. It kept dropping. West
Virginia was safe. Ohio showed us ahead. Then the ticker said

19

25,000 votes had been "mislaid in Ohio." They turned out to be Dewey votes. We were once more behind in Ohio, but not far behind. Tennessee was safe.

The Truman lead continued to drop in Illinois. The Republican downstate vote was inexorably creeping upwards. In Ohio the "mislaid" votes were questioned. It seemed maybe they weren't "mislaid" after all. The news brought a cheer. But— Thurmond cost us Louisiana. Mississippi was long gone. Alabama was going.

At midnight Truman still led in the popular voting. But his position in the electoral vote was behind Dewey. The fight was so close that we now had literally hundreds milling outside. McGrath's big table was crowded. Doris Fleeson, oftentimes a critic of Truman but always a liberal, was now sitting front and center eagerly taking notes. India Edwards had slipped her in. If the rest of the press—excluded from the inner room—tumbled, there'd be hell to pay.

Brightman pointed her out to me and said, "That's a good omen."

But the Truman lead in Illinois was dwindling. Ohio was close but the question of the "mislaid" votes was vexing. We looked close, but if those votes were Dewey's we weren't so close.

Colorado began to come in and Truman was leading. The atmosphere was tense. Dewey's reporters were drifting to Democratic headquarters. The big crowd was now at the Biltmore instead of at the Roosevelt. Young David McGrath, who had been holding down the door to McGrath's quarters, was now reinforced by policemen. Even the police department of New York were beginning to think we had a chance. One cop said: "They've taken Boss Tom's belt and shoelaces away from him." He laughed.

McGrath was showing no strain. He methodically placed his calls and took the reports that streamed in. But Jim Sauter was losing his air of detached calm. As he handed in the latest reports from Illinois he was sweating, his face was flushed, his

20

hand shook. The lead in Illinois was still dropping but not swiftly. Some scattered returns came in which for a moment reversed the trend.

Howard was on the telephone, talking for the twentieth time to Arvey. His face brightened and for the first time he showed real emotion. He looked at his wrist watch. I matched his gesture. The time was 5:40 A.M. Then he looked at me, but he spoke to Sauter: "Jim, you can take it easy on those Illinois returns. We've got Illinois. Close, but we've got it for Truman and it's a landslide for Douglas and Stevenson."

In a moment the news spread through the crowd like a ripple and bounced back as a wave. The cheer brought the door open despite the resistance of the three brawny cops who were tending the door. The press wanted to know what had happened. I went out and told them Jack Arvey had just informed the Chairman that Illinois was in the Truman column. There was a rush to the big board where the result still looked inconclusive. Most of the newsmen shrugged it off, preferring to wait for the ticker to confirm it. But a few brave souls bulletined their offices.

For the first time Truman was ahead in the electoral vote, but not far enough ahead. Truman needed either Ohio or California to attain an electoral count above the absolute majority of 266 that was necessary. If Ohio went Republican we'd still have a chance in California. Even if California was lost too, it appeared we'd have a chance to have the election thrown into the House of Representatives where each state would have one vote. In other words it now appeared that Truman was the odds-on favorite.

Hal Boyle of the Associated Press, who had been assigned to the Dewey headquarters, stopped me in the hall. There were only about twenty-two or twenty-three people left over at the Roosevelt, he told me.

Later he was to write as follows: "After midnight deepening alarm swept over the gaily bannered room. The face of the crowd was a slow-motion study of confidence changing from sur-

21

prise to doubt, from doubt to disbelief and then on to stunned fear and panic."

Brightman, Hal Leyshon and I held a quick get-together. The consensus was that there should be a statement. McGrath said tersely, "Still too early. Wait for Ohio."

In Ohio the lead was fluctuating. The California reports had slowed, waiting for the mountain counties. But we had a chance for California. Ohio was close. It might go either way. But California . . . if not Ohio then California.

That "mislaid" bundle of Dewey votes was plaguing the headquarters. It was plaguing the newsprinter, too, for each report that came over the printer was qualified by some reference to the "mislaid" ballots. Finally, it was nine-forty in the morning. The sun was bright through the windows. The crowd, hunched at the board, was immense. All of the press were here, waiting for the dramatic moment of victory. Arizona was ours. New Mexico was ours. We were leading in Idaho. Nevada was ours. Iowa was now solidly in the Truman column. Minnesota behind Hubert Humphrey was in line.

Howard raised his hand as he picked up the telephone, his Celtic sense of drama holding the crowd breathless. Then he began speaking out loud, repeating what he heard through the telephone:

"The Secretary of State of Ohio . . . 9,360 precincts of 9,710 show Truman 1,403,000; Dewey 1,390,000. The precincts still to come are from Democratic districts in Cuyahoga County— Cleveland. . . . Thank you for calling."

The cheer that followed McGrath's words was tremendous. Then McGrath held up his hand for silence. "That's Ohio. We're going to be all right. We got it. We have at least 270 electoral votes. Maybe it'll be more."

The press was insistent. I asked McGrath, "Can we do a statement now?"

Howard was smiling. "Take your time, Jack. Savor it. Work

22

on it but take your time. You can be sure that Mr. Dewey will take his in conceding."

Suddenly there was champagne. "Chip" Roberts, the old Democratic wheelhorse from Georgia, had bought. And the corks were popping. But no one drank. They waited while Dorothy Vredenburgh made the call to Kansas City. They were quiet as McGrath took the receiver and spoke into the phone. "Thanks, Clark [Clifford]. Thank you. No, I don't deserve what you say but I appreciate it. Where is the Boss? . . . Okay . . . I'll call him."

But he didn't make the call for suddenly, almost magically, the President was on the phone. Howard listened, smiling broadly. "Thank you, Mr. President. Nobody deserved to win more than you did, Mr. President." He held up his glass; the wine shimmered effervescently in a shaft of sunlight. Nodding to the crowd surrounding him, he said, "Your staff is drinking to you, Mr. President . . . From the bottoms of our hearts we drink to you."

The glasses were raised high, but before the toast was drunk there came a universal: "And to you, Mr. Chairman."

The crowd stayed quiet as McGrath went on talking to Harry Truman. He spoke quietly and we all strained to hear. Then, "Here's India, Mr. President. She wants to congratulate you."

India Edwards took the phone. She was almost incoherent. "The best man won. The best man won," she repeated. "Congratulations, Mr. President, and kiss Mrs. Truman and Margaret for me." She gave the receiver back to McGrath and he gravely hung it in its place. He turned to me. "Now let's have a statement."

To the assembled crowd of staff and party leaders he said, "To each and every one of you: Thanks. Without your wonderful efforts it couldn't have been done."

McGrath took the prepared statement claiming final victory and at 11:10 A.M. read it to the press. Four minutes later as he was still answering questions on his own statement, he was handed a telegram. He looked at it and his face beamed. Holding up his hand for silence, he announced, "Gentlemen, I have here a message that will make your stories conclusive.

"This is a message addressed to Harry S Truman, President. I will read it slowly, for you may wish to copy it down word for word.

" 'My heartiest congratulations to you on your election and every good wish for a successful Administration. I urge all Americans to unite behind you in support of your efforts to keep our Nation strong and free and establish peace in the world.' Signed," said McGrath proudly, "by Thomas E. Dewey."

Then we were walking away from the rostrum where the victory statement had been given, where Dewey's conceding message had been read. McGrath, an undemonstrative Irishman, put an arm round my shoulders. "It was a great thing. A wonderful thing. All of us have given much from our souls to the victory. Thank you—and you understand what I am saying."

I was tired. No sleep for forty-eight hours. But beyond that, months and months of fatigue, disappointment and bone-chilling labor. Out of this came a final remark: "And the President, Howard? He understands too how these things came about?"

"Yes," said McGrath. "Possibly he understands better than any of us how these things are done."

CHAPTER 2

TRUMAN knew how it was done. He knew; for much
of it, most of it, was his doing. He had hammered
out victory across the weary miles, up and down the country,
crossing the wide plains and crisscrossing again, telling the story
of the Republican "do-nothing" Eightieth Congress.

From Labor Day to Election Day, the miles added up to
more than 30,000 and his speeches numbered over 300. [*I traveled 31,700 miles by train in 1948. My speeches were 356 prepared ones and about 200 more off the cuff.—HST*] His was an
offensive mission, to take to the American people the warning not
to be fooled by the catch phrases, the eye-filling slogans, the fables
about "the team," Dewey's team. Above all, he told the facts
about his own program for peace abroad and abundance at home.

Yes, Truman knew. And, knowing, he realized that the winning was the result of many men working long hours, tirelessly,
faithfully, to elect a President in the firm belief that such a
course was good for the country.

Thomas E. Dewey had taken his "team" talk and his speeches
calling for "unity" across the nation too. Not so far as Truman
—Dewey had traveled 18,000 miles and given 170 speeches.
He had seen the gleaming promise of the White House so close
that it could nearly be touched, only to have it vanish, as all
dreams vanish.

25

Most people expected a Republican landslide in 1948. Dewey might naturally have believed he could coast into the Presidency, that his fight was won when his nomination by the Republican Party was achieved.

He learned, however, that the American people love the underdog, that they will steadfastly back a fighter, that they weary of the unexciting and the static.

Truman's campaign was not one but many. There was the campaign he himself waged so well across the country; there was the other campaign he waged from his desk in the White House, formulating the programs for which he fought with the Eightieth Congress.

There was the campaign before the Democratic Convention, the campaign fought in the offices of county clerks and of election boards, where people were registered to vote, where party organization was whipped into shape.

There was the campaign fought by labor and the campaign fought in the farm country and the campaign fought from headquarters in the Biltmore in New York, and the other campaign fought from the train. It was a vast, complex meshing of plans, work and situations.

It was an election campaign unlike any other that had ever been fought in the history of the United States. It was a campaign that will never be paralleled, for never again can the manifold details of fact and circumstance fall into conjunction with man, time and destiny.

Political infighting gets few headlines for itself. Yet obscure body blows delivered without fanfare can do much to set up an opponent for a political knockout.

In a congressional election year, upwards of 750,000 elective jobs, at all political levels short of the Presidency itself, are in contention. Assuming conservatively that every office to be filled will be sought by at least the incumbent and one contender, this means approximately 1,500,000 candidates. In addition, most candidates will have a campaign manager, a treasurer and sev-

26

eral workers. Thus the total number of people directly affected by such an election will number conservatively some six to eight million people.

In 1958 contests for the office of Governor will be held in thirty-three states. Thirty-two Senators will be either elected or re-elected as the case may be, and the 435 members of the House of Representatives will lay their jobs on the line. New state legislatures will be elected in the thirty-three states having gubernatorial elections; and literally hundreds of thousands of judges, mayors, city councilmen, school-district members, sanitary trustees, coroners, county boards, sheriffs, county treasurers and others will be chosen.

In 1954 the total who went to the polls was, in round numbers, 42,000,000. In 1956 the total was almost 60,000,000. In 1958 the total vote should be some three to four million higher than 1954, the last national election that was held when the office of the Presidency was not at stake.

Additional millions of citizens, through neglect—i.e., failure to register—or through some change in residence or because of other legal requirements, will not be able to vote. Many of these, nevertheless, will follow closely the progress of the campaigns. Others, young people who are not quite of voting age, and the million or so inhabitants of the District of Columbia who have no vote, will also be following the course of the election, particularly as it affects the political make-up of Congress.

During the campaign the citizenry will be informed by radio, television and the press. Despite the fact that many people consider radio an obsolete form of communication, there is a total of some 143,500,000 sets in use, with 53,000,000 homes having at least one set. There were 42,000,000 television sets in use in 1956.

Daily newspapers in the United States number approximately 1,761, with a metropolitan list of some 200 covering the 130 major cities of over 100,000 population. In addition, there are 8,500 weekly newspapers of general circulation.

Statistically the number of column inches devoted to politics in an election year would be staggering. The amount of time during which TV and radio transmitters carry political news of one sort or another would also be fantastic. Even more fantastic in my opinion is the amount of misinformation given the public by communication media, and the number of times the news editors and reporters who work for these outlets of information either do not get the story or, having got it, fail to print or air it.

This is the arena of the political infighting that marks a political campaign. Within that arena many blows are given and received. And, just as when you watch a televised version of a championship prize fight, many of the best blows are so obscured as never to be seen at all.

Now stretch your television camera lens. Imagine a prize fight where the principals number hundreds—candidates in the races for Governor and for national congressional seats alone; where no one hesitates to wear a horseshoe in the padding of each glove; where the trainers and managers are expected to club the fighters any time they get into reach; where even the audience may get into the fight on the slightest pretext; and where someone sitting on the outside with no interest in the match at all may do something which may change all the rules—like Russian scientists launching an earth satellite.

Thus you can see that simply following the campaign is in itself enough to tax the powers of observation and discernment of the onlooking voters. To be conscious, too, of the political infighting and assess the results of that infighting is clearly beyond the powers of the average voter. Yet it may be in the infighting that the damage is done that allows the clean-cut knockout blow to be delivered right out in plain sight of all.

Never was this better illustrated than in the historic campaign of 1948 for the office of President of the United States. Harry S Truman delivered the classic long right to the jaw which registered the knockout. In the background were J. Howard McGrath, then a United States Senator, and the late Gael Sullivan, Executive Director of the Democratic National Committee, using the thousands upon thousands of Democratic Party members around the country to beat a less publicized but rib-shaking tattoo on the Republican body politic.

Harry Truman's accomplishments are well known, for if ever a man contributed to his own election it was Harry. He epitomized the whole Democratic campaign—epitomized it and to a great extent *was* the whole campaign. But the fact that he did so was no accident. It was a carefully planned effort to show the people the Democratic candidate in person; to allow his own personality and words to high-light the fight.

The reasoning was simple: In Truman we had a sincere American, a natural leader, a man of decision, a man who had no fear of saying for what he stood, a man of such personality that he could be recognized by every other American for what he was—a simple man of the people. Truman's success was no accident!

That he was so effective paid tribute to the judgment of the leaders of the Democratic Party who were able to recognize the "Man from Missouri" for what he was in the darkest days of political despond following defeat in the congressional race of 1946, when a Republican Congress was voted into power in apparent repudiation of the Democratic President.

Political infighting of course is not confined to one man or one group of men. Many times the best blows are struck by a bystander who may not contribute another single action to further the campaign. Many times, too, the blow that hurts is delivered by coincidence and not by design. But to gain the most from coincidence and from the one-time aid of a sharp-tongued or sharp-eyed friend, an atmosphere must be created which tends to bring such incidents forth. And each incident must be used.

The creation of political atmosphere is no casual thing. It must continue day in and day out. The forces that create it must be fed short pithy stories, wisecracks, sharp contrasts pointed up in few words. American politics is a rough-and-tumble free-for-all with the bludgeon far too often being the only apparent

29

weapon. But, paradoxically, no weapon succeeds better than the chuckle or the outright belly laugh at the expense of a candidate. [*Ridicule is a wonderful weapon!*—HST]

Many times the work of creating atmosphere is hindered by the necessity of carrying on two- or three-front wars, involving sharp disagreement with people normally within your own party. This was particularly true in 1948, when Wallace and Thurmond were splitting off segments of what normally would have been Democratic strength. The combination of trouble on the right, guerrilla warfare on the left and a grand assault on the center is what made the Democratic victory in 1948, to some, an incredible thing. But again, the success was no accident! For leadership of the party early recognized the problem, assessed the situation as perilous, then moved to meet and solve it for victory.

That there was a victory confounded the press and many of the political pundits of both parties.

A good part of this book, then, is the story of the political infighting of that campaign as seen from ringside. I was an instrument, a weapon, in the hands of the party leaders and as such took part in much of what helped to set up the situation for Harry Truman's knockout campaign. I'd like to tell some of it, most of which has not been told in detail before.

Early in March 1947 there was unrest and gloom in the Democratic Party. The 1946 elections had been the first major defeat in fourteen years. The Republican slogan of "Had Enough?" had been all-conquering. The situation seemed to presage an inevitable change in national administration at the first opportunity. The opportunity was to come on November 2, 1948.

Democratic Party chieftains, called "Big City Bosses" in the Republican press, were gloomiest of all. Many of them were muttering that defeat was inevitable. Organization of the party was at an all-time low. One Democratic Senator had called for the President's resignation in view of the pummeling he had taken in losing the congressional race.

30

Early in March, Carroll Reece, the Republican National Committee Chairman, had precipitated an open row by editorializing in the GOP party organ that Republican members of Congress should play on the Republican "team" and follow party leadership. He criticized those who didn't help block for the leaders who, he said, were carrying the "party ball."

This drew a counterblast from the then Republican Wayne Morse of Oregon among others who made a blistering attack on Reece as a tool of Big Business in its effort to get a major tax reduction. There were also rumblings of a change in labor law which only a few weeks later was to emerge as the Taft-Hartley Act. Congressman Knutson of Minnesota was promising a twenty-per-cent tax reduction "across the board."

Harry Truman, President of the United States, was engaged in two major efforts. He was weighing a historic decision to intervene in Greece and Turkey, filling a vacuum left by the decline of British power. On March 13, Truman appeared before a joint session of Congress and enunciated the Truman Doctrine —calling for $400,000,000 in aid to Turkey and Greece to keep those countries from toppling into the orbit of Russian Communism.

He was also proving that his feel for people, his sense of history, was far greater than that exercised by any of his advisers. On an official visit to Mexico as American Chief of State, Truman was of course formally feted everywhere he went. In the course of a trip through Mexico City, he was taken to view a monument to the heroes of the Battle of Chapultepec. These men had fought gallantly against Winfield Scott's American Army in 1847 to keep the Mexican West Point from falling to our invading troops.

When Truman, acting from "feel," spontaneously paid honest and abiding tribute to the memory of those young Mexican heroes, the guards who perpetually stand watch over the monument wept at their posts. All through Mexico there went up such a storm of *"Vivas"* that the world of the Americas was stunned.

It was an early straw in a wind of approval from people, a straw that many observers failed to credit.

To me, writing free lance in the study of my home on Hemion Road in Suffern, New York, the whole thing was academic. The whole thing, that is, except the Truman Doctrine. I considered this the most important step taken by the United States in the area of world affairs since the Potsdam Conference where I had been military spokesman. At Potsdam I served under three bosses, as behooved an officer of an allied force: Truman, Churchill, Stalin.

During that conference amid the ruins of Berlin I had come to know Charles Ross, Presidential Press Secretary, very well. I had served immediately under President Truman's eye and greatly respected him as President, of course, but even more as a man.

Later I had been drafted to fill a post in government immediately at the close of the war, when I was under army orders to go to China. I took the job with Stuart Symington, now United States Senator, at the Surplus Property Administration for a stipulated six months' period and resigned when the six months were up.

Now I wanted to contribute more toward helping, if I could, the Truman Doctrine achieve its goal. I called Ross at the White House and asked for a job either in Turkey or Greece where I might be useful. Charlie was cordial and said he would discuss it with the Boss.

So on a cold, blustery Sunday late in March my wife called me in from my snow shoveling to answer a telephone call. It was the postmaster in Suffern: "I was called to the office from my home, Colonel Redding, because there's a letter here for you from the President of the United States!"

I said, "Fine."

What I said, or perhaps the way I said it, apparently did not seem right to the postmaster. "I do not," he said, "ordinarily come in to the post office on Sunday. But a personal letter from the President . . ."

With lowered voice I acknowledged that this was indeed important. He waited. So did I. Then I asked if he could open the letter and tell me what it contained.

The postmaster was shocked. "I couldn't do that!" But he went on, "I'll deliver it personally and consider it an honor."

Truly impressed then, I said, "No, I'll come down." But he would not hear of it and within a few minutes arrived carrying the letter reverently. Inside was a note from Charlie Ross saying the President would see me at "your convenience, on Monday at ten o'clock."

I went to Washington and was in Charlie Ross's office a quarter of an hour before ten on Monday morning. Ross was tall, thin and a little stooped. His face looked leathery and a little tired. He looked like a plainsman—an aging Bat Masterson in store clothes. He said he had discussed me with the President. The President recalled my previous service and wanted to talk to me.

At ten o'clock on the button I saw the President. He was friendly and remembered me favorably. He had decided that I was the man for the job, he said. Then we shook hands and I was ushered out feeling a little bewildered. I didn't know what the job was!

Merriman Smith of the United Press, an old friend and a good one, whispered, "Are you all set?"

He knew what was going on. I didn't, but not wanting to let it be known that I didn't, my answer was a careful one: "I guess I'm in."

Back into Ross's office. Charlie asked, "How'd you make out? All set?"

"Yes, when do I leave?"

"You'd better go right now."

"Right now? But I haven't packed."

"Packed!" Ross looked at me as though I were slightly insane. "Where do you think you're going?"

"Well, I don't know . . . Athens, I hope . . . I . . ."

Ross came closer to loud laughter than I ever saw him before or after. "You're not going to the Near East. You're going over

33

to the Mayflower to see Gael Sullivan. If he buys, you'll be the new publicity director of the Democratic National Committee!"

I was ushered out of the White House still in a fog and made my way to the Mayflower. There I was promptly shown into Gael Sullivan's office in the committee headquarters. Here I was, about to be considered for the key post of publicity director for the Democratic Party at a challenging time in history, and I hadn't even been a candidate for the job, actually hadn't known the job was open or about to be open.

I knew Gael from Chicago. We shook hands. "Long time no see," said Sullivan. I agreed.

Vibrant, dynamic—these were words that Gael Sullivan loved and they fitted him. Medium-tall, slim, well-built, he had dark wavy hair and the handsome black Irish look. His voice was rich and, well, vibrant, and when he talked—made a speech—he had a trick of pausing, then leaning forward and thrusting his jaw out and up like Mussolini.

Sullivan said, "Ross tells me that I'm to choose you as our new publicity director. When can you go to work?"

And that's how this newspaper type came to be the man charged with directing the publicity effort of the Democratic Party in the campaign for President that was to make political history.

CHAPTER 3

THE TRUMAN DOCTRINE for the defense of Turkey and Greece had triggered the action which placed me in my new position; but not having been concerned with partisan politics I had paid little attention to the opposition to the plan. Yet here I was tossed willy-nilly into the midst of a red-hot political controversy which had been brought about by the President's proposal.

It had not occurred to me that the courage to face up to the problems of a world-power conflict—either hot or cold—had to be backed up by a different sort of courage: the willingness to take such action in the face of a domestic political threat. Now on the inside of the political picture I could see the problem of domestic politics and its threat to the President's future.

Harry Truman wanted to be elected President. He wanted the office on his own, not as a substitute called off the bench by death. Even as he pondered the need for action to save Greece and Turkey from Russian domination, Truman knew that taking such steps might seriously divide his personal support at home. This division would not be between American Communists and non-Communists, but, in the main, between honest Americans who feared bold action might bring on war and those who saw more clearly. The appeasers were willing, honestly enough, to

35

defer action in the hope that if they closed their eyes tightly the threat to peace would go away. It was to these mistaken but peace-loving Americans that Wallace largely appealed.

Further, there were those within the Administration's political circle who would have postponed action, not because they failed to see the Russian danger to international order, but because they saw a threat to their own positions of power within the government. Harry Truman pondered the problem, but he was able to withstand the cautious counsel of some political advisers, to appraise the situation more clearly than the appeasers. I believe that he never allowed his decision to be influenced by the possible harm that might be done to his own ambitions.

Shortly after the President appeared before a joint session of Congress to ask authority for his program of aid to Greece and Turkey, former Vice President Henry Wallace, as expected, took a role in direct opposition. A full-page advertisement in the New York *Times*, paid for by the Progressive Citizens of America, bitterly attacked Greece as "not Democratic," Turkey as "no ally," and said the whole Truman proposal would lead to war. The four basic points of the Wallace argument were summed up in the ad as: (1) President Truman's proposals divide the world into two hostile camps and head the country to war. (2) American dollars and American men should not be pledged to aid kings and emperors. (3) The full power of the United States should instead be placed behind the United Nations. (4) Our confidence should be placed only in a world partnership creating peace for all peoples.

About the time this advertisement appeared, Gael Sullivan precipitated controversy by writing to Carroll Reece, proposing that the heads of the two national political committees sign an open document pledging support of party machinery to the Truman Doctrine.

Senator Vandenberg of Michigan took the floor in the Senate to condemn Sullivan's action as endangering the bipartisan foreign policy of the nation. Many Democrats in the Senate openly agreed with him. Reece did not miss the opportunity piously to lambast Sullivan for "playing politics."

As this pot boiled in the press, Sullivan openly damned Wallace for going outside his party. Thus another burner was heated and the political reporters in Washington did a war dance on Sullivan.

While I tried to digest the problems posed by these items, the announcement was made to the press that a new publicity director had been named. Sam O'Neal, the retiring director, had the misfortune of having been on the job during the congressional election debacle of 1946. He had the additional handicap of a personality difficulty with Bob Hannegan, then Democratic National Chairman as well as Postmaster General of the United States. He was unable to talk over his problems with Hannegan.

Things finally reached a point where O'Neal could communicate with Hannegan only by going through Hannegan's speech writer, Joe Berger, who was part of O'Neal's staff. It was an untenable position, one that could be handled only by resignation. O'Neal had turned in his resignation, undated, along with an expression of willingness to stay on as long as it took to get a replacement. Now he expressed the wish to complete the work incident to the Jefferson Day Dinner, which was to take place immediately after the first of April.

This was agreeable to all, but I was asked by Sullivan, although my official tenure didn't begin until the first of April, to stay in Washington for the few remaining days of March to help him get out of his Wallace problems.

Sullivan accepted an invitation to appear on "Meet the Press," Sunday, March 31. The questions asked were easy enough through most of the half hour on the air until Bert Andrews of the New York *Herald Tribune* asked the pertinent question: "What about Wallace?" And he added, "Senator Pepper?" The Senator had sharply attacked the President's program on the floor of the Senate a few days before.

Sullivan did not box. He answered specifically and to the

point: he would not ask either Wallace's or Pepper's support in 1948. Thus further fuel was added to the anti-Sullivan fire, for his answer was taken to mean that Wallace and Pepper were being read out of the Democratic Party. Sullivan was right, in the case of Wallace, but the time was not ripe.

Walking back from the Trans-Lux Building down Fourteenth Street in Washington to the Raleigh Hotel where Sullivan was staying, we discussed the program. "How did it go?" he asked me.

"It went all right," I answered. "The only thing I could see that might cause a problem was that Wallace-Pepper quote."

"I don't think so," Sullivan replied. "If Hannegan said it, or the President, it would be important. But not me."

He underestimated his position. The heat engendered was terrific—a sort of geometric progression from the other incidents. The newspapers deplored the incident, meanwhile building up the controversy. Members of Congress condemned Sullivan. There was talk of a visit to the presidential "woodshed" for a "paddling."

The really serious repercussion, however, came from the tender senatorial sensibilities of Alben Barkley of Kentucky, the Senate Minority Leader, who demanded that Sullivan apologize publicly to Senator Pepper. Barkley took the position that a United States Senator could not be "bullied" or "threatened with expulsion from his party" for statements made on the floor of the Senate. He stated that a United States Senator must "speak from his conscience" in addressing the Senate and must not be subjected to political pressures. Fortunately this item never reached the press. The White House was perturbed, however, not only by the public furor as expressed in the press and what was considered "unfortunate timing" in the attack on Wallace, but also by the inclusion of Pepper in the controversy and, most of all, by Barkley's reaction.

On April Fool's Day Sullivan was depressed.

"I was right," he declared to me. "I'll resign before I'll apologize."

38

We took the first of the long-distance soundings which were to become a regular practice. We called Hannegan, of course, as the boss of the committee. His advice was to "sweat it out." Then Mayor Ed Kelly of Chicago took time out of the election-day voting for his successor, Martin Kennelly, to talk at length with Gael, his protégé. "Sit tight," Kelly counseled. "If they want you to apologize, that's unreasonable—but do it! Do what you have to do, but don't resign."

Bill Malone of San Francisco was next. He too counseled moderation. Then Dick Neuberger in Portland, Oregon: "Sit tight!" There were others. All expressed the same sentiment: "Don't resign!"

Having considered this unanimous advice, Sullivan backed down on his threat. He called Senator Barkley and stated his willingness to apologize to Senator Pepper. Barkley was pleased and told Gael to call Pepper himself.

Pepper was generous. He did not want a public apology, he said, but a private discussion of the problem might be helpful. They agreed to have dinner together, alone, for this purpose. When he returned from this session, Sullivan was radiant.

He told me, "The Senator was friendly and held no grudge." Sullivan had apologized for criticizing what Senator Pepper had stated on the floor of the Senate, and Pepper had professed to see the whole thing as a tempest in a teapot. The Senator had also stated that he was a Democrat and certainly would feel very bad if he were not asked to support the Democratic ticket in 1948. He had also "mildly" mentioned the Wallace part of the episode, saying that Wallace, he thought, was a strong man in the party and should not be cast lightly aside.

The President called Sullivan in and talked to him very reasonably about the necessity of co-ordinating his actions with those of the Administration. Neither the wording of the reprimand, nor the manner in which it was delivered, was stinging. Sullivan did not reveal the subject of this meeting to the press as he made his exit. But later in the day, at the regular presidential press conference, President Truman, in answer to a question, said he had asked Sullivan to make arrangements for "better co-ordination" of his political actions. He laughed off a quip about "woodshed spankings," and that appeared to be that. After the conference, Merriman Smith called and told me of President Truman's statement. He asked, "Are you the 'better co-ordination'?" I evaded the question.

But that was not to be all, for the rivalries brought about by Sullivan's ambition to be National Chairman of the Democratic Party nurtured sniping. Hannegan was ill. A big man, a former football star from St. Louis University, he still had the frame; but the muscles were beginning to go and hypertension, the ailment that killed him, showed in a ravaged face. It was no secret that he intended to resign—and soon. There were others who wanted the Hannegan mantle and they were willing to fight tooth and nail to get it.

The recurring troubles with John L. Lewis and the United Mine Workers were brewing again. The possibility of a coal strike hung over the nation's industry. It was true that there was then in effect a federal injunction restraining Lewis and the mine workers from striking, but no one was willing to bet that Lewis would honor it.

Further complicating the picture was the Communists-in-government issue which was beginning to make its way into the headlines. President Truman had announced his loyalty program, which I personally considered harsh and an invasion of the rights of citizens. I have always distrusted secret police. In Europe during the war against the Nazis, I had learned to abhor the Gestapo, and my experiences in Berlin where I had seen the Russian MVD operate had hardened that feeling.

Gael Sullivan was in agreement with me but he was unwilling to make an effort to modify the "too harsh" program. After a long talk I asked if he were agreeable to my discussing the matter with Tom Clark, the Attorney General. Sullivan assented.

Clark listened to me patiently. He conceded that the power of

40

economic life and death given to governmental agency heads over their employees was "a very considerable step away from the ordinary concept of law." But he told me that the problem of Communists in government was greater than the issue I had raised. He felt that the feared abuses would be held down by good administration and need work no harm on the rights of citizens. On the other hand I argued that any citizen threatened with what would amount to an economic life-or-death sentence had a right to be confronted by his accusor. I felt too that the raw files of the Federal Bureau of Investigation were not sufficient evidence of disloyalty to warrant such serious action as depriving a citizen of his livelihood. I got nowhere.

As we parted, we discussed for a moment the political problem of Lewis' defiance of the Supreme Court. It was my feeling that imposing severe penalties on Lewis was politically "not good." But as Clark put it, "Lewis has left us no way out." Again I could not help but feel respect for the President who was willing to compromise his political position with labor rather than allow the sovereign powers of the government to be infringed. There was no room for action in this field for me as a political agent.

On the issue of the loyalty program, I asked permission to discuss the matter with the President and was given an appointment for that purpose.

When the President saw me, his mood was very serious. The problem of disloyalty in government was one he had wrestled with at length in his own mind. "If there are disloyal persons in the employ of the government," he told me, "they must be eliminated. I believe the issue has been blown up out of proportion to the actual number of possible disloyal persons we may have. But the fact is that one disloyal person is too many." (The above is a paraphrase of his actual words.)

The President agreed that an invasion of the rights of some citizens was possible under the loyalty program but felt that good administration would prevent such an invasion. The whole matter would adjust itself as it went along. Besides, he said,

41

the government as an employer had no obligation to employ anyone who the government felt was objectionable for any reason—
including drunkenness, dishonesty, lewd or immoral habits *and*
disloyalty. There the matter rested.

There were other pressing problems. One of the most serious
and one which was to grow more serious as time passed was that
of party finance. Almost immediately after taking office as
Director of Publicity, I was pressed to cut staff. I knew very
little about the holdovers from Sam O'Neal's tenure but felt that
they had a right to prove themselves to me and did not deserve
arbitrary dismissal. For many years the National Committee
publicity staff had consisted of only a director and a secretary
in political off years and was beefed up only for the actual
campaign.

This policy I felt to be outmoded, particularly when we were
trying to recover from a severe defeat and build to a successful
campaign in 1948. Sullivan agreed. George Killion, possibly
the most able of the treasurers of the National Committee, felt
otherwise. Killion, of course, watching the steady drain of dollars from the committee treasury, was breaking his health to
keep up the inward flow of contributions. His was a difficult
position.

Included on my payroll was Charley Michelson, the old
genius of the Democratic Party who had contributed so much
to the New Deal successes under Roosevelt. Michelson, now aged
and infirm, was unable to appear at the office. In fact he was so
weak that the strain of a discussion lasting more than half or
three quarters of an hour tired him completely. Actually his
pay, only a few thousand dollars a year, was a pension.

The proposal was made by Killion and the decision passed on
to me by Sullivan to cut Michelson off the payroll. This decision
I instantly opposed. I told Sullivan, "There're two reasons why
I can't go along. The first one is that I talk every day to Michelson on our problems and get helpful advice from him. The sec-

ond reason is the more important: if we fire Michelson we'll bring down on our heads the worst blast of publicity possible. We'll be called ingrates. We'll be pictured as the very archetypes of the soul-less-corporation concept that the Democratic Party stands against. We just can't do it."

Gael agreed. So did Killion when we discussed the matter. So Charlie Mike was undisturbed in his last days. I don't think he knew the matter was even discussed. Michelson was a great mind. Weak and infirm though he was, he delighted to sit and talk out political problems as they arose. We had but one serious difference. He felt that I should identify my name with actions taken by the committee. I felt that the proper role of a publicity man was to identify action with his principals—in the present instance, President Truman, Bob Hannegan and Gael Sullivan. On this subject Charlie Mike snorted at all my arguments, saying that I would be more effective for the committee if I would sign political blasts with my own name.

During the last years of Charlie Mike's life I made it a practice to see him at least once a week and sometimes oftener. He was a truly great Democrat.

Another more difficult problem was that posed by John Maragon. Early in April 1947, Merriman Smith and Tony Vaccaro, the Associated Press White House man, called at my office in the Mayflower. Both men had a deep and abiding affection for President Truman. This they explained was the reason for their call. They wanted to discuss Maragon. Did I know him?

I did not. I knew nothing more about Maragon than I had read in Drew Pearson's column concerning some of Maragon's alleged manipulations in perfume from Europe.

The two newsmen explained that they knew and liked Maragon as an individual, but Maragon was *persona non grata* to the President and to Charlie Ross. He had been ordered not to enter the White House but he persisted. Inevitably, they warned, Maragon would be investigated. Better have nothing to do with him.

43

My answer was that I didn't know Maragon and had nothing to do with him, but that I could not take any action to bar him from my office without specific evidence of wrongdoing or on orders of my superiors. I had to take this position, but after the two reporters had left, I told my secretary, Claire Jones, that I didn't want to see Maragon if it could be avoided. Unfortunately, Maragon heard of this and resented it.

Hannegan came to Washington from his home in St. Louis. Rumor had it he was about to resign. Actually this was not yet true but there was a spate of stories in the papers concerning his possible successor. Sullivan's name led all the rest.

Staff problems had handled themselves. Both Julian Stein and Joe Berger, Hannegan's speech writer, had resigned on their own initiative and over my protests. Edgar Brown, Charlie Mike's old 1932 office boy, since grown to active publicity-man stature, left to take a job on Capitol Hill. Sam Brightman, my associate during six months with the Surplus Property Administration, and before that my executive officer in General Bradley's 12th Army group in Western Europe, had joined the staff as assistant publicity director, sponsored by Senator Barkley.

Hannegan, Sullivan, Brightman and I sat down to hammer out objectives. Bob Hannegan started off by laying down a general rule of thumb for all publicity activity: "Don't do anything unless it advances the cause of President Truman's election. We do not want publicity for the sake of publicity. So on every proposal you make, first try it against this rule."

Concerning possible Republican candidates: "It'll be Dewey again," said Hannegan. "But Dewey will have to run on what Taft does in the Congress. Actually, if the Republicans were smart, they'd run Taft. He'd make a better candidate and would probably be harder for us to beat simply because he would fight harder. Don't make the mistake of underrating Taft. Many people think he'd be easy to beat. But that's because they see in his nomination the simple matter of a clear division between the parties. The fact is that Taft is a fighter and willl make a ter-

44

rific fight for what he represents. Dewey will be 'me too' all over again. He'll tend to beat himself. Just remember, if Dewey is the candidate, as I think he will be, he'll have to run on Taft's program. Hit Taft hard and often; maybe we can stop him from getting the nomination and at the same time embarrass Dewey."

Afterward I was often asked by newsmen, when we had hit particularly hard at Taft: "Why? He's Mr. Republican. He'd be the easiest man to beat." The explanation has never been made until now.

The position of the daily press was outlined: "There's a lot of affection for Truman among the reporters but the papers are dead set against us. We'll have no paper of importance that will tell our story."

Hannegan objected. "They'll print the news."

I agreed to that but pointed out the difference between telling our story and printing the news. "The papers will run the Republican story and print the news about us. What we need, if we can get it, is a mouthpiece of our own. But that's hopeless."

To this Hannegan finally agreed.

I went on, "For this reason we should decide now to make our greatest effort directly to the people. We can do this best in two ways: First, as far as standard publicity efforts are concerned, we should make our principal effort by radio. By radio we can tell our own story in our own words. We don't have to go through a whole series of people from reporter to editor who try to condense and interpret the story we tell.

"Besides, I think we can get the jump on our Republican friends by radio. We can hit anything that moves if we get the offensive. The trick will be to have them explaining and answering what we have to say. We should never answer them. Let them do the explaining!"

"How will you get the jump on radio?" asked Hannegan. "How can you get the jump on them anywhere?"

"The issue is Big Business and the high cost of living. We'll accuse them on this issue, indict them and find them guilty.

45

Their position is so bad that they can never avoid answering us and when they explain, they in effect admit they have something to explain."

"All right."

"The second way to carry our story is to go directly to people by word of mouth. We have an advantage, it seems to me, in that the Democratic strength is concentrated and allows us to use the word-of-mouth means of communication to best advantage. In the South the vote is ours. In many areas of the North and West our vote is the big-city vote. And we have organization there. We can use that organization to tell our story, building by building, block by block."

"True enough," said Sullivan. "But organization is not as strong as many people think. The Democratic Party has been running on FDR's coattails so long that the organization thing is largely a myth. If we're going ahead on a word-of-mouth program, we'll have to work first to get organization."

"We'll have to work on organization anyway," Hannegan interposed. "That's your job, Gael. You know it. I know it. And the best way to create organization is to give the workers in the precincts something to do. Redding's plan would do just that. So we'll work on organization."

This decision meant that a vehicle to reach party workers had to be created. It had to be terse, readable, eye-appealing—not pretty but compelling. And above all it had to be cheap. Sullivan proposed a newsletter, "something like the Kiplinger letter." Hannegan winced. He considered Kiplinger's newsletter an organ of big business.

A clip sheet, we agreed, wasn't the answer because such a sheet addressed to newspapers would again subject our copy to the willingness of editors and publishers to print what we said. It would be the same old story: if printed, it would be a watered-down version. More likely it wouldn't be printed at all, particularly at this time when the campaign had not yet got "hot."

Sullivan finally overcame Hannegan's objections to the news-

46

letter format and we agreed to go ahead on that line. It was to be aimed at precinct workers in the big cities and at the county chairmen and their workers in other areas. The purpose was to give them material that they could use directly on voters in their districts and precincts.

We didn't propose to make them think, merely to give them material which they could use without thinking. Actually the issues were so simple that thinking was not necessary. Feeling, emotion—that was the formula!

"Well," Bob said, "that's something for Redding and Brightman to work on." Then he attacked another point which obviously had bothered him. "The Cabinet doesn't seem to think that there's anybody named Truman. I'm going to do something about that. It's about time Cabinet officers recognize the fact that they hold their offices at the pleasure of the President, and the policies they talk about in their speeches are not theirs but the President's."

He was going to take up that point at the Cabinet meeting the next day, he said. He expected to get some action.

The matter of a party organ had already caused dissension within the committee staff. Creekmore Fath, Sullivan's assistant, had proposed that the *Democratic Woman's Digest,* a monthly magazine covering the distaff side of the party, be taken over by the publicity division and converted into a general political vehicle for the committee. I had resisted the change, pointing out that the *Digest* had acceptance as a woman's publication; it would be difficult to persuade readers that the magazine had been changed. Unfortunately neither Mrs. Chase Going Woodhouse, Director of the Women's Division of the Democratic National Committee, nor her assistant, Mrs. India Edwards, was present.

In turning down the magazine as a general party organ, I had said the format was not right for such a purpose and that it was published too infrequently—once a month—to be effective.

Fath and Sullivan accepted my judgment. But they went on to suggest that the magazine should be read by the publicity division from a policy standpoint, "Just to make sure we don't have any divergences showing up that might be embarrassing."

This conversation was almost immediately reported to Mrs. Woodhouse and Mrs. Edwards. But the whole sense of it was garbled in the reporting. The following day I was called by Mrs. Edwards' secretary and politely asked if I could drop by Mrs. Edwards' office. "India is lying down with a headache," the secretary said, "or she'd come to your office."

An hour later I went to India's office to be greeted with a tremendous blast. Trying to take away the *Woman's Digest* . . . trying to build an empire . . . trying to undercut the women's division. In conclusion, India said, "You keep your hands off the *Digest!* Understand?"

An explanation that we weren't contemplating doing anything about the *Digest* would be taken as a sign of weakness. If the matter was allowed to stand as it was, the claim would be made that I'd backed down. It was a case of damned if I did and damned if I didn't. I contented myself with saying that the publicity division would oversee the content of the book for political policy "as planned" and beat a retreat.

Actually, the whole contretemps was brought about by a gross misrepresentation to Mrs. Edwards as to what had occurred among Fath, Sullivan and myself. The matter was never discussed again, but I am sure that India later found out the facts. I must say that overseeing policy in the *Digest* was never a difficult problem, for the book under Mrs. Edwards' direction never erred in this respect.

It seemed that all the political infighting was being done on us. The Wallace-ites were screaming all over the world, literally, that Truman was leading the world to war; there were vexing problems of internal dissension within the committee, and the difficulty of beating off rivals for Hannegan's job as National Chairman.

Hannegan went to work on the Cabinet. He bulled through a

pact whereby every Cabinet officer agreed that neither he nor a subordinate of his would make a speech without mentioning Truman. Then Hannegan came back to me with a request, "Get me a man to research the President's public announcements and speeches for quotes to be used in speeches by Cabinet officers."

Hannegan said, "Some of these people had the gall to say that the President had nothing to do with what they had to say. Now they admit that he does. But I'm going to call time on them."

Hal Leyshon was recruited from New York for the job. He formulated a tremendous "Truman file." All the President's speeches since he had taken office, and even before, were broken down into quotes on almost every conceivable subject, then coded and placed in order.

Now Hannegan called in Leyshon and outlined the agreement with the Cabinet. He said, "I want you to make a report to me weekly. I want it in a book. The report is to cover each and every speech made by a Cabinet officer or one of his assistants: when you were informed of the need for speech material, the date you supplied that material, a copy of the quote you supplied. I want the date of the speech itself. And then I want a copy of the actual speech that was made, with the Truman quote marked out in red pencil—if the quote was used. If the quote you supplied was *not* used and there was no other Truman quote contained in the speech in question, I want that fact noted. With that material each week on every Cabinet or Little Cabinet speech, I'll be in a position to make these people dance."

The project was carried through—and successfully. It took only one or two readings from the "report" at Cabinet meetings, before the President entered the room, to convince other members that Hannegan was ready and willing to fight on the issue. From then on we had no problem.

Later we made speech-material releases from the Truman file, giving a chronological record of what the President had said on such subjects as "peace," "Christmas," "the high cost of living," the various phases of "agriculture," and the "Truman Doctrine."

This material proved valuable in our project of using party organization in a block-by-block, word-of-mouth campaign.

At one time the President's own speeches became a matter of great concern. There was no particular reason for it, nothing you could put your finger on, but suddenly people were talking about Harry Truman's "terrible" speeches. There seemed to be almost general agreement that his speaking voice had no guts, that he spoke without conviction, that his voice lacked timbre; in sum, he was just a "lousy" speaker!

The actual problem was the contrast between Truman's speech manners and those of Franklin D. Roosevelt. In the comparison Truman came off badly. Most of the criticism seemed to be among Democrats but, amusingly enough, even Republicans who had hated Roosevelt were making the same comparison.

The criticism, meaningless at first, gained in strength. Those who opposed the President carried it further, saying, "Too bad we don't have a Roosevelt. Truman says things as if he doesn't mean them." From there, the opposition took the final step, inferring that Truman *was* merely mouthing things written for him, things which were counter to his personal beliefs. Instead of dying down, this wave of criticism grew and did real damage to the President's prestige.

And the criticism was difficult to combat because it was partly true. President Truman was not an accomplished speaker. He was not giving a good account of himself when he addressed the nation. It wasn't because he lacked conviction. Anyone who knew the President knew that, but truth doesn't necessarily put down criticism.

The same comments kept cropping up in our organization meetings with party leaders from all over the country. They were openly critical of the President's speeches and they were the ones mourning the loss of Roosevelt most bitterly. While we were pointing out shortcomings in organization work in their states, right down to the precinct level, they were answering that it was Truman's fault because he didn't have the magic voice that Roosevelt had had.

During the Roosevelt years, leaders didn't have to work at organization because the great man in the White House was able to carry the people with him. Organization was not vital.

Understanding why our own people were griping about the President's speeches was one thing. Doing something about it was still another.

Hannegan and Sullivan asked me what I thought.

"The difficulty is that you're trying to picture the President as FDR," I told them. "You're expecting the impossible. He isn't FDR. He isn't anything like him. Roosevelt was an Eastern aristocrat, educated at Groton and Harvard. Harry Truman is a Midwestern farmer.

"But that's not all of it. The same thing is being done, probably subconsciously, by all the people around the President. They want him to be Roosevelt, too. Maybe the President, himself, without realizing it, is trying to force himself into the Roosevelt mold.

"It's a mistake. No one can make him over into a Roosevelt and we ought to stop trying. Our speech writers are putting together fine Groton and Harvard phrases, beautiful language that FDR could roll out for the people to admire. But when they try to put that same sort of language into Truman's mouth, it doesn't sound right.

"The answer is that although Truman hasn't the virtues of Roosevelt as a speechmaker, he does have a virtue of his own. He naturally talks like a Midwesterner. He uses language that wise guys in New York may call 'corny'; but every listener in the Midwest knows exactly what he means. Further, he's been in politics almost all of his life. He's been a United States Senator, and before that a county judge. He had to run for those offices. He must have had to make speeches. And he must have done all right. He was elected.

"Why don't we try to get him to throw out all the old Roosevelt ghostwriters and start fresh from a Truman base?"

To give an instance of the routine being followed, the President had consented to listen to recordings of his voice. He would hear playbacks of his speeches while so-called experts pointed out alleged mistakes. This is always a disconcerting experience, for your own voice on a recording comes through reedy and high-pitched. It never sounds right.

Further, when you practice a speech, rehearse it and change words and whole paragraphs to fit real or imagined faults in delivery, the result is a script without life and a speech that has no conviction or feeling.

Public-speaking professors may howl about this but I have learned that people do not listen to words and construction in a speech so much as they listen to the over-all meaning and feeling. Minor slips in pronunciation and faulty parsing of a sentence generally go unnoticed. For example, President Eisenhower at press conferences has answered questions off the cuff with a fine tone, with all the appearance of saying something important. Reporters, at the time, were completely satisfied. It was only when they read back their notes that they would ask, "Yeah, but what did he say?"

I drew up a memorandum for Hannegan covering these points, and then added my views on other subjects which Hannegan had not requested. First the point was strongly made that Truman should speak naturally; that the writers concentrate on the President's *own* style so that he could give his speeches in an easy, natural manner. Then I recommended that the recording machine be dispensed with.

Then, pointing out that for campaign purposes the greatest assets Mr. Truman had were his own forthright manner and his smile, I suggested putting the President on the rear end of a train and exposing him to as many people as time and spirit would allow.

"If people see him in person," the memo continued, "they'll

vote for him. His personality, his smile, his manner of approach, his sincerity all come through perfectly. People will trust him. Trusting him, they'll vote for him."

This was a concept which Sullivan and I had discussed at length and to which Hannegan subscribed wholeheartedly.

When completed, the memorandum was dispatched to the White House via Hannegan. Portions of the recommendations, particularly those regarding the use of train platforms as a campaign device, somehow leaked to the press. The result was considerable speculation about this campaign technique; some of the newsmen sucked their thumbs and came up with what they described as a raging controversy in presidential circles between the pro-train people and the anti-train people.

There was in fact no such controversy. Almost every political leader recognized the virtue of the plan. The only opposition was that voiced at a later date by the Secret Service, who feared danger to the President. This, of course, had nothing to do with politics, involving solely the President's personal security, for which the United States Secret Service is responsible by law.

Results of the memorandum were soon in evidence.

Recordings and playbacks of Truman's speeches were stopped.

The President made several talks where he spoke off the cuff in his natural manner. This "new"—actually the old—manner of speaking was hailed as tremendous. People took bows in all directions as being responsible for the President's new technique. Truman finally became known as a very effective speaker, all because he started to talk like himself and not like someone else.

And I don't need to remind anyone of the fact that the 1948 campaign was made from the rear platform of a train.

CHAPTER 4

THE RETURN of three world travelers and the birth of a new publication made headlines in the opening days of May 1947.

From Moscow came Secretary of State George Catlett Marshall, fresh from the bitter wrangling of the Foreign Ministers Conference. The conference had opened weeks before with great hopes of bringing about some sort of *modus vivendi* between the East and the West; but it had collapsed on procedural disagreements and had accomplished nothing. This failure pointed up the need for the Truman Doctrine if the free world was to be saved from further aggression by Russian Communist power.

Second to return to the United States was Henry Wallace. During his tour of Europe he had been the guest of Communists in France. In England, he had proposed Senator Claude Pepper as candidate for President on a third-party ticket in 1948—an honor which Pepper gracefully declined. Wallace had made some twenty-two speeches in Europe, speeches critical of President Truman and American foreign policy. His arrival created a great stir. He "reported" to the American people by radio, renewing his criticism of the Truman Doctrine, again saying it would lead to war.

In Washington, Wallace held a press conference attended by

54

more than one hundred news correspondents. In his column Lowell Mellett wondered at the "friendliness" displayed toward Wallace by the press. Mellett expressed the opinion that Wallace was viewed by many as a "hedge" against war. According to Mellett, the extreme position taken by some Congressmen in the debate over aid to Greece and Turkey scared some people into thinking that perhaps the Truman Doctrine did mean inevitable war; that it was being used as a vehicle to advance the cause of a "war of prevention."

Mellett went on to say that while there was much confidence in Wallace's personal integrity, the feeling was prevalent in the country that Wallace should not have gone abroad to criticize American foreign policy.

The third traveler, who attracted very little attention at first, was former Governor Harold Stassen of Minnesota who landed at Idlewild after an 18,000-mile, sixteen-country tour as an avowed candidate for the Presidency. Stassen had gone abroad to study the effects of our foreign policy on the world and to ready himself for the high office he confidently said he expected to win.

Stassen didn't try to compete in the press and on the radio with Wallace and Marshall. He saved his fire for several days until public interest in these distinguished travelers had died down. Then he released the transcript of an eighty-minute interview with Josef Stalin he had had on April 9 in Moscow.

The transcript of the interview had been translated into English from notes made by Stassen's secretary who was also present. Later it was checked with the Russian interpreter, Pavlov, whom I had met at the Potsdam Conference. Release of the interview was agreed to by Stalin.

The document was sensational. Here was a possible next President of the United States who was able to secure a face-to-face session with the Russian dictator. Stalin had told Stassen that he foresaw no war between the United States and Russia. He also expressed the opinion that Russia and the United States could "co-operate" in keeping the peace; that they could "co-exist."

Stassen in one stroke took the headlines away from Wallace and Marshall.

In this atmosphere the Democratic National Committee modestly brought out the first issue of its own publication, *Capital Comment*. The news had been so filled with the returning travelers that I did not anticipate much comment on *Comment*.

I was wrong. The infant publication, a newsletter in the Kiplinger format, created a national sensation that brought the apologists for Big Business up screaming, and even took the play away from Stassen.

The four-page newsletter was designed with a simple heading, a drawing of the Jefferson Memorial and the title in hand-drawn capitals on each side of the picture. The opening paragraphs were aimed at aiding Sullivan's project of spurring party organization.

"Elections are won at the grass roots," was the opening line; and the newsletter continued, "Organization upwards from the grass roots is the key to success in 1948." Pointing to the need for putting up candidates in every local election to spur interest among voters and workers alike, *Comment* set a goal of registering two out of every three potential voters. It was stated that the 1946 election, which Democrats had lost, was a "minority election" since only a minority of eligible voters had cast their ballots.

Such talk was harmless enough. But on the bottom of page one came the shocker. For the first time we hit at the cost-of-living issue, the theme that Hannegan had decided on.

"Prices are soaring" was the opening, and President Truman was hailed as the only leader who sought to cut back prices. It was pointed out that President Truman had little real authority, that he had to depend on "moral suasion" in his efforts to roll back prices. A "concentrated publicity campaign" by Cabinet members was being conducted at the direction of the Pres-

ident, *Capital Comment* said, to put heat on "basic manufacturers."

"These are the real culprits," said the newsletter. "Retailers
in general are willing to co-operate; they are exposed to the
wrath of the buyer and they respond to pressure. . . .

"But retailer's cuts provide only slight alleviation. Only if
basic manufacturers like steel, automobiles and the manufacturers of durable goods come up with substantial price slashes
will any real savings be passed on to the consumer."

There was more along this line with a table contrasting prices
on June 18, 1946, just before price controls were removed, with
those of March 1947, less than a year later. After quoting
Chester Bowles, former economic adviser to the President, who
said that "Republican irresponsibility" had cost the American
housewife and businessman eight billion dollars in unnecessarily
higher prices, the article concluded by advising party leaders to
pin the guilt in the right place.

In the same issue Senator Taft was assailed for his part in
what was termed the "shabbiest show of the week." While it was
Senator Taft who had led the fight to discontinue price controls,
he was now seeking to escape the responsibility. He had expressed "qualified agreement" with the President that prices
were too high.

The little newsletter came off the press smoking-hot. Gael
Sullivan received the copy from the printer while I was attending a meeting at the White House between the President and
party leaders from Ohio. Gael bustled over to the White House
with a sheaf of the letters and passed them out to White House
news correspondents in the lobby of the west wing.

Shortly thereafter I came out of the presidential meeting,
ready to give a guarded version of what had occurred in the
conference. I was surprised to find no press awaiting me.

Tabbed as "thought-control" clinics by the press, these party-
leader conferences were designed to bring about a closer relationship between the President and his party. They had been

57

creating considerable news interest, but this time I waited around for the newsmen in vain.

Some big story must be breaking, I thought, and went back to the committee offices where I found the news ticker banging its bulletin bell. The story of the day was on *Capital Comment*. Our attack on basic manufacturers was featured, the phrase, "the real culprits," appearing in the lead and recurring throughout the article.

The first story was hot enough, the follow story even hotter. I was amazed and pleased, especially since I had not anticipated such furor.

Soon the press corps were all over me. Was this to be the theme of the Democratic campaign? Did we really believe that basic manufacturers were the culprits behind the high cost of living? Was this the beginning of a new attack on business? Why were we attacking Big Business? Were we going back to the tactics of the New Deal? And, finally, who had written this thing? Had the President seen it? Had it been cleared with congressional leaders?

Capital Comment had proved newsworthy!

Then Charlie Ross called to tell me, "Come right over. I want to talk to you." He was obviously upset and that upset me. Walking over to the White House, I speculated as to what kind of a hanging they'd give me.

When Ross heard my voice outside his office, he came charging out. Thrusting a copy of *Comment* at me, he demanded, "Have you seen this?"

"I wrote it," I admitted.

"You wrote it?" He looked at the signature on the back page. "Gael's name is signed to it."

"That's right, but I wrote it."

"Gael was giving these out right here in the White House Press Room and I didn't know a thing about it," he told me indignantly.

That was unfortunate, I agreed. It had happened because while I was attending the presidential meeting with the Ohio

58

group, Gael had seen *Capital Comment* come in from the printer's. In his enthusiasm, he had started to distribute them prematurely.

"But," I explained, "the fact is that I wrote it. It was going to be distributed anyway. The responsibility was mine."

Somewhat placated, Charlie led me into his office. What was worrying him was the fact that the President had been stressing a nonpartisan approach to national problems and the content of *Capital Comment* indicated something less than non-partisanship. Ross feared that this would be taken as another instance of lack of co-ordination between the White House and the committee.

I reminded Ross that the decision to follow this line of attack had been taken by Hannegan, Chairman of the National Committee, and I thought he had discussed the policy with the President. It seemed to me that the nonpartisan approach had failed. The Republican congressional leaders had taken this attitude to mean that the President was agreeing to rubber-stamp whatever they did in the name of nonpartisan policy and, consequently, the policy had backfired. I told Ross that Hannegan accepted this view.

Ross went along with my explanation and asked to be kept informed in the future.

"And please," he requested, "don't hand these things out in the White House. Keep politics over at the committee office!"

I promised not to hand them out personally at the White House but pointed out that the newsletter had to be mailed to the news correspondents, who would get them in their White House Press Room.

"These are the men who write most of the political stories," I said, "and we have to reach them where they can be reached—in the White House. But I won't hand out the newsletter personally, and you'll get one of the first copies so you'll know what's going on."

Later I talked over the matter with Sullivan. Delighted with

59

the excitement caused by the first issue, he gloated, "The party workers will be looking forward to seeing the thing. We couldn't have got a better break."

Agreeing with this, I nevertheless asked Gael if he sensed any significance in the reaction at the White House. He asked what I meant.

"Didn't you get the feeling that much of the excitement at the White House was aimed at you personally? One of the principal complaints was that you passed out copies of *Comment* in the White House. I think your fences need a little mending!"

Gael became thoughtful. "It was all right if you did it. It was all right if Hannegan agreed to it. But it was bad if I did it. That's what you mean?"

"It looks that way."

In grim silence, Sullivan retired to his own office.

There were aspects of humor in the violent press reaction. Particularly amusing was the plaint of Frank Kent that this dastardly document "had been signed in black sprawling characters by Gael Sullivan." This seemed to be the ultimate in criticism as far as Mr. Kent was concerned and there he rested.

Our first newsletter was principally important in that it followed the precepts of the Hannegan-Sullivan policy. We had stressed organization. We had struck out at the high cost of living. We had attacked Taft. All of this had been done in language aimed at the ordinary party worker in the hustings. The political workers in the field responded. Almost immediately we began to get mail, bags of it.

Most of the letters were complimentary. Much of it carried items which the writers felt would help the party if printed in the newsletter. There were a few letters of criticism, some blind, others constructive.

There were doubts as to whether the news interest of the letter could be sustained on a weekly basis. But this problem was solved for us. The Republicans and their "do-nothing Congress," as *Capital Comment* dubbed it, provided plenty of am-

60

munition. Senator Taft was a particularly easy target, for, in his position as Majority Leader, he was constantly making news.

On May 10 we returned to the attack. Hardest hit in this issue was the "reactionary dream world where all true Republicans dwell." We gave an analysis of the results of a poll that had been printed in *The Republican*. To determine what the working staff of the Republican Party in New York thought were the principal issues facing the nation, questionnaires were sent to Dewey-Republican political workers in New York State—3,500 of them. The results were made to order for us.

As *Capital Comment* stated: "Ignoring such top issues as prices and foreign policy, Republican 'Statesmen' plump 90 per cent for control of unions and strikes, and reduction of government spending as the two primary issues of the day.

"Next in importance to Republicans is limiting the Presidency to two terms.

"Finally after these three dream-world issues, comes the housing shortage with only 54.4 per cent of the Republicans calling the issue urgent."

Capital Comment gave us the means to reach our party workers; in addition it brought us newspaper publicity. For these two reasons the publication was of tremendous value, particularly as we found Democratic political workers throughout the country responding to the material in it.

This acceptance was evidenced most dramatically after our attacks on Taft. In attacking Taft for his publicly stated views and for his actions as Majority Leader of the Senate, we found that the use of coined words of ridicule was very effective. For instance, the word "tafter" was used to damn any Republican who gave evidence of yielding to the pressure of lobbies, particularly the real estate lobby.

This led to another coinage, "tafting," used to describe anyone who was actively carrying out a Taft policy. Finally we used "taftwits" as a word of opprobrium describing any persons who agreed with the Ohio Senator. It became quite a game as Democrats over the nation wrote in to suggest further ramifications of this litany of disapproval. Some of the suggestions were too hot to handle, but the fact that we were getting correspondence in increasing volume indicated that the idea was taking hold.

According to newsmen who were in daily contact with the Ohio Senator, Taft was beginning to react personally to the barbs.

Now I was called to the White House by the President. Referring to the newly coined Taft words, he asked me not to use them further. He recognized Taft as acknowledged leader of the opposition and disagreed with the Ohioan on almost every point; yet, the President said, Taft had integrity and he honestly and firmly believed that what he was doing was right. The President found the ridicule of Taft distasteful and asked me to discontinue it in *Capital Comment*. The order was tactfully delivered but no misunderstanding was possible.

There was no argument, of course. If the President didn't want us to call people "taftwits," we wouldn't do it. But the thing had caught on already and the fact that it was discontinued in *Capital Comment* did little to discourage the game.

Capital Comment lost none of its zip. If we couldn't use the Taft words, we could use others and we did. The paper crackled in every issue. After the first few issues, Sam Brightman did much of the writing and his vitriolic pen sustained the pace.

That party workers used material from *Capital Comment* was proved by the rent-control issue. The rent-control law would expire on June 30. Obvious Republican strategy, Mr. Taft included, was to repeat their price-control maneuver: wait until the last minute; then, on June 30, place an unworkable bill on the President's desk. The effect was to force the President either to sign a bad bill or to let rent controls expire the next day.

This was a low blow. It deprived the President of his right to consider legislation for ten days before either signing or vetoing it, as provided in the Constitution.

In *Capital Comment* we asked for a concerted drive by Demo-

62

crats to force early action on the extension of rent controls, avoiding such a last-moment quandary.

Earlier consideration of the legislation by the Congress would also allow time for debate, and debate would clarify who was for what. Then, if Congress and its Republican leadership persisted in their strategy, the voters who were caught in the rent squeeze would know who was at fault.

Comment called upon Democrats at every level to take action. Democratic mayors were asked to get resolutions on the issue from their city councils; state legislators to present resolutions for forwarding to Congress; party leaders at the local level to initiate taxpayers' petitions and arrange local rallies in co-operation with veterans' groups, churches and other organizations; and, we emphasized, "Women's clubs can be decisive."

The response was immediate and, because the rent-control issue was important to everyone, the response was not along partisan lines. Not only Democrats, but also dissident Republicans and independents were stirred. The issue appealed to veterans, laborers, young voters just getting started in the business of providing a home for a new family, and all those who sympathized with the millions caught in the rent squeeze. Congress was inundated with mail.

And the Democratic Party had provided the leadership in a national protest which was politically nonpartisan.

The same thing was accomplished on the school-lunch issue. The Eightieth Congress reduced school-lunch program funds from $75,000,000 to $45,000,000. It meant cutting milk off the lunch programs in hundreds, even thousands, of schools. Again the Democratic Party, using *Capital Comment* as a vehicle, was able to bring about a national protest headed by Parent-Teacher Associations, farm groups, social welfare groups, and mothers and fathers by the millions. Local Democratic leaders were in the forefront of this wave of protest.

The Democratic Party again found itself in the welcome political position of leading the people in protest on good and valid issues.

By the same technique, ammunition was provided in the rural areas enabling our farmer-Democrats to take positions of leadership in what would become a farm revolt that was of tremendous importance in the 1948 campaign.

Of major importance in our organizing drive, *Capital Comment* provided a means to spur party leaders at the local level and furnished the political ammunition they needed. Precinct and ward leaders, some of whom had become discouraged and disinterested, suddenly found the work rewarding, and the problem of recruiting workers disappeared. The entire organization picture brightened immeasurably.

CHAPTER 5

THE PRESSURE was increasingly heavy. I had a
room on the fifth floor of the Mayflower Hotel and
my office was on the second floor. Many days I didn't leave the
building, eating my meals either in the restaurant or at my desk.
Sullivan worked at all hours, starting promptly at eight o'clock
in the morning and winding up anywhere from midnight to three
in the morning.

The heart of a political publicist's work is reading the newspapers. To get this done within the Sullivan schedule, I had to
get up and start reading by six. I began to lose weight, as well as
sleep, and developed a fine set of dark circles under my eyes.

One morning in mid-May, Sullivan requested a draft of a
speech he was to deliver at a Jefferson-Jackson Day Dinner in
California. He had specific ideas on what he wanted to say. For
once, he was going to swing directly at the Wallace group. I cautioned against it, feeling that this dignified the opposition within
the Democratic Party and would be taken as a sign of worry.

Gael listened, finally agreed. Then, always mercurial, he announced, "Well, I won't go to the dinner."

He sent a telegram to Jimmie Roosevelt, then state chairman
of the party in California, informing him that it was impossible
to attend the dinner, which was only a couple of days away.

Soon Roosevelt was calling from Los Angeles to protest Gael's decision. He pointed out that tickets to the dinner had been sold on the basis of Sullivan's being main speaker; and Jimmie's mother was to be there, along with all of the hierarchy of the Democratic Party in California. "It's going to look bad," Roosevelt warned, "if you back out at the last minute."

Gael was worried. To me he said, "People out there say Jim Roosevelt is flirting with the Wallace crowd. According to them, he's surrounded with Los Angeles liberals and he's against Truman. If I go, there may be trouble. But if I don't go, maybe there'll be trouble too."

There were other factors governing Sullivan's decision not to attend. He was wary of crystallizing the opposition to Truman in California. If at the dinner an attack was made on the President or on the program to aid Greece and Turkey, Gael felt he would have to answer. This would pin-point the split.

Now Roosevelt insisted that Gael keep his commitment, saying that failure to attend would be taken as a slight to Mrs. Roosevelt. The horns of the dilemma were equally sharp.

Sullivan sought advice. He called Hannegan but was unable to reach him. Ed Kelly thought Gael should go. Most of those to whom Sullivan put his problem followed Kelly's reasoning that, having accepted the invitation in the first place, he was committed. Finally Gael once more reversed himself and so informed Roosevelt.

Carroll Cone of Pan American made arrangements for us to fly out in Juan Trippe's converted B-23 bomber. I was to go along and we planned to stop in Chicago to pick up Mrs. Sullivan. At the last minute Bob Shaffer, a personal friend, joined the party.

The trip west was uneventful. In Chicago a delegation of Democratic leaders came to the airport to greet us. Among them was an old friend, John Casey, Superintendent of Midway Airport, and I enjoyed the half-hour visit with him. Our talk had no political significance, but in recalling the trip I remember this as the last really pleasant moment.

We set down in Los Angeles at the Municipal Airport about eleven o'clock at night. Mike Fanning, Los Angeles postmaster, was there to drive Gael and me to see Ed Pauley, a wealthy oilman and the Democratic National Committeeman for California. He and Jim Roosevelt were bitter rivals for power in California.

Mrs. Sullivan and Shaffer went on to the Ambassador Hotel.

At Pauley's home was a large conclave of conservative Democrats who foresaw nothing but trouble from the dinner. Frank Scully and Pauley were the two most prominent men there, but a score or more others whom we did not know were also present. They all urged Sullivan not to go to the dinner. The invitation to speak, according to them, was a plot to entrap Sullivan as executive director of the Democratic National Committee, within a movement for Wallace, at a dinner the theme of which would be criticism of the Truman Doctrine.

Though it was close to three in the morning in Washington, I was urged to call Charlie Ross and ask for instructions.

I was reluctant to make the call. I said I didn't think Ross would appreciate being brought into the problem. I also felt that the whole thing became much more important if the White House was injected into the matter. But I was overruled. The "spanking" administered as a result of the Wallace-Pepper episode and the letter to Carroll Reece had left its mark; Gael didn't want to take any action without clearing with President Truman.

When Ross answered the telephone, he was impatient. He made the same points that I had made to Sullivan and, while I was in solid agreement, I could not, in loyalty, say that I had already advanced this argument. I could only press for some statement of position by Ross as representing White House opinion. I had a bad twenty minutes on the phone and the result was what I had expected.

"You're there on the spot," said Ross. "You know what the situation is. You make the decision. It isn't fair to the President to bring him into it personally. It's your problem and your decision."

That was that.

In Pauley's presence and with Scully sitting near by, Sullivan asked me, "What should we do?"

"There are two alternatives," I answered. "You can stay and take it, or you can get out of town. You don't want an open break with Roosevelt so if you're sure that he plans a Wallace coup, you can't attend. But if you don't attend, you've got to make your absence something which he can accept. In other words, you've got to fix it some way so that Roosevelt can save face."

"I won't attend," Sullivan told Pauley. "I'll get out of here right now. Redding will stay and handle the press and explain to Roosevelt why I couldn't stay for the dinner."

I blinked, but there it was.

Ed Pauley saw us to the car. Pauley asked if I thought he should duck the dinner too. On the contrary, I told him, he should go, sit at the head table as planned, but get involved in no controversy.

"If it gets hot, make no comment," I cautioned him.

Mike Fanning took us to the Ambassador Hotel to pick up Mrs. Sullivan, the Sullivans' luggage, and Bob Shaffer, who had gone to bed. As the car was being loaded, Sullivan gave me instructions.

He was going to Palm Springs. The next day I was to get the private plane and pick him up there. It had to be done secretly, for the story was to be that matters on the Hartley labor bill pending in the House of Representatives had made it necessary for Sullivan to fly back to Washington.

By five o'clock in the morning I was alone in a bungalow on the Ambassador Hotel grounds, with five bedrooms and a baronial sitting room. I felt like a die in a dice box.

I took the precaution of educating the bell boys with a couple of five-dollar bills that Sullivan and his party had gone to Washington. I felt sure some slue-foot newsman would be questioning the hotel staff before many hours passed. I talked to our pilot, rousing him from a sound sleep in his room at the Biltmore. He agreed to be at the airport at noon, ready to go.

I ordered some breakfast. It was too late to get any sleep, so I composed myself in the huge sitting room, waiting for the story to break wide open.

My plan was to wait until about ten, then call Roosevelt and break the news. After that, if things went according to plan, the press would descend upon me and I'd tell them my story.

About six the telephone rang. It was Ed Pauley. There was sand in the gearbox. Frank Rodgers, a reporter for the Los Angeles *Daily News,* knew about the meeting the night before, had actually been in the house.

"But," said Pauley, "Frank's all right, a nice fellow. He won't print the story."

His reasoning was a little loose, I thought. Being a nice fellow had nothing to do with not printing an exclusive story.

It developed that there was some hope that Rodgers didn't know the entire story. He knew Sullivan had been in the meeting, that there had been a call to, or from, Washington. And, of course, Rodgers, as a competent reporter, knew that those in the meeting represented the opposition to Roosevelt in Democratic state politics.

I determined to sweat it out on the planned line, but I realized that Rodgers was probably calling Roosevelt right then for a reaction. So there went a ten-o'clock curtain on my little show.

I called Ross. I briefed him on the problem, told him the White House would not be brought into the matter and explained how I planned to handle it. After a sound sleep, Charlie was more gracious than at my earlier call.

"I'm sorry," he apologized, "for talking to you the way I did. I realized after I hung up that you knew the problem, that you called me because you had to. You wouldn't make a mistake like that on your own."

69

I outlined the circumstances in detail and Ross was amused. "Maybe you'd have been better off if you had gone to Athens," he chuckled. Maybe Ross was right!

About eight, one of Chet Holifield's aides came in. Chet is one of the influential Democratic Congressmen from Los Angeles. It was obvious that his man knew Gael was no longer there, but I gave no information, merely thanking him for his offer of help. If it had been Congressman Holifield himself. I might have talked freely, but I saw no percentage in talking to an aide.

Then Roosevelt called. I didn't know Jimmie at that time, so I had no compunction about telling him my fabricated story. He was displeased and told me so.

Next the members of the press, six of them, came down on me like wolves on the fold. And I was the lone shorn lamb.

"Where is Sullivan?"

I looked at my watch. "Nearing Washington National Airport."

"Nuts!"

I looked hurt.

"Why is he ducking this dinner? Is this a split with Jim Roosevelt? A slight to Mrs. Roosevelt? How's she going to like this?"

"He's not ducking and the answer to the second question is no. As for Mrs. Roosevelt, I happen to know that Gael Sullivan thinks she is one of the great women of America. There's no truth to any talk of a slight to her. I'm sure the first thing he'll do in Washington will be to call Mrs. Roosevelt and make his explanation."

"What is the explanation?"

I tried out my labor-bill story. There were doubtful looks.

"You sure," queried one newsmen, "that Sullivan isn't hiding here in the bungalow?"

"Yeah," said another, "if he's gone why do you need five bedrooms?"

"I like movie starlets," I told him, "and I like lots of room." Then, with a grand gesture, I invited the press to search the joint. They did. It was obvious they didn't believe the story but since they were unable to shake it, they left.

The telephone rang again. It was Gladwin Hill, Los Angeles correspondent of the New York *Times*. He had been a war correspondent in Europe, where we had become friends. He wanted to come out and talk. Would I be there for a while? I said I would.

Five minutes later he knocked on my door. He'd called from the lobby and, after calling, watched the bungalow doorway to see if anyone skidded out. Later I found out that he had managed to check the long-distance telephone calls I had made but got no information other than to whom they were placed.

"Is Gael really gone?" he asked.

"Yes."

I told him the story about the labor bill.

"I don't buy that story," he said. "I think he's ducking and he's still out here somewhere."

He watched me but I sat tight.

"His plane's still at the airport." It was supposed to be a bombshell.

That was easy. "Sure, those fellows in the crew flew until late last night getting us out here. Naturally they couldn't turn around and fly right back again. Besides, the plane needed servicing. Gael's party went commercial and I'm taking the private plane back myself after the crew gets some sleep."

It was a reasonable story but he still didn't believe me.

"You know, if Sullivan's ducking you can't keep it shut up forever. It'll break sooner or later."

Shrugging, I told him that he was right on the beam. "That's the very reason why you ought to believe me. You know I've been around enough to know that. I'd be silly to try to fool the press on a simple matter like this. The answer is that I'm not fooling."

Hill was shaken but still doubtful. We fought the war over again for a time and then he left.

I called Frank Rodgers at the Los Angeles *Daily News*. "I

71

wish I had realized last night that you were a newsman," I said. "I had a story to give out and you could have had it exclusive."

"Yeah," he said, "I know."

"Just had a press conference here at the bungalow at the Ambassador," I said, ignoring the ominous tone of his answer. "I told the boys about Gael going back east last night."

Frank was interested in spite of himself. "You did? You told them that?"

"Sure." I took a deep breath. "Sure. After all, he's going to be around Congress all day today on the Hartley bill and some of the newsboys back there would be asking questions anyway. So I told them."

"You did?" Now he was uncertain. "You mean he didn't just duck out on the dinner?"

"Hell, no. Where'd you get that idea?"

"It wasn't hard. But can I quote you on this?"

The answer was, of course, "Yes." After a few more questions which cleared up the story from his standpoint, Rodgers rang off.

I found myself wringing wet from perspiration, took a shower and then called Ross at the White House to give him a guarded version of the results of the little plot.

I headed for the airport, where the plane crew was waiting. The bomber was still in the hangar, and we had company—four news photographers. They didn't want me. They were waiting for Sullivan.

At my request, the pilot filed an open-flight plan and the big plane took off. Less than an hour later we swooped into the old air force field at Palm Springs and picked up Gael, Mrs. Sullivan and Shaffer.

After the take-off I went to sleep and slept right through a thunderstorm. Later Gael told me he had never been so frightened.

"There was lightning all over us, even running up and down the wings."

"Was there a smell of brimstone?"

Gael looked at me, puzzled. "Well, yes. Now that you mention it, there was a strange smell."

I didn't tell him that what he smelled was ozone which is always present in electrical disturbances.

Instead, I said, "When you smell brimstone, you know the Devil is near. And I spent all morning lying like the Devil. He was probably looking over his new boy!"

CHAPTER 6

WE HAD GAINED NOTHING in the whole California dinner fiasco—not even definite knowledge that Roosevelt was planning to support Wallace—if he was.

True, we had been able to stave off a possible split; but our vacillation irritated Jimmie Roosevelt, for it was, of course, impossible to keep our movements concealed for long. However, by the time the truth was known, it was no longer worth a story.

The National Committee could not afford to take sides in California, for it was a vitally important state if Governor Dewey was to be the Republican candidate in 1948. If Dewey, as a native son, carried New York State, we had to carry California partially to offset New York's forty-five electoral votes.

At about this time the President enhanced his position by state visits to Brazil and to Canada. In both places he was enthusiastically received. In Brazil an incident occurred which might have had tragic consequences. On a motor trip into the mountains back of Rio de Janeiro, the President's car skidded on a turn with a precipice yawning on one side and a granite wall rising on the other. The driver of the President's car was an expert and no damage was done except to the nerves of the Secret Service men and the newsmen following the President's car.

74

At home the President spoke before a farm group in Kansas City where he damned Congress for cutting large sums from the Interior and Agriculture department budgets. The money had been earmarked for public power, reclamation and soil conservation. It was an important speech. The New York *Times* editorially applauded the President for his forthright stand and castigated the Republicans for what it termed "senseless" cuts.

Meanwhile in the House Ways and Means Committee, Republican Congressman Walter Ploeser of St. Louis opened fire on the farm co-operatives, demanding an end to the co-ops' tax-exempt status.

Thus the President, with an assist from GOP Congressman Ploeser, rammed home the opening wedge in the campaign to split the farm vote from the Republicans. Steve Harrington, of Brown & Bigelow, then a Democratic fund raiser in Minneapolis, immediately began to sound out the farm co-operative associations, and the results were encouraging.

After a six-day compromise session of the House-Senate conferees, the Taft-Hartley bill emerged as the final, somewhat modified version of the Republican anti-labor legislation.

At the same time there emerged a tax-reduction bill, based on the Republican formula of greater cuts for the wealthy and fewer for the average working man.

How the Republican leaders were ever persuaded to let these two explosive bills come to a head at the same time is hard to explain. But the fact that they did was grist for the Democratic mill; and that mill ground exceeding fine.

The tax bill was passed by a substantial margin but, after passage, it was conceded that there was little chance that the presidential veto would be overridden.

The Taft-Hartley bill was a different matter. In the House the vote on the Hartley bill had been 308-107. But we thought we might have a chance to muster enough votes in the Senate to sustain a veto. And here we had one breath of hope: on a motion to recommit the Taft bill, Democratic opponents of the bill mustered thirty-five votes in favor. If those votes could be held, an attempt to override a presidential veto would fail.

Every night there was a strategy meeting in the Carlton Hotel, generally attended by Lewis Schwellenbach, the Secretary of Labor, Under-Secretary of Labor Dave Morse, Clark Clifford, Oscar (Jack) Ewing of the Federal Security Administration, plus a revolving group of other interested leaders.

On the nights when there was no meeting of this labor group, I was attending other sessions, the most important of which was a group of Southern Democrats worrying about the upcoming report of the President's Commission on Civil Rights. It was an odd contrast of the ultra-liberal labor group on the one hand and the conservative Southern leaders on the other, all Democrats.

However, Taft-Hartley was the problem of the moment. On June 4, the House passed the modified version of the Taft-Hartley bill 320-79. Two days later the Senate voted for the bill 54-17. It looked very bad. But there was still hope of making that 35-vote total on the motion to recommit stand up to sustain a veto.

Now, with the legislation on the President's desk, work really began. It was somewhat amusing to watch the GOP candidates maneuvering. Stassen came out for the Taft-Hartley bill almost immediately. Governor Warren and Governor Dewey hesitated. Eventually they recognized the truth: it wasn't possible to hedge on the issue.

Finally aroused to its danger, labor was rallying its masses. In New York Mayor Bill O'Dwyer and Senator Murray of Montana addressed a crowd of 60,000 at Madison Square Garden. Rallies in Chicago, Pittsburgh, Allentown, Johnstown and in literally scores of other industrial cities loaded the congressional mails with petitions and resolutions. But the flood of labor opposition did not stem the tide; in fact, the tide seemed to swell against labor. Votes began slipping away.

A most serious factor in the erosion of our thirty-five votes was a series of wildcat strikes in the coal industry that broke out in protest against the Taft-Hartley bill. They could not have been more poorly timed. They inflamed anti-labor sentiment and, as the wildcat strikes spread, the possibility of upholding a veto became less and less likely.

The weather was hot; tempers were hotter. President Truman became "that man" in the White House, just as Roosevelt did before him.

Truman made history with his veto of the Taft-Hartley bill. He pointed out the faults of the bill in strong, well-reasoned language. At a luncheon with Senators he explained further his reasons for a veto. Finally he sent a letter to Minority Leader Alben Barkley calling for the veto to be sustained. No President ever worked harder to sustain his veto.

It looked as if we might hold thirty of the thirty-five votes we hoped for. Since a full vote of the Senate was unlikely, thirty-two votes, a constitutional one-third of the total Senate membership, might prove to be enough. However, the extra two decisive votes would have to come from Senator Elbert Thomas of Utah, who was in Switzerland attending a conference of the United Nations International Labor Organization, and Senator Robert Wagner of New York, who was on his deathbed.

There also was a possibility that bringing Senator Wagner into the Senate chamber on a stretcher to cast his vote might, in view of his enormous prestige as author of the Wagner Act, swing other votes against the Taft-Hartley bill.

First I called Senator Thomas in Geneva. Would he fly home to vote if I could get a special plane? He would! I called the Air Force and asked for a flight to be set up from Paris to Washington. The Air Force was willing to co-operate with a senatorial request, but . . . I assured them that the plane's operating costs would be paid.

Then we had the problem of getting the Senator from Geneva to Paris in time to make the transatlantic flight. To complicate matters a tremendous fog closed in over Western Europe. Orly

Field in Paris was socked-in. No commercial flights were being made. Then an Air Force officer volunteered to make the flight from Paris to Geneva and return on a combination GCA-ILS basis, if Senator Thomas was willing to take the risk. GCA, Ground Controlled Approach, and ILS, Instrument Landing System, were both in a doubtful stage of development at that time.

Senator Thomas was willing, with one proviso. We had to assure him that his vote could reasonably be expected to be decisive. I promised that we would not require him to make the flight unless we were convinced we had at least thirty votes without him. Meanwhile, the Air Force set up its planes on a stand-by basis.

Senator Wagner was yet another problem. It was not generally known that the Senator was on his deathbed. His passing was merely a matter of time, dependent on how long his remarkable vitality could keep him alive. Senator Wagner was a man of iron resolution. Through his son, now Mayor of New York, the Senator replied that he would come to Washington for the vote, "If my vote is the decisive one."

Young Wagner was indignant and protested that this would kill his father, but in the end he bowed to his father's will. We decided to charter a special train. The Senator would be loaded into the car through the windows and taken out the same way on arrival in Washington. We arranged for an ambulance with oxygen to be at Union Station ready to take this gallant man to the Capitol.

Heartless? Yes. But the whole plan was predicated simply and wholly on the willingness of the Senator to take the risk. We had been told that the attempt might kill him. We were also told that the Senator was willing to die, if die he must, in casting the deciding vote.

The deadline for departure of Senator Thomas was midnight of June 26. Fog still lay over western Europe; it would have to be a GCA-ILS flight with all the attendant risks.

I sat in my office in the Mayflower with a wire open to Geneva and Paris; the telephone costs were fabulous. Gael was on the Hill making a last-minute check of our chances to muster the needed thirty votes.

Midnight came with no decision, but Gael was still hopeful. We decided to wait until two o'clock in the morning, knowing we could get a delay in the Senate vote if Senator Thomas were actually on his way. In New York arrangements for the special Wagner train were set. The Senator could leave the city as late as noon and still be present at the voting.

One o'clock, one-thirty, two, two-fifteen.

Gael's voice, tired and discouraged, came over the phone. "Tear them down," he said. "Tear them down. It's no go. We've lost ground instead of gaining. No use killing one Senator and risking another for a lost cause . . ." His voice trailed off. Then he said briefly, "Wait for me. I'll be right in."

I cancelled all arrangements, and after a short ten minutes Sullivan was in the office. He had little to say. We sat around for about two hours grunting at each other and finally gave up.

The next day the United States Senate overrode the President's veto of the Taft-Hartley bill, 68-25.

The defeat seemed like the end of the world. Yet, in retrospect, I realize that vote probably was one of the major factors in President Truman's election in 1948. An already aroused labor movement became embattled.

In upstate New York, J. Russel Sprague, the Republican National Committeeman for New York, introduced Governor Thomas E. Dewey to a silk-stocking audience as "the next President of the United States." Dewey did not protest.

We had the Taft record firmly before the people with Dewey almost certainly committed to run on it. The Hannegan strategy was paying off.

CHAPTER 7

THE PRESIDENT had made his record on the Taft-Hartley Act and on the Knutson tax cut. These two vetoes brought approval from millions of people. Furthermore, organized labor knew how hard the Democratic National Committee had tried to defeat the hated Taft-Hartley Act.

The tax veto was upheld. A Gallup poll had shown that a majority of the people were willing to forego a tax cut if a substantial payment was made on the national debt. However, the main factor in defeating the bill was the controversial formula for the cut—favoring the wealthy.

Meanwhile the Democrats had lost still another legislative battle: the attempt to preserve a really effective rent-control law. The real estate lobby put over a bill which permitted landlords to raise rents by 15 per cent.

We pointed out to the voters that through the Republican tax cut a stenographer earning $2,500 a year would gain only $67 in take-home pay on a full year basis. The Republican mock rent-control bill would raise her rent by at least $75 a year. This combination caught on.

Rent hogs all over the country found loopholes in the so-called rent-control law as soon as it was passed. They went wild. In New York 50-per-cent increases in rent were common and some went as high as 125 per cent. In Denver a man making $170 a month found his rent raised to $240. In St. Louis, boosts up to

200 per cent were reported. In a Los Angeles apartment house the landlord raised rents from $45 a month to $125. In Philadelphia a hotel raised its rent to permanent guests by 400 per cent.

The National Association of Real Estate Boards wrote its members: "It is important that every realtor understand the law so that we may take full advantage of its privileges."

The combination of proposed "soak the poor" tax cuts, the anti-labor Taft-Hartley Act, the "rent-control" law resulting in tremendous raises in rents across the country, plus the Real Estate Boards' blatant bragging, made potent reading, particularly for people in the lower and medium wage brackets.

To tell this story, the Democratic Committee also took full advantage of every opportunity to put Democratic speakers on the air in radio debates. It appeared that Republican spokesmen were hard to come by, however. On many shows we had to forego our chances to appear because the Republicans could not produce a man to debate on their side.

Senator Taft was the one exception. He believed in what he stood for and was willing to stand up and be counted. But the strain was beginning to tell on him. His temper became increasingly short, culminating in a real tantrum in the Mutual Broadcasting System studios.

The occasion was a radio debate between Democratic Senators John Sparkman of Alabama and Joseph O'Mahoney of Wyoming, and Republican Senator Taft and former Senator John Danaher of Connecticut, to be followed with a fifteen-minute telephone poll made in an agreed area. In this instance the subject of the debate was: "Are the Republicans in Congress doing a good job?" The poll area was Pittsburgh. Result: 62 per cent of those polled voted "no."

When Taft saw the trend of the poll, he lost his temper. To Mutual officials who tried to placate him he said the whole thing was a Democratic plot, aided and abetted by network officials who had refused to allow him to talk first, and last. Then he said the poll wasn't run properly. Then he blamed me for "fixing" the poll. Finally he stormed out in a towering rage.

The results of this poll were particularly galling to the Republicans because, after the previous week's debate on the question, "Is the Truman Administration doing a good job?" voters in the poll answered in the affirmative by 57 per cent.

Late in July we decided the time had come to go directly to the American people without having to find some Republicans with which to debate the issues on the air.

I asked the National Broadcasting Company for a half hour of sustaining time on which to hold the first nationwide political meeting in history. NBC refused.

The Columbia Broadcasting System was unable to find time available, a more polite turndown. But the American Broadcasting Company agreed to give us the time, on September 3. The period allotted was excellent: from 9:30 to 10:00 P.M. Eastern Standard Time.

Sam Brightman and I started to build the show. We gathered speakers from various parts of the nation, all of them important. We asked them to talk on basic issues. To get a technically perfect program, timed to the last split second, we ghosted all of the scripts and sent them to the participants for review or change with the stipulation that they could neither lengthen nor cut them.

This part was simple enough. But to make news and influence public opinion, we needed help from the party. Through *Capital Comment,* press releases, telephone calls, telegrams and other forms of communication, we promoted Democratic meetings in 2,981 counties across the country, set up for the express purpose of listening to the broadcast. In Ohio, listening parties had been arranged in every one of the 8,800 precincts in the state. The number of people who sat in on a meeting—three, five, ten— didn't matter. As I recall, the largest meeting was in Ohio: 150 persons, with speeches by local leaders before and after the broadcast.

82

We were using every public-relations technique and all media to focus attention on our program. It was an adaptation of a basic principle of war: concentration of force.

The night of the broadcast, the show clicked along beautifully. Each speaker's spot came to a close right on the button. Switches from studio to studio in different cities were made with dispatch and precision.

We had issued a press release about the broadcast, hailing it as the first nationwide political meeting of the air and including, as a backup, full scripts from each of our seven speakers. Our publicity results far exceeded even our own rosy expectations. The Baltimore *Sun* had it on page one with a five-column head. The New York *Times* had a column and a half reading out of page one. The Washington *Post* broke the story in a two-column head on page one and used a total of about a column. The Chicago *Tribune* carried the story big, inside. The Scripps-Howard newspapers, rabidly anti-Democratic, carried a full column nationally. The wire services used the story, quoting liberally from each speaker on national wires; and all news services carried regional stories leading with our regional speakers.

The *Times* told the story of the broadcast in detail: "The broadcast, first nationwide radio political meeting in history, originated from seven cities."

Acting as master of ceremonies, Gael Sullivan opened the program by introducing Mayor William O'Dwyer of New York, who declared the people would not let "the Republican Party turn back the clock." The show shifted to Helen Gahagan Douglas in Los Angeles, who scored the Eightieth Congress for "ordering an investigation to see if prices were too high when every paper's advertisements told the truth."

Hubert Humphrey, then Mayor of Minneapolis, declared that "the full story of the Eightieth Congress will show the farmer of America has suffered more at the hands of reaction than any other group."

Senator John Sparkman of Alabama came from Birmingham

to denounce the housing policies of the GOP. "The veterans," he said, "will take Congress away from the real estate lobby in 1948 and return it to the people."

Next Sullivan called on Marshall Hanley of Indianapolis, president of the Young Democrats, who outlined an "organize to win" campaign for young party workers.

Speaking from Philadelphia, Senator Francis J. Myers of Pennsylvania said the "Republicans seek to drag the nation back to the dog-eat-dog economy of the Harding and Coolidge administrations." He concluded by accenting the necessity for registration and voting.

The last speaker was Senator Brien McMahon of Connecticut. Broadcasting from Washington, he declared that the "nationwide unity of purpose resulted from sound policy devised and advanced by President Truman," and warned of the dangers of an atomic war if there was a breach in our bipartisan foreign policy.

Not only did we get a tremendous press, there was also a very successful secondary play on radio newscasts. Seven radio stations in Wisconsin alone rebroadcast the show during the following week. In all, twenty-three rebroadcasts were made.

Exclusive of the Roosevelt fireside chats, no single political radio show had ever made such an impact. We were so pleased we made up for internal consumption a press book that showed us in every daily paper in America, plus a considerable advance play in weeklies and biweeklies. We estimated that in some form our program—either the show itself or news stories or other radio shows about it—had reached sixty-three million Americans. *Time* Magazine reviewed the show extensively in their radio department and quoted Sullivan as "saying happily, 'We have a technique we'll use again and again.' "

By this time we had the initiative by radio, and our field organization was functioning with a word-of-mouth campaign. It would be bragging to say that all this was the single-handed work of the National Committee. First, of course, we had the President aggressively creating a splendid program and defending it in such a way as to make the very best record for the Democratic Party. Then we had the Republicans themselves, with incredible stupidity, adding to their already bad record.

It was practically impossible for Bill Murphy, the Republican publicity chief, to take the offensive. And when he did, Carroll Reece, his spokesman, was continually putting his foot in his mouth. Typical was the reaction to Reece's criticism of President Truman for not being just a rubber stamp for the Eightieth Congress.

"Reece," editorialized the New York *Times,* "is an albatross around the neck of the Republican party. There should be a longer interval between what he says."

Finally Senator Taft himself was adding to the Republican dilemma. For instance, at Senate hearings on the Marshall Plan, Taft, opposing the plan on the basis that the United States economy could not stand the load, said, "Apparently the President and the Administration are abandoning talk of keeping prices down in favor of spending abroad that will keep them up."

The press reported the comment and then criticized Taft as an "isolationist." At a press conference the next day President Truman denounced Senator Taft by name as an exponent of "the boom-and-bust" school of economics.

Taft lost his temper and rejoined with a bitter tirade which revolved around the statement that the President was trying to "veto the law of supply and demand."

The honors were even. But the impression made on the nation was one of the President trying to bring about good times at home and peace abroad; and, in contrast, Taft bad-temperedly talking about high prices in a way that seemed to approve of them and, in general, deriding that which Truman was supporting.

I am sure that Taft was espousing economic theories in which he really believed. But he was in an unpopular position and his stubborn insistence on having his say continued to hurt his chances and the chances of any other Republican.

CHAPTER 8

UNDER THE STIMULUS of Sullivan's pressure, the organization drive was making headway. First impetus came through the so-called "thought-control clinics," which brought in different state Democratic leaders every week to meet with the President. The ostensible purpose of this meeting was to bring about a closer relationship between party leaders and the man in the White House.

Actually the White House visit was the lure that brought these men and women into Washington where Sullivan could get at them with his organization plans. Not many people would come to Washington for the mere purpose of talking politics, especially when much of the talk verged on criticism of their own efforts. But the prospect of a visit with the President brought them.

As a prestige builder it was a natural. To enhance that prestige, no stones were left unturned. State newspapers were informed from Washington when the invitations went out. Stories were released again when the group arrived in Washington. Pictures were taken and sent back to the home-town papers. And almost always members of the group were interviewed by the White House press when they came out of their presidential conference. All this was balm for the political ego.

Attendance of such political bigwigs as Ed Kelly from Chicago, Mayor Dave Lawrence of Pittsburgh, Bill Malone of San

86

Francisco, Frank Hague of New Jersey, and other well-known men made the conferences sure-fire national political stories as well. This meant a healthy traffic in news stories about Democratic activity.

After the White House build-up, state and local leaders would adjourn to the committee offices where Sullivan and I would tackle them on organization and on publicity materials. These meetings were unsung and unnoticed, but they were a vital payoff.

When finally seated at the conference table with Sullivan, a state political leader's almost automatic reaction was to make patronage demands. This was the signal for Sullivan to lower the boom.

Prepared charts of state, city or county in question—charts which showed dropoffs in the Democratic vote in 1946—were whisked out and put on a display board. The figures were analyzed. The answer to the patronage demands was, "Why? What have you done?"

As an example, when Pleas Greenlee, the bombastic, red-faced state chairman from Indiana, arrived in Washington, he spouted off to the Indiana newsmen in the capital that he would get "more postmasters" and followed with a general list of all the other things he was going to "demand." In the White House he took the floor during the visit to the President to make more of the same "demands." At the committee meeting afterward, he continued his campaign.

But when the charts came out and the figures were presented for cold analysis, Greenlee's demands collapsed. He became quiet. After the situation had been spelled out in detail, he shrugged. "I guess that answers what I had to say about jobs. But," he promised, regaining some of his aggressiveness, "we'll organize. We'll turn out a vote. I'll be back. And when I do come back, I want those jobs!"

Sullivan was too smart to let such a man go away empty-handed. After all the shouting was done, when the "organize"

87

lesson had been driven home, he privately released what patronage he could so that everyone went home happy.

We worked out with the members of each group the use of publicity material. Circulation of *Capital Comment* boomed. Further, in meeting these leaders face to face, we were able to assess them; determine how to evaluate their reactions, their manner of reporting political situations. The result was not only better organization and more widespread use of publicity materials but also an improved intelligence and communications system within the party.

We began to expand our system of asking for advice from party leaders on current issues by telegram or by telephone or, if time permitted, by letter. If it was a letter, it was always sent air mail, special delivery. The response to this was wholehearted and enthusiastic.

The fruits of this effective organization work showed up immediately, particularly in better response from leaders and in vigorous registration drives.

There was a secondary result, for Sullivan. His campaign to succeed Hannegan as National Chairman, when Bob resigned, made progress. Party leaders from the states were flattered by his requests for advice. In general, they were solidly in his corner.

Of course Sullivan realized this support was more apparent than real, for while a party is in power the national chairmanship is only technically an elective office. Actually the chairman is personally selected by the President and the choice is confirmed by the National Committee in a *pro forma* vote. Sullivan tried to use the approval of party leaders to "influence" President Truman and those around him in the White House so that when the President was ready to make a selection, Sullivan would be the natural man to choose.

Others were competing for the job and there were signs that Sullivan's star was not waxing. Secretary of Agriculture Clinton

Anderson was an open candidate for the committee chairmanship. Bill Boyle of Kansas City was mentioned, as were Paul Fitzpatrick, New York state chairman, and Oscar Chapman, Under Secretary of the Interior Department. There were others.

Sullivan's bid for power was dramatic and imaginative but, as it turned out, doomed to failure.

An accident involving a drunken driving charge finished him as a candidate. The fact that Sullivan actually was not drunk, did not even drink, made no difference. The charge was made and the story was printed nationwide and never successfully refuted.

The incident occurred in the early morning hours on a Sunday in the late summer. Gael left Washington by car, driving to New York where he spent several hours in conference with New York leaders. After dinner with Toots Shor, a close friend, Gael started out for his summer place at Narragansett Pier, Rhode Island. It was nearly eleven o'clock when he left New York. He had had only a few hours of sleep the night before, no rest during the day and, by that time, had some 275 miles and several hours of political conferences behind him.

Nearing his destination, he dozed at the wheel. After unconscious seconds, he awoke to find headlights from an oncoming car glaring in his eyes. He wrenched the wheel, grazed the other car and went into the ditch, scraped along a stone wall for about a hundred feet and stopped.

No one was hurt. Damage to the two automobiles was superficial. Local police arrived and took both drivers into the station to fill out an accident report. Gael was in shock and his replies were incoherent. When his identity became known, he was called a drunk. He denied it and then refused to say anything more until he had an attorney. Later he explained to me that he knew the local township was violently pro-Republican and he feared that he was being framed.

But his refusal to explain and to demand an alcohol test cost him dear. He was put in a cell and a local correspondent for the Providence *Journal* turned in the story. Of course, the charge of drunken driving was never proved but Sullivan had his license suspended for "reckless driving."

The national press did a scalp dance over Sullivan. The fact that drunkenness was not proved never caught up with the original charge printed in the papers. Sullivan's enemies in Washington and his rivals for the national chairmanship made hay in the White House. Ross called me and asked if the story were true.

Late Sunday afternoon I went to the White House and gave a complete report on the entire incident. My talks with Shor and others in New York developed the fact that he had not been drinking during the evening before the crash. From my personal knowledge Sullivan had not had even one drink in five months. But personal assurances from me were not enough to repair the damage. Sullivan was judged and found guilty and his sentence was to be passed over for the chairmanship.

Not long thereafter Hannegan made up his mind to retire. He stanchly demanded that Sullivan be given the post to succeed him, but was overruled. The night the decision was made, Hannegan came to the committee office about nine o'clock after an afternoon and evening session with the President. Bob was in a towering rage.

As soon as he saw me, he burst out, "You, Redding, you're going to be the next presidential press secretary."

I couldn't credit my ears. Not knowing anything of what had happened, I asked, "Has Charlie Ross resigned?"

"No, not yet. But you're going to be the next press secretary."

I took a deep breath. "Bob, there's nothing I'd like more than to be press secretary to the President. But Charlie Ross is my friend and I wouldn't touch the job unless he asked me to take it. No other way. I'd quit first!"

Hannegan stared at me. "Do you mean it?"

"Yes."

"Well," he said, "I guess that tears it." And he turned away.

He never discussed the matter with me again. I never knew what had triggered his offer of the job. I never even knew whether he had the offering of the job. And, of course, I never said anything to Ross about it.

A few nights later Hannegan broke the news to Gael that Senator J. Howard McGrath of Rhode Island had been selected by the President as the new chairman. Since he had never been mentioned in speculations about the job, the news came as a complete surprise to me and to most others.

Hannegan and Sullivan telephoned national committeemen in all of the states. I sat down at the typewriter and banged out first a formal call for a meeting of the National Committee; next, put out a bulletin to the wire services that the committee meeting was being called; then wrote a story that Hannegan was resigning and the President had selected Senator McGrath to fill his shoes.

I listened as Hannegan called leader after leader, telling them of the upcoming committee meeting, of his own decision to resign and of the selection of McGrath to succeed him. Then Hannegan concluded his conversation with each one, "I want you to promise me that you'll vote for McGrath. I want to tell you that this is the President's urgent wish."

Sullivan then picked up the phone to add his own plea for votes for McGrath. Each time he did so, I could feel the knife turning in Gael's wound, but his voice never wavered.

It was long after midnight when the task was completed. Hannegan and Sullivan talked for a few minutes. Then Gael came into my office and on my typewriter tapped out his resignation. He took it back in to Hannegan.

I sat down at the typewriter and wrote out my own one-line resignation, took it in and laid it down on top of Gael's longer one. Hannegan read both letters.

To me he said, "Take this back. No one is going to do anything with it. You can't quit. I appreciate the offer as a genuine compliment to me and to Gael; but your loyalty is to the President, not to me. It isn't necessary for you to make the gesture. Just sit tight."

To Gael he said, "The boss won't take it, Gael, but you've got to offer it."

"Has anyone told McGrath that he's the guy?" I asked. Hannegan looked up, then laughed as he said, "No! I was supposed to do it and, making all these calls, I forgot. The President will talk to him but I've got to get hold of Howard and have him call the White House if he hasn't already."

He picked up the telephone and called McGrath. "Howard, have you heard the news? . . . Oh? . . . You have? . . . You've talked to the President? . . . Well, fine! And congratulations . . . It's a tremendous responsibility and I know you're the man to do the job."

I signaled to him and he covered the mouthpiece. I said, "Tell the Senator that the press will be all over him. If he wants, I'll call a press conference for tomorrow in his office or here at the committee office, as he prefers. That will ease the pressure."

Hannegan nodded, turned back to the telephone. "Howard, you ought to have a press conference tomorrow. You call it or, if you like, I'll have Redding do it. . . . Okay, Jack will get on it right now. Good night."

The next morning McGrath met the press in his Senate office. I was present, feeling isolated and ineffective, for I knew McGrath only casually.

The Senator outlined the President's request. Of course he was accepting. It was a great honor.

"I told the President," he added, "that I would take on the responsibility only on condition that Gael Sullivan, my old friend from Rhode Island, stay on in his present post as Executive Director of the committee. The President agreed that we could not afford to lose Gael's services and he will so tell Sullivan today. I sincerely hope that Gael will not insist on his resignation

92

being accepted. He has too much to offer the Democratic Party."

When the press conference broke up Senator McGrath asked me to stay behind. "We'll confer later," he told me. "I don't want to make any changes in staff—at least not at present."

My response was perhaps prompted by temper. "My resignation was turned in too. I hope you'll act on it quickly." Then I left. It had been a rough time.

CHAPTER 9

ONE OF SULLIVAN'S accomplishments for which, ironically, he got little credit, was the reconciliation between Alexander Fell Whitney, President of the Brotherhood of Railroad Trainmen, and President Truman. It was a hat trick that no one would have believed possible, for the close friendship between Whitney and Truman had changed to bitter enmity.

This enmity grew out of the railroad strike of 1946. The President had gone before a joint session of Congress to announce that, in the face of a railroad strike which had stopped the wheels of the nation, he was seizing control of the railroads and was asking legal power to draft railroad employees into the United States Army. This dramatic statement was interrupted by Secretary of the Senate Les Biffle, who delivered a message to the President on the rostrum. The message informed the President that a settlement of the strike had been effected.

Whitney charged that the President had known of the settlement before he started to address the Congress; that the dramatic interruption was prearranged, and that the President was a "ham actor."

President Truman characterized Whitney as "un-American" and as an "enemy of the people." Whitney, in turn, said, "You can't make a President out of a ribbon clerk."

In a voice quavering with rage, Whitney told a press conference: "The trainmen will spend every penny in their treasury [some forty million dollars] to defeat this man for President." That was May 1946. In March 1947, Walter Monroe, formerly an assistant to Mr. Whitney, resigned his federal post as a labor conciliator in the Mediation Service, to return to the Brotherhood of Trainmen in his old role. His purpose was to bring about, if possible, a reconciliation between President Truman and Whitney.

Monroe told Sullivan, "There's no reason why these two men should be apart. The difference comes from the action of some of his advisers who bungled that strike situation. It's up to you and me to bring about a settlement."

Gael grasped at the opportunity. For weeks Gael, Monroe and I schemed to arrive at some basis for a settlement which would allow both men to forget the past and to do so with no loss of stature. There was a great deal of i-dotting and t-crossing but finally we reached what looked like an agreement in principle.

Monroe took what we had hammered out back to Whitney. Gael undertook to sell the proposal to the President. Both were successful.

The basis for agreement was simple: merely to forget the past and start afresh on the problems of the next presidential campaign where the true interests of the trainmen lay—with the Democratic Party.

Then in August, at a dinner on the Washington Hotel roof, Whitney told Gael, "This is fine. I'll go along all the way. I hope Harry will do the same. But one thing—" and he shook a finger under Sullivan's nose— "I will not take the initiative!"

That seemed to stymie the project. How could we explain a meeting as not being the result of Whitney's "initiative" and at the same time keep it from looking like weak supplication on the part of the President? There seemed no answer and for a time the project lapsed.

While this was in suspension, the problem of the site of the Democratic National Convention in 1948 came to a head. There was a prospect that Philadelphia would put up $200,000 if the Democrats selected the Quaker City. But there wasn't a definite offer. Atlantic City had made some vague gestures but really didn't mean it. The timing of the convention would place it right in the middle of the summer resort season and the Atlantic City hotels didn't need the business then. Chicago showed no interest.

We needed competition that would transpose the tentative Philadelphia proposal into a hard proposition. Hannegan was in San Francisco. He had the idea that if San Francisco got into the act, we could force a firm bid from Philadelphia.

I was called in and told of the difficulty, then asked if San Francisco would make a good convention site from the publicity angle.

My answer was no. The time differential was too great. We'd lose much of our public attention simply because the time difference of three hours would put our newsworthy events at unworkable hours for effective press and radio coverage.

But we could do it if we had to?

If we had to, I agreed.

Gael said, "Hannegan has an offer of $150,000 and six thousand rooms. Can you arrange for a story on it?"

I called my close friend, Clancy McQuigg, then night city editor of the San Francisco *Examiner*. It was eight o'clock in the morning in Washington, and 5:00 A.M. in California. I told Clancy of the San Francisco bid and suggested, "Hannegan is at the St. Francis Hotel. Get him up. He'll talk."

"Anyone else got the story?" McQuigg asked.

"No, it's exclusive if you get Hannegan now."

"If I get him out of bed, will he talk?"

"He'll talk," I assured him, "and if you hit him for it, he'll hold any announcement until after your home edition tomorrow."

Within ten minutes a reporter and a photographer were hammering on Hannegan's door. The *Examiner's* exclusive story created a stir and accomplished the objective. For a time, I had qualms, feeling that perhaps I had sold my friend a phony. But when the National Committee met in Washington to make the decision, San Francisco did make a solid bid through Mrs. Elinor Heller, the Democratic National Committeewoman from California. Philadelphia topped Mrs. Heller's offer with its $200,000 check, and the higher bid was accepted.

To return to the Whitney project, Walter Monroe had kept on with his attempts to persuade Whitney to relent. The effects of the Taft-Hartley Act, the rent-control law and other Republican legislation finally changed Whitney's mind. We held another dinner session, again on the Washington Hotel roof. This time Whitney signified his willingness to "go all the way."

Meanwhile Howard McGrath had become Chairman of the National Committee. Sullivan and McGrath agreed to call on the President to make the arrangements. They met no opposition at the White House and the meeting was set for the following afternoon.

Whitney agreed that he would go to the White House and make his bid for peace, then he was to return to the National Committee offices, now in new headquarters in the Ring Building, for a press conference. He had indeed consented to "go all the way."

Whitney and Monroe were to go to the White House together while McGrath, Sullivan and I stayed at the office for the press conference to follow.

At the last minute Whitney made a change in the plan. "Monroe will go to the White House and wait for me there," he decided. "I'll go over alone."

The white-haired, blue-eyed, fiery Whitney was a proud, devout man. His language was picturesque, and he was a fighter with a keen sense of the dramatic. He was also a stubborn man and it was a very large and bitter pill he had agreed to swallow.

He walked to the White House. At the east entrance he stopped but he didn't go in. Instead he continued walking, first toward

97

the Potomac and then all the way round the White House grounds. Arriving at the east entrance again, he paused but then resumed walking. Once more he completely circled the White House grounds.

Later he told Monroe and me: "I was rehearsing what I was going to say. I realized that to do the right thing I'd have to make some form of an apology. And I had to phrase it and pray over it before I could get up my courage."

Finally, having completed two circuits of the grounds, he stalked into the White House proper. He was ushered immediately into the President's office. But let me tell it as Whitney later told it to me:

"The President was the most gracious man I've ever seen. When I entered the room, he got up from behind his desk and came to the door. He offered his hand and said, 'It's good to see you, Al. You're looking wonderful.'

"I was all ready with my little speech, all ready to apologize. But Harry Truman was too big a man. He wouldn't let me do it.

"Before I could start into the speech I had rehearsed, he waved it aside. 'Let's not waste time discussing the past,' he said to me. 'Let's just agree we both received some bad advice. Instead, let's talk about the important things—the future, the campaign and the rights of labor.'

"I had walked in there," Whitney told me, "red-faced, expecting to humble myself, embarrassed. But Harry Truman was too big a man to let me be embarrassed."

The two men talked for about half an hour. As the talk neared an end, the President rose from his desk. Stepping over to Whitney, he said, "Al, I remember back in Missouri, when I was running for the United States Senate and there wasn't a soul who seemed to care whether I made it or not, that one organization and one man came forward to help. It was the Trainmen and the man named Whitney. I've never forgotten that."

There was a little more talk as these two men who had been

friends for years settled their differences. As they parted, both men were literally in tears.

[*John Steelman was the man responsible for sending word to the Senate on the railroad settlement in 1946 and was prominent in the reconciliation proceedings with Whitney.*—HST] In the hallway outside the President's office, Whitney was waylaid by the White House correspondents. He brushed them aside saying brusquely that he was meeting the press at the Democratic National Committee offices where he would be prepared to answer questions. Until then he had nothing to say.

One reporter, more aggressive than the others, demanded loudly, "I thought, Mr. Whitney, that you once said you would spend forty million dollars to defeat this man whom you've just talked to and who you say will be elected President once more. And now you're going to help him?"

Whitney shook his white mane and roared, "If I were a young man like you with the great opportunities that exist in the newspaper business before me, I'd stay away from the morgue and past history and get in on the development of new news!" He went on, "I'm telling you that Harry S Truman will be the candidate of the Democratic Party and he will be elected President. I propose to devote my time and effort to bringing that about because I think his election is in the best interests of the nation."

We held a press conference, but Whitney had said his piece. However, the matter was threshed out at length at Democratic headquarters with McGrath and Whitney sitting together at the head of the conference table and scores of newsmen facing them.

This story was developed in more detail here but there was little essential change from Whitney's White House declaration.

The reconciliation was a dramatic success, a strategic political triumph and helped immeasurably in the campaign which followed. For Whitney never reneged. He campaigned up and down the country, speaking, arguing, fighting, always for Truman and the Democratic Party. He contributed money personally—not much, for Whitney was not a wealthy man—and, more important, he raised money in large sums from friends and associates.

As a sidelight to this incident, Ed Lahey of the Chicago Daily *News* broke a story the next day to the effect that the payoff "exacted" by Whitney from the President for his change of heart was the appointment of Walter Monroe to the National Mediation Board. Monroe read the article and was incensed.

He called Sullivan, saying, "This story is an outrage. You know it and I know it. I want you to know that I'm calling A. T. Burch, editor of the Chicago Daily *News*. I'll denounce the story as a damn lie and demand a retraction."

Gael let Monroe finish his piece and then said, "Don't be hasty, Walter. There's something you don't know. After the meeting I took Mr. Whitney to the railroad station. He told me he thought that you should get some recognition for your services. I suggested the National Mediation Board and he thought that was good. He didn't exact it from me and he never mentioned it to the President. But I did. And the President agreed."

Monroe refused the job. He said, "I did what I did because I thought it was only right and honest. These men had no business being apart. I want no reward and I'll take no reward. And I'll not be put in the position of confirming the Chicago Daily *News* story."

So, at Monroe's insistence, the plan was dropped. Later Monroe was offered a place on the National Labor Relations Board but he also refused that.

CHAPTER 10

WITH A NEW Chairman and the convention city selected, the political fire burned hotter and hotter. Secretary of State Marshall had made his historic speech at Harvard calling for massive aid to Europe—the Marshall Plan—in June. But no enabling legislation had been enacted by Congress during its first session. Inflation was becoming a major factor in the national economy but the Eightieth Congress did nothing about this either.

President Truman called a special session of Congress for November 17 to consider these two important matters which bore so greatly on the safety and welfare of the nation.

The Marshall Plan proposal further excited Wallace and his left-wing, peace-at-any-price followers; it became increasingly evident that there would be a third-party movement headed by the former Vice President. Trouble also had developed on the right. The President's Civil Rights Commission had made its report and the South was up in arms.

The President's popularity, as marked by the Gallup poll, was high, with 56 per cent saying the Administration was doing a good job. But the dissatisfaction within both left and right wings of the Democratic Party, engendered by Wallace and the civil-rights issue, started a downward trend.

At committee headquarters, the pounding on Senator Taft

101

increased. He was now "Mr. High-Button Shoes" and his some-what remarkable statement that "employment in 1950 should be at about the same level as in 1900" was hailed by Democrats as evidence that he had just heard of the sinking of the battleship *Maine*.

In contrast to the incessant pressure on Taft as the leader of the Republican Party, Tom Dewey of New York was being given the "damn with faint praise treatment."

The handling of a Dewey television speech, in which he came out wholeheartedly for ski trails, was typical. We used extensive quotes from the comments of radio critic John Crosby who said, among other things: ". . . Dewey exhibited himself briefly . . . last week in a speech concerning proposed amendments to the state constitution. It was the sort of speech which Mr. Dewey, a man keenly reluctant to become pinned down on the larger issues, does very well.

"The Governor spoke spiritedly on the needs for an amend-ment to permit the state to construct ski trails in its forest pre-serves. 'The health of the citizenry,' he said, 'would be greatly enhanced if they were permitted greater access to winter sports.' "

Crosby remarked that Dewey "still sounds a little stuffy, and his talks, smooth as they are, remain oddly unexciting."

We quarreled good-naturedly with Crosby, saying, "Stuffy? Uninteresting? Why, even Stassen hasn't stated his program on ski runs. Dewey has finally scored a first."

Dewey on the art of cooking was headed: "Dewey wears no man's bib." And we revealed he had come out four-square for better-cooked home meals.

Deadly serious was the response to Republican attempts to change the tax-exempt status of farm co-operatives. Howard McGrath assured the farm co-ops that the Democratic Party was unwavering in its support of the principle of co-operative buying and selling that had improved the small farmer's ability to bar-gain for better prices. Later Secretary of Agriculture Clinton Anderson, in a full-dress speech made after a conference with

102

President Truman, gave all-out support to the embattled co-ops.

Off-year election campaigns were now being waged with the two national parties making few claims before the voting. In Kentucky, Democrats were making a strong campaign to recapture the Governor's office which was held by a Republican. Earle C. Clements, later a Senator, was the Democratic candidate and seemed to be well out in front in the race. At the last moment he suddenly suffered the well-known Democratic ailment of lack of funds. In Washington, Gael Sullivan raised a cash contribution of $20,000 which had to be taken to Kentucky immediately to pay workers' expenses at the polls and to pay for a series of last-minute statewide radio appeals. I was given a fat envelope containing the money and was asked to get it to Senator Barkley, who was in Kentucky masterminding Clements' campaign.

My solution of the problem was to give the envelope in turn to Sam Brightman and tell him to take it to Barkley. With some trepidation about traveling overnight by train with so much cash on his person, Brightman delivered the money safely.

Later the group of contributors who had made up the cash fund protested that they had heard nothing about the money's use and implied there was some question whether the money had ever been delivered. Fortunately Senator Barkley was in his Washington office. While the contributors' session was still being held, I produced the Senator. He verified receiving the money, told of the use to which it had been put, credited the money with saving the election for the Democrats and then wound up by gravely thanking them.

That settled that. But the experience strengthened my belief that the election laws of the United States should be changed so that party officials would not be forced to handle large sums of cash outside the usual channels of finance.

In fact, I don't think that a political party should be in a position of begging for funds to carry out its function. This system seems to place a price tag willy-nilly on the party record.

103

I think that the federal government should handle the finances of the major parties, either financing them directly or holding and disbursing all of the money collected by the respective finance committees. The present system places money-raising under a cloud of suspicion and intrigue, with the possibility of corruption always present.

Despite financial difficulties Earle Clements was elected in Kentucky, and the Democrats' other gains in the state gave positive evidence of a Democratic trend. It was argued that there was little basis for such a conclusion, Kentucky being normally a Democratic state. But just across the Ohio river, in the usually strong Republican state of Indiana, the results were almost as dramatically in favor of the Democrats. In this off-year balloting, Democrats won 53 city elections while losing in closely contested elections in 49 cities. Net Democratic gain was twenty-five mayors. In Ohio and Pennsylvania the results were similar.

It is true that these elections were mostly local—the largest statewide election was in Kentucky—and were fought to a great extent on local issues. But it was also a fact that the larger issues posed by the actions of the President and the Republican Congress had a strong influence on the voting.

We made claims to the press and over the radio as to the significance of the elections, and those claims were not too modest. But in the quiet of the committee's offices in Washington, a more sober and objective analysis of what these elections meant to our political policies was being made.

At the same time other events made headlines in the nation's newspapers, events which helped in judging the trend.

Because the Jews felt the Democratic Party showed a lack of forcefulness regarding the problem of Israel, our position was weak with them. This weakness was exploited by Wallace and his backers, the Progressive Citizens of America. We had not been hitting directly at Wallace for we felt that the Communists and fellow travelers who were joining his supporters and seeking to direct them would eventually destroy him. Wallace's Jewish strength, however, was outside the problem of Communism.

We were heartened by two events. First, President Truman was offered the honorary chairmanship of Brotherhood Week, sponsored by the National Conference of Christians and Jews. This was a sign of confidence of a solid sort. Second, the Progressive Citizens of America, holding a rally for Wallace in Philadelphia, were picketed by a tremendous group of anti-Wallace citizens. The demonstration and counterdemonstration nearly developed into a riot. The strife was deplorable, yet the evidence of a strong reaction to Wallace as a "fellow traveler" was encouraging.

Best side show of the period was the Brewster-Ferguson committee hearings in which these two GOP stalwarts undertook to cut down to size another Republican, millionaire Howard Hughes of Trans World Airlines, the Hughes Tool Company and RKO Motion Pictures. Highlights of this protracted hearing included an investigation of the operations of Johnny Meyer, highly paid publicist for Hughes, who had a happy proclivity for arranging parties for such government officials as might have business with Mr. Hughes.

The testimony was sensational and some of the names brought out were newsworthy; but in tackling Howard Hughes, Senator Brewster caught himself a tartar. Hughes was not one to sit still and take it. He opened fire on Brewster, calling him a "stooge" for Pan American Airways, TWA's chief competitor.

On the Hughes payroll was the publicity firm of Carl Byoir & Associates of New York. Byoir's vice president, Bill Utley, took personal charge of the drive to carry the fight to Brewster.

Utley and I were old friends, having worked together in Chicago on the publicity department of the World's Fair in the thirties. During the Landon campaign in 1936, Utley was hired by the Republican National Committee. Later he went with Byoir. He came to me at the Democratic National Committee and asked for help against Senator Brewster. I was delighted.

Thus we had a happy teaming up, behind the scenes, of a Democratic publicist and a Republican publicist in an effort to discredit a pair of Republican Senators, in the interest of a prominent Republican contributor who was engaged in an over-all trade war with still another Republican, Juan Trippe, President of Pan American.

Brewster, his efforts nullified by Hughes's counterblasts, finally gave up under pressure. Shortly thereafter, I met the Senator in the lobby of the Statler Hotel in Washington, following a White House Correspondents' dinner. Mutual friends offered to introduce us.

Senator Brewster drew himself up. "I know about Mr. Redding," he said. He did not offer to shake hands.

As he turned away, I said, "Ah, yes, I know about Senator Brewster. The Senator has the Pan American publicity man, Julius Klein, running Senate investigations for him from his Senate office."

Brewster reddened but offered no rejoinder. In the words of an atrocious pun, "Juan Trippe was enough."

The Johnny Meyer epic reminds me of the classic remark made by Senator Warren Magnuson, Democrat of Washington, in his 1956 campaign for re-election. The Senator's opponent had been commenting on Magnuson's status as a bachelor, while the Republican candidate was always pictured as a "saintly" type who never went out with the ladies. How he had managed to marry was not specified. Nothing was said that was really shocking or slanderous but the implications were broad. Finally Magnuson began to lose patience.

While the Senator was speaking at a Seattle rally, a heckler rose to embarrass him.

"How about this chasing after skirts?" demanded the heckler. "Now the Governor doesn't . . ."

Maggie answered without a hint of rancor in his voice: "When

I was a little boy at my mother's knee, I was taught always to beware of a man who doesn't like women."

Magnuson's bachelor status was no longer an issue in the campaign.

In late December, Sullivan asked me to go to Nebraska with him where he was to deliver a speech to a Democratic fundraising dinner in Omaha. Then Chairman McGrath asked us to arrange to meet him in Chicago and go on to California.

"We've got to settle the party's problems out there," he said, "or we'll lose California by default."

Sullivan was against going. Still fresh in his mind was the dinner episode of the spring. But he recognized the truth of what McGrath had said and acceded. I bound up my old scar tissue in silence.

The day before we were to leave, McGrath, after long conferences with the White House and with leaders across the country, gave orders for committee policy in the future, based on his analysis of what had happened in the past months.

He felt, he said, that the party organization program had been enormously successful. Registrations were up in all areas, and the drive was continuing. New party workers had been easy to secure and were filling the void that had been left by the inactivity of those who had become tired of politics.

The publicity program, he said, had been effective. *Capital Comment* had demonstrated its worth and would be continued and its circulation increased. We would carry out the recommended policy of expanding the working staff of the Publicity Division to increase its capability. The policy of opposing Taft to make it tough for Dewey would be continued.

"The work of the Publicity Division on the issues of rent control, taxes and the high cost of living has been most successful," he said. "As a result of pounding on these three issues, the Republicans have been convicted in the eyes of the country

107

of being the party which has been against ordinary people. We have been singularly successful in this field."

"Senator, speaking of the Publicity Division," and I produced a letter which had been sent to me by his office, "this letter you referred to me was written to you by an editor of a North Carolina paper. It has to do with the Publicity Division. What the man wants is my job. It seems to me this is not something properly to be referred to me."

McGrath looked at me with a twinkle. "Sure, it should be handled by you, Redding. Tell him 'No.' You're the Publicity Director around here and we're not in the market for another."

I was gratified but I had one more point to raise.

"Mr. Chairman," I said, "Pleas Greenlee of Indiana is outside. He won in Indiana in November. Some time back he was told to organize and then ask for patronage. Now he's here and he told me, 'I did organize! I did win! Where's the patronage?' He came to see me. I have no patronage. Will you talk to him?"

McGrath laughed. "Of course, I'll talk to him. Pleas did a fine job in Indiana and he's entitled to ask for recognition. And I'll give him what he wants."

108

CHAPTER 11

Sullivan's Omaha speech was an unqualified success. As usual he kept his audience spellbound with a steady outpouring of ideas delivered in staccato style. His method was to stand up and fire thoughts, ideas, exhortations in a continuous stream. There was no build-up to a single climax.

Listeners everywhere were overawed by Gael's dynamic volubility. The explanation was simple enough when you knew the secret. Gael was an omniverous reader and it was his habit to mark a passage in a book or magazine that took his interest. The following day Marylee Buchly, his secretary, typed out the quote or story on an index card. These cards were then given to me for speech-writing purposes.

Usually Gael appended a note to the current batch of cards asking me to comment. I learned that if I heeded this injunction I would find myself involved in a long ideological debate. In general, I ignored the invitation because of the pressure of other work; but occasionally I deliberately provoked such discussions, for Sullivan was an interesting, stimulating thinker.

To write a speech for Sullivan it was only necessary to gather together a group of these cards on related subjects and proceed from there, quoting liberally. He preferred simple sentence structure and the wide-open copy—that is, short sentences and one-sentence paragraphs all punctuated with lots of exclamation points. The speech he liked best was one in which I linked about a score of these idea cards with a few bridge words. I re-read this particular speech only recently and it did go very well.

Gael knew that the type of speech he made had to be short or his audience tired of following his intellectual gyrations, so we wrote for a time limit of not more than twelve or thirteen minutes.

Howard McGrath, as I was finding out, was the direct opposite of Sullivan in his speeches. Despite the fact that they had been teammates on the Providence College debating team during their undergraduate years, there was a world of difference in their manner of approach to a speech.

Sullivan preferred a set speech. McGrath liked to talk extemporaneously. Even when Howard had a prepared text, he rarely followed copy for more than the opening paragraphs: then his tongue would take flight. Newsmen, used to getting releases from which they could file stories in advance, found themselves forced to follow McGrath's every word, for what he said frequently made a better story than the text he abandoned.

It was difficult for the press to adjust to this. It was equally difficult for me as publicity man. Prepared speeches are usually given more space in newspapers for the reporter can write more fully for an earlier edition. At a political dinner or rally, the principal speaker generally talks last. And morning editions of the papers are either on the press or about to go to press when he takes the stand. If a story is written from a prepared speech, it's frequently already in the paper by the time the first word is read. But when the reporter has to wait to see what is actually said, there is so little time the chance for a story is often lost.

Also, McGrath liked to build to a single blazing climax coming at the very end of his address. He could bring a crowd to its feet cheering, as well as any speaker I've ever heard. Yet, because he wouldn't follow prepared texts, we were not getting the publicity mileage that we should.

Eventually a plan was worked out where we made a one- or two-page release in advance on several issues which McGrath

110

would cover in the early moments of his speech. In this way reporters had an opportunity to write advance stories; and frequently they were able to add a new lead from the ad-lib portions of the talk that followed.

McGrath worked hard when he spoke. He had an uncanny ability to phrase and parse his thoughts as he went so that subject and verb always met in the right place. The flow of thought was brilliant and fresh. But his speeches took enormous effort, and when he concluded he was drenched with perspiration.

After Gael's speech in Omaha, we rushed to the depot to catch a train that would connect with McGrath in Chicago. I had with me a specially fitted suitcase containing a portable typewriter and a radio. It was a handsome gadget which Bob Hannegan had given me; but the combination of a heavy goatskin bag, typewriter and radio made it about as heavy as a single piece of luggage could be. And no porters were available at that hour in Omaha.

We joined the McGrath party in Chicago, as planned, and boarded the Super Chief for Los Angeles. McGrath preferred train travel to flying. To those of us who were accustomed to the speed of a plane, it was a long ride; but it gave us an opportunity to discuss some of our problems.

One of these problems I found a little amusing. It seemed one of our ambassadors had taken on a rather large load of liquids at a cocktail party given in honor of the President of a South American republic. Having drunk too much, he made some rather amateurish passes at a dark-eyed beauty who was present. Much to his chagrin the beauty turned out to be the daughter of the honored guest.

The difficulty facing Jack Peurifoy, then Assistant Deputy Under Secretary of State, was to get this indiscreet gentleman home without scandal and to find another ambassador to replace him.

Sullivan pointed out that the erring gentleman was one on whose appointment as ambassador he had not been consulted.

He claimed that there'd have been no such difficulty if the committee had more to say on the appointment of ambassadors.

More serious were the discussions we had on the California problem. McGrath felt strongly that Dewey was the next candidate on the Republican ticket. Boss Tom was a proved vote-getter in New York State, and to counter his strength in New York, we needed California.

The trouble was that under California's cross-filing law, candidates for state office always filed on both the Democratic and Republican tickets. If a man could win both nominations in the primary he didn't need to run in the election. Thus it was often impossible to determine on any particular issue whether a man was a Democrat or a Republican. Consequently, party responsibility, in the way of a party record, had little to do with whether an individual was elected; and with little party responsibility there was a corresponding lack of party discipline.

As a state, California generally went Republican despite the fact that Democrats had an edge of more than a million in party registration. Of party organization there was little discernible trace. In a statewide campaign, Democratic efforts ordinarily consisted of a loose confederation of local political chieftains, strong enough in their localities but primarily interested in local successes.

It was true that Bill Malone in San Francisco had knit together a tight organization, but this was only in the north. In the southern section of the state, while there was a great preponderance of registered Democrats, liberals in the main, they lacked organization and coherency.

"Jimmie Roosevelt," said McGrath, "has been building his organization in the South. There's never been anything like that before in the area. I don't know how effective his organization is but it's the only one."

Sullivan was strong for Malone in the north but saw no strength below the line of the Tehachapis, the mountain barrier which separates northern and southern California into rival areas.

Gael agreed that what organization there was below the Tehachapis belonged to Roosevelt.

As I listened to the discussion I felt that McGrath was planning a course of action by trying out and clarifying his ideas on us.

I had my portable radio set up with the antenna fastened to the train window with vacuum cups. As we talked, a news broadcast came on from a West Coast radio station. The big story was that Wallace had declared his intention of seeking the Presidency as the candidate of a third party. He was going to put his name on the ballot in as many states as it was possible under present law.

The newscaster also speculated that United States Senator Glen Taylor of Idaho might leave the Democratic Party to be Wallace's running mate.

McGrath looked at Sullivan and me. "I've been expecting it," he said. "But I think we had to play it the way we did. I didn't want to drive him into a third-party movement, but he went anyway.

"Henry Wallace is slipping before he's well begun. A lot of people were supporting him on the basis that he was a hedge against war. But many of them are beginning to worry about how he stands with the Communists. They'll be leaving him in droves now that he's declared."

Sullivan added, "People don't like to throw away their votes. When they get into the booth, those that have stuck that long will back away at the last minute. No one likes to bet on a sure loser."

McGrath nodded. "Remember this. After the election is over and all the votes are counted, Wallace won't get more than a million votes in the entire nation."

On the morning of December 31 we checked into the Biltmore Hotel in Los Angeles. Jimmie Roosevelt boarded the train on the outskirts of the city and rode in with us. He had cars waiting at the station to take us to the hotel. Jim was cordial to Gael and to me but more intent on McGrath than on us lesser fry.

Arrangements had been made for everyone for New Year's

113

Eve parties. The McGraths, their son David, and Sullivan headed for dinner at Romanoff's, with several engagements to follow.

My refusal to tag along earned me a suspicious glance from our hosts, but I did have a previous engagement. Sy Bartlett, one of the better film writers and an old friend, had invited me to a party at Sam Spiegel's. He promised the most fantastic extravaganza in the true Hollywood tradition. This I wanted to see. I was not disappointed, finding myself honored among two thousand other guests. It was a big evening but probably I should have stayed with the Roosevelt party, as the reasons for my absence were not understood.

The next morning I found two tickets for the Rose Bowl game under my door, seats next to the Grand Marshal's box on the fifty-yard line. The Grand Marshal was General Omar N. Bradley, Chief of Staff of the United States Army—my old boss in Europe. Again I missed the Roosevelt party. I went to the football game, hangover and all, with Joe Lawler of Universal Pictures. And once more my absence from the activities arranged by the Roosevelt group was viewed with suspicion.

On the day after New Year's I attended an incessant round of meetings with one small group after another. The setup was designed to give McGrath a quick view of the Democratic situation in southern California. Roosevelt, tall, slim, balding, not handsome but with a tremendously charming smile, was omnipresent. He it was who introduced each group. He was at McGrath's elbow being helpful at every instant. It was a truly impressive example of how to handle a VIP.

The next day was given over to meetings with the Pauley-Scully-Fanning group of conservative Democrats. Here we found ourselves dealing with individuals rather than with *an* individual. There was no dominant personality among the conservatives; in fact, the uniting factor seemed to be a negative one: opposition to Roosevelt.

That night I wrote a statement for McGrath in answer to

114

Wallace's third-party announcement and telephoned it back to Washington for release.

In part, McGrath's statement read: "Wallace will not attract true liberals . . . because liberals understand that a third-party movement . . . will serve only to assist the forces of reaction.

"Republicans see in this a chance of winning not on merit but by confusion."

On Wallace's proposal that we abandon the bipartisan foreign policy, he said, "This would bring a complete surrender to the demands of the Communist states and a shameful abandonment of . . . the free peoples of the world.

"A vote for Wallace . . . is a vote for things for which Stalin, Molotov and Vishinsky stand.

"Major danger in the Wallace campaign is that it will obscure the fact that the voter has three choices in 1948:

"(1) To throw away his vote on Wallace.

"(2) To vote for Republican reaction and four years of Taft bumbling.

"(3) To vote for President Truman and a Democratic program of true progressive liberalism to go into effect on January 1, 1949.

"The issues are that simple!"

The following day McGrath scheduled separate meetings with Roosevelt and Pauley. Roosevelt was state chairman, but under the party's system, the state chairmanship in California rotates from year to year between the northern and southern portions of the state. Thus, Roosevelt was slated to become merely a deputy chairman to a northern Democrat.

Prior to the meeting with Pauley, McGrath told me: "The only organization out here is Roosevelt's. It makes sense to go with him. He offers the only chance to win votes. We'll get more in the way of contributions from Scully and Pauley and their friends. But they don't have votes and it's votes that will win, not money.

"The problem is Pauley. He's a friend of the President, a

115

close friend. If I ask him to stand aside to make room for Roosevelt as National Committeeman, I may offend him mortally. If he is offended, he may well appeal to Truman, and the President stands by his friends. Then we'll all be in the soup. But we want votes and we'll have to take a stand. I want you here while I talk to Ed."

McGrath opened the conversation with Pauley circumspectly but finally wound into his spiel. The upshot of it was an appeal to Pauley, as a personal friend of President Truman, to stand aside and give Roosevelt a chance to try to win the state for Truman.

Pauley seemed to have suspected something of the sort and registered no surprise. When Howard had finished, Pauley asked, "What you want is for me to drop out as National Committeeman in favor of Roosevelt?"

McGrath took the jump. "Yes."

"You'll regret it," Pauley predicted.

I took a breath. It seemed like an ominous opening. But Pauley only repeated, "You'll regret it. Roosevelt will let you down. He's more interested in Roosevelt than in Truman. When the going gets tough he won't be where you want him.

"But," Pauley continued in a very low voice, "I might be wrong. I don't think so, but perhaps you see things more clearly. If what you want is for me to withdraw as National Committeeman to make room for Jim Roosevelt, I'll do it."

"That's what I want."

"You've got it."

"Thank you, Ed," said McGrath. "I know how hard this is for you. Believe me, it's even harder for me to ask it of you. But I truly believe that the only way to win California is to consolidate our strength in one place. To my mind, Roosevelt has what organization there is and therefore he's the logical man to handle the job. It has nothing to do with personalities."

Pauley listened without comment. Then, as he arose to go he said, "You'll regret it, but you have my resignation and you can give the job to Roosevelt." Then he was gone.

116

Sullivan came in shortly afterward from a luncheon with a group of movie moguls, where he had been drumming up contributions. Told of McGrath's action and Pauley's agreement to resign, Sullivan said, "I'm afraid of it. I'm afraid of it."

Later Roosevelt arrived for his appointment with McGrath. Sullivan had gone again and I sat in the back of the room while Roosevelt and two or three of his people talked with Howard. Suddenly there was mention of the Jefferson-Jackson Day Dinner which Sullivan had ducked. McGrath expressed bewilderment.

Roosevelt asked, "You mean you haven't heard about Sullivan's run-out, his trip to Palm Springs, his flight in the night?"

"No," said McGrath, "I know nothing about it."

Roosevelt looked at me and grinned. Then he gave a long and detailed account of the affair as he saw it. I sat tight. McGrath listened patiently, then turned to me. "Is this all correct?"

"Main outline, yes," I agreed. "As to point of view, well, I've heard it told from the other side."

"That's all behind us," McGrath told Roosevelt. "I'm glad to know your side of the story but that's history. We're going ahead now."

He then outlined his plan. He did not, however, tell Roosevelt that he had requested Pauley to stand aside; he merely indicated that Pauley had made the decision himself. In this manner McGrath saved Pauley the embarrassment of having been deposed with his opponent's knowledge.

Roosevelt was pleased. Instead of being relegated to a secondary role, he would remain in a statewide position within the party as National Committeeman. It was a signal victory.

We were off once more for Washington and home. McGrath was very pleased with the results of his maneuvering. Sullivan was glum.

The last hour or so on the train, McGrath, alone with me, brought up the incident of the dinner in the spring.

"Was Roosevelt right about the dinner?"

"I don't know," I answered. "Last spring I would have sworn he was wrong. But today I don't know. It didn't look to me like

117

Jimmie was hot for Wallace. In fact, it looked the other way around. I don't think Wallace has any real strength out on the Coast. If I'm right on that and Roosevelt knows it, then he won't be for Wallace."

McGrath was thoughtful. "Why didn't I know about the dinner?"

"I can't speak for Gael. For myself, I thought you'd heard about it. I thought everybody in the world knew about it. But I didn't bring it up because it would look as though I was trying to prejudice you against a course of action you were set on. It was better, it seemed to me, for you to make your own decision without a lot of talk from me on a matter which was probably no longer important."

"Logical," said Howard. "Makes sense."

CHAPTER 12

At Senator McGrath's suggestion we reorganized and expanded the publicity division. I remained as director, but I was deeply enmeshed in policy work with McGrath and Sullivan so it was necessary to have someone in charge when I was out of the city or otherwise occupied. Sam Brightman was made associate director of publicity and executive director of the division.

Hal Leyshon, who had completed the Truman file, was retained as New York publicity representative of the committee, for the period prior to our move to New York for the campaign.

We required additional help to carry out our policy of stressing radio in an effort to talk directly to the people. First I asked Bill McAndrew of WRC in Washington to take the job, but he decided his future lay with NBC and turned it down. Bryson Rash, then a newscaster for ABC, had been radio director in 1946, but we didn't ask him in 1948 simply because we felt he would turn an offer down in favor of staying with the network.

Finally we settled on Ken Fry, who had resigned from the Voice of America as chief of its radio broadcasting service. Fry was an old friend whom I had known in Chicago when he was director of special events for NBC. He agreed to join us, even though all we could offer was assurance of a job through Election Day.

119

About this time Gael Sullivan asked me to hire Fred Blumenthal who had worked for Chester Bowles at the Office of Price Administration. Blumenthal was a young, energetic newsman who had operated as a liaison between columnists and Bowles. I was doubtful about Sullivan's proposal because there seemed little room on our staff for a special liaison man with columnists.

But Gael had another reason. Bowles had succeeded to the leadership of the liberal wing of the party, taking over the allegiance of many who had previously looked to Wallace for inspiration.

Bowles did not approve of many of the President's decisions, particularly on Palestine and in the field of labor, and on occasion had been openly critical. Consequently the situation was strained, not only between Bowles and the President, but also between Bowles and the National Committee.

Sullivan, an admirer of Bowles, felt unable to discuss matters freely with him because such conversations might be misunderstood, either as an admission of presidential weakness or as personal disloyalty to the President.

Sullivan's idea was that we would hire Blumenthal and let him learn things we wanted Bowles to know. Then, Gael reasoned, Blumenthal would leak this information to Bowles and our problem of communications would be ended.

On this basis Blumenthal was hired. But, as an avenue of "leaks," he was a bust. He was too loyal to the President and the National Committee to tell even his idol, Bowles, what was going on. After about a month of this "failure," I told Sullivan his plan was no good.

In the meantime Fred had demonstrated his value as a staff man so he was kept on, ironically enough "even though he was trustworthy." However, Fred did supply a solution to the problem of communication with Bowles when I took the bull by the horns and suggested that on specific items he tell Bowles unofficially, but with our consent, what was happening.

120

We hired another man about this same time, a good writer and an excellent liaison man who made a fine appearance. Within a few days he was handling difficult assignments, even in the White House. Because of this ability, I asked him to submit to a security clearance so that he could work freely at the White House. To my astonishment he turned up with a criminal record, having served time for passing bad checks; and the Secret Service informed me they couldn't have him around.

With this dictum in hand, I asked him to come into my office.

On the defensive, he said, "I know what's happened. I knew it was going to happen as soon as you wanted a security check. So I'll make it easy. I quit!"

He was bitter and I didn't blame him, but I had no recourse but to accept his offer. We went in to McGrath's office and I explained the case, winding up by saying that I had personal faith in the man but had no choice. McGrath was sympathetic and tried to help him get a job elsewhere.

A little later Edward R. Murrow of CBS, an old friend from wartime Britain, asked me to lunch. When we met, he was accompanied by Joseph Evans, a former New York *Herald Tribune* editor and *Newsweek* foreign correspondent. I had known Evans in London in 1942. Murrow wanted me to take on Evans in some capacity for the duration of the campaign.

I had no doubt of Evans' ability but I wanted to discuss the matter with Sam Brightman, for it was Brightman who would deal with Evans if he were taken on. Brightman was enthusiastic. Here was a trained, expert newsman ready at hand. He wanted Evans at once.

So Evans was brought in and he did an excellent job. After the campaign was over, I backed him for the position of secretary of the Inaugural Committee in Washington, and still later for a foreign assignment with the European Recovery Program.

Another addition to the staff was Don Pryor, a former CBS news commentator, who had been cut adrift in one of the recurring economy drives of that network. Pryor was assistant to Ken Fry and, at the end of the campaign, went with the United Nations.

A young reporter recommended by Brightman was hired to help in preparing news releases and to do leg work. He was Julius Dushay. Later Julius worked for the official newspaper of the American Federation of Labor, and, still later, won a Nieman Fellowship at Harvard University.

A final addition to the staff was another radio man, Wally Gade, who was brought in at Ken Fry's request to help put together radio recordings for shipment to party organizations in the field.

One other personnel change which occurred in this period involved appointment of Neale Roach as managing director of the Democratic National Convention. Roach is one of the finest professionals in the political business. When the time came to appoint a manager for the convention, McGrath asked my advice. I recommended Roach, who at that time was an assistant finance director of the National Committee. Roach did such a good job in 1948 that he was selected to be convention manager again in 1952 and in 1956. In the last year he resigned shortly before the convention opened after a disagreement with National Chairman Paul Butler.

Meanwhile the name of General Dwight D. Eisenhower kept cropping up in the news as a possible Republican candidate for the Presidency in 1948. His position as a candidate, even if not avowed, was compromised by the fact that he was still Chief of Staff of the Army.

He also made the mistake of proposing, at what was supposed to be a private dinner with Pennsylvania Republicans, that businessmen should help in the fight to curb inflation even if they "had to forego profits for a year." His Republican hosts cooled rapidly on the General as presidential timber; and, to prevent development of an Eisenhower boom for the Republican nomination, "leaked" the story. Interest in the Eisenhower candidacy

122

in the big-business circles of the Republican Party waned immediately, and Eisenhower was reported as "disgusted" with politics.

He himself said that he felt that "being a general was not the right training for the Presidency." This was taken at its face value for a time, but was finally assessed as a shot aimed at a MacArthur boomlet which was then on the horizon. This Eisenhower denied, but most politicians, reasoning that Eisenhower could hardly expect to survive a MacArthur Administration as a presidential hopeful, took the denial with a grain of salt.

But at this point Eisenhower was little more than a name in political gossip columns. There was more important news in the papers almost daily.

The Navy had ended segregation. This was hailed by Negro leaders as "the greatest social advance resulting from World War II." It also brought grumblings from the South, grumblings which underlined resentment for the report of the President's Civil Rights Commission.

Joseph Keenan, Secretary of the Chicago Federation of Labor and a wartime vice chairman of the War Production Board, was named Director of the American Federation of Labor's political arm: Labor's League for Political Education. His job was to work against members of Congress who had voted to inflict the Taft-Hartley Act on labor.

Still another problem was Palestine. Britain had warned the United Nations that she would end her mandate over Palestine on May 15, 1948, or sooner. Terrorist gangs were bombing and killing first Jews and then Arabs in reprisal. To complicate a difficult situation, a Communist coup in Jerusalem was feared by Ernest Bevin, Great Britain's Foreign Secretary.

On domestic issues Senator George D. Aiken of Vermont, chairman of the Senate Agriculture Committee, was drafting new farm legislation. His plan was reported to eliminate fixed parity for farm crops and substitute a system of sliding parities. The Republicans began to hear rumblings from the farm belt on that,

123

dissatisfaction which had already begun as a result of attempts of some Republicans to eliminate the co-ops' tax-exempt status.

With farm revolt against the GOP beginning to show on the horizon, Senator Taft ventured west on a political foray to capture convention votes. He was now an outright candidate for the nomination for President on the Republican ticket.

As Taft took off on his western trip, the market broke. The break on the big board was promptly followed by falling grain prices in Chicago's commodities market. For several days in a row the price of wheat and other grains dropped the legal limit in a day. With the farm belt openly worried about losses resulting from the grain price break, Senator Taft chose this moment to attack President Truman for trying to maintain the price of grain by government buying at 90 per cent of parity. This action, said Taft, proved that the President was trying to keep prices high.

The statement unintentionally underlined Truman's concern for the farmer, but the Ohio Senator went blithely on his way. In Omaha, Taft made a full-dress farm speech to a livestock association. In it he declared that he was for some sort of plan for a lower support level for farm crops: something under 90 per cent, with "perhaps" the government taking interest when the price of wheat reached the 90 per cent of parity level but not actually supporting the market until prices fell substantially under that level.

It was obvious that Taft had embraced Senator Aiken's farm plan, and the Midwestern farmers were displeased not only with Senator Taft but also with the Republican Party under his leadership.

Elsewhere in the world, Western Europe was hungry as a result of a bad crop in 1947, and shivering in the bitter winter that followed, with coal shortages making sub-zero temperatures seem even lower. The people were ripe for Communist activity. The Marshall Plan was Truman's answer to the problem, as aid to

124

Greece and Turkey had been the answer a year earlier. In Washington, Senator Arthur Vandenberg announced that the program of aid to Europe would be ready in the Senate Foreign Relations Committee by April 1.

In contrast to Senator Vandenberg, Taft was still inclined to isolationism. Suddenly Governor Dewey gave strong support to the aid program. He proposed, however, that the Administration get out of the program and leave it in "competent" hands for, he said, only in this way can the program be effective in stemming the march of Communism. This was a complete reversal of Dewey's usual noncontroversial stand and showed he was willing to fight for his party's nomination.

Russia underlined the urgency of the program. With bewildering speed, Czechoslovakia was taken over by an internal coup. Italy and France seemed in danger of taking the same road. In India Mahatma Gandhi died.

Against this background the Democratic Party's fund-raising dinner was held, headed by Wilson Wyatt, former Housing Expediter and chairman of the Americans for Democratic Action, an anti-Wallace liberal group, who had split with the White House on housing policy. Bringing Wilson Wyatt and the ADA back into the Democratic picture in an active role was a definite plus, sparked by Sam Brightman, who had worked with Wyatt briefly at Housing. At Sam's suggestion, I convinced Chairman McGrath that Wyatt should be invited to be chairman of the Jefferson-Jackson Day Dinner. When McGrath put the question to Wyatt, he was pleased to accept.

Mrs. Perle Mesta was co-chairman. Mrs. Mesta, famous as "the hostess with the mostest," was a close friend of India Edwards and a great admirer of the President. She did an outstanding job then and later in a fund-raising role for the Democratic Party.

In this welter of historic events and political fence-mending, came a new challenge in the form of a boom for Senator Van-

125

denberg as Republican presidential candidate. Highly respected for his part in the engineering of an effective bipartisan foreign policy, Vandenberg was a towering figure. There was a distinct possibility that Senator Taft and Governor Dewey might fight each other to a standoff in the Republican National Convention. If this occurred, Vandenberg's nomination could result. It was reported by a number of news columnists that if Dewey couldn't make it himself, he would throw his support to the Michigan Senator.

And Vandenberg was no Stassen. If nominated, he would not be tarred convincingly with the Taft leadership record, for Vandenberg had supplied striking leadership of his own within the Senate. Furthermore, during the build-up phase, Vandenberg would be safe from sharpshooting from Democratic propagandists, for he was far too precious to the Administration's foreign-policy plans to be subject to partisan attack. The matter never was taken to the President, for we knew full well what Harry Truman's response would be. All that could be done was to hope that the internal warring in the Republican Party would destroy Vandenberg as a candidate.

There was hope that Vandenberg might take himself out of the race. But this was shattered by an authoritative story in the Alsops' column—and Vandenberg was known to be friendly to the brothers Alsop—to the effect that the Senator would accept the Republican nomination on two conditions; first, that he would be President for one term only; and second, that he would engage in no barnstorming campaign.

Condition one, we felt, was a definite plus for the Vandenberg candidacy for it would place the Senator in a sort of Cincinnatus role of a leader being sought by his country for a specific emergency.

Condition two would no doubt hurt him with the Republican chieftains, for they were anxious to leave no stone unturned in their drive for the Presidency; and any candidate on the GOP

126

ticket would have to make a strenuous campaign to satisfy this requirement.

Problems were multiplying for the Democrats. We had the leftist Wallace chipping away at our liberals. We had definite political pains growing out of the Palestine issue which we were unable to touch. The civil-rights storm was gathering force and seemed ready to break upon us at any time. And we had a "hands-off" candidate in the shape of Senator Vandenberg who was a truly formidable possibility.

CHAPTER 13

THE REPORT of the President's Commission on Civil Rights had stirred the country, and congressional leaders, particularly from the South, were showing signs of being restive. In an effort to bring about unity between the National Committee and the legislators on Capitol Hill, we made attempts to tie Democrats in Congress closer to the Democratic program. Our first move was to bring the administrative assistants of the Democratic members of the Senate into a unit with which we could co-operate.

I was host to a dinner at the Mayflower Hotel at which we tried to launch this project. But the effort failed in the crosscurrents of conflicting interests between Southern and Northern Senators and the wilderness of politics in the individual states.

Still hopeful, we tried another gambit in the House of Representatives where we attempted to bring about an organization of young Democratic Congressmen whom we could spotlight. Here, contrary to what might have been expected, we found a willingness to co-operate among representatives from the South. Among those who seemed eager to take on the projected organization were William Jennings Bryan Dorn of South Carolina, John Bell Williams of Mississippi, Hale Boggs of Louisiana, and Olin E. (Tiger) Teague of Texas.

128

This evidence of interest by the young Southerners seemed to worry liberal Northern Congressmen. They seemed to suspect the Southern group of plotting something. In vain we tried to explain that the little group of young Southerners in Congress, whom we felt to be "comers," could and would stay out of the welter of issues which bade fair to split the Democratic Party. After much talk, the idea subsided without action.

Actually the idea was doomed to fail even though it was well conceived. Events were shaping to a fight between Northern and Southern Democrats and no amount of romancing would prevent it.

There were those who professed to believe that the report of the President's Civil Rights Commission was a political gag which would not be implemented. I will confess that, as a political propagandist, I hoped they were right. But knowing the deep-seated convictions and courage of President Truman, I knew they were wrong.

Sure enough, early in February there came a barrage of telephone calls, from newspapermen at first and from politicians later, asking what was up. There was a rumor that some sort of special presidential message to Congress was in the works. No one seemed to know exactly what it was, except that it was presumed important.

I called Ross at the White House and he refused to discuss the rumor on the telephone. Instead he invited me to come right over.

In Ross's office he showed me a copy of the projected message. It was on civil rights. It was strong. Reading it through, I could only say, "Whew!"

Ross had been watching me for a reaction. Now he asked, a little sharply, "Don't you like it?"

"Me? I like it very much. There's a lot of people around who won't, though."

Now that I had seen it, Ross cautioned me against discussing

129

it with anyone. He didn't want anyone finding out about the message prior to its delivery to the Congress, for, he felt, this would only bring pressure on the President.

"He won't give on the thing," said Charlie. "He's made up his mind. There's no use trying to talk him out of it."

So I went to a movie, the first one I had seen in almost a year. I didn't take in much of it, but the darkened movie house allowed me to escape questions which might have been embarrassing.

When I came out, the President had delivered his message and the story was in print. I was disappointed to see the newspapers, even in the first stories, treating the message as "creating" a controversy, rather than discussing its merits.

"We believe," the President declared, "that all men are created equal and that they have the right to equal justice under law.

"We believe that all men have the right to freedom of thought and of expression and the right to worship as they please.

"We believe that all men are entitled to equal opportunities for jobs, for homes, for good health and for education.

"We believe that all men should have a voice in their government and that government should protect, not usurp, the rights of the people."

With these simple words the President wrote a creed of American democracy—the faith in mankind that lies deep in the hearts of Americans. This creed was sent to Congress as part of the civil-rights message in which the President bluntly and honestly cited unpleasant facts about our country. Then he outlined a ten-point program of federal legislation to correct them.

The President wrote, "Today, the American people enjoy more freedom and opportunity than ever before." Yet, he added, there still are examples of discrimination in our nation, and he set this goal for correcting them: "We cannot be satisfied until all our people have equal opportunities for jobs, for homes, for education, for health and for political expression, and until all of our people have equal protection under the law."

130

Specifically, the President asked Congress to pass legislation designed toward the following objectives:

1. Establishing a permanent Commission on Civil Rights, a Joint Congressional Committee on Civil Rights, and a Civil Rights Division in the Department of Justice.
2. Strengthening existing civil rights statutes.
3. Providing federal protection against lynching.
4. Protecting more adequately the right to vote.
5. Establishing a Fair Employment Practice Commission to prevent unfair discrimination in employment.
6. Prohibiting discrimination in interstate transportation facilities.
7. Providing home rule and suffrage in presidential elections for the residents of the District of Columbia.
8. Providing statehood for Hawaii and Alaska and a greater measure of self-government for our island possessions.
9. Equalizing the opportunities for residents of the United States to become naturalized citizens.
10. Settling the evacuation claims of Japanese-Americans.

The President concluded his message with a moving plea that we lead the world to peace by the strength of our example in living one with another in truly democratic freedom. It was the plea of a man who believed that our democracy is not merely a library of laws and resolutions but is the flesh and blood and heart and soul of all Americans.

The President said:

The position of the United States in the world today makes it especially urgent that we adopt these measures to secure for all our people their essential rights.

The peoples of the world are faced with the choice of freedom or enslavement, a choice between a form of government which harnesses the state in the service of the individual and a form of government which chains the individual to the needs of the state. We in the United States are working in company with

131

other nations who share our desire for enduring world peace and who believe with us that, above all else, men must be free. We are striving to build a world family of nations—a world where men may live under governments of their own choosing and under laws of their own making.

To be effective in these efforts, we must protect our civil rights so that by providing all our people with the maximum enjoyment of personal freedom and personal opportunity we shall be a stronger nation—stronger in our leadership, stronger in our moral position, stronger in the deeper satisfactions of a united citizenry.

We know that our democracy is not perfect. But we do know that it offers a fuller, freer, happier life to our people than any totalitarian nation has ever offered.

If we wish to inspire the peoples of the world whose freedom is in jeopardy, if we hope to restore hope to those who have already lost their civil liberties, if we wish to fulfill the promise that is ours, we must correct the remaining imperfections in our practice of democracy.

We know the way. We need only the will.

The newspapers played the story of the civil-rights message in its controversial aspects and paid little attention to its serious side. And, as the reaction built up, the play was often contradictory. On the one hand, the press said the message was a bid for votes in the big-city Negro centers; then, sometimes in the same story, it was predicted this action would break the solid South and bring about the Democratic downfall.

How they could have it both ways was not explained. Few papers gave the President credit for being anything other than a politician, shrewd or stupid as they felt the move might be from the standpoint of politics.

Politically, the message cost the party dear. It did break the solid South. Almost as serious, it cut the party off from a large source of its contributions.

Thus, as the Washington *Post* said editorially, the Democrats "have been advancing with their wings in the air. Now they are gravely imperiled on each flank. To the left harassed by Wallace and his pink-coated partisans. To the right they are not only menaced by the heavy dragoons of Big Business in cuirasses of gleaming gold and bristling plumes fashioned from the stubs of innumerable checkbooks, by isolationist ambushes and by the Parthian warriors of fanatical constitutionalists; they are also threatened with the defection of some of their own best-disciplined and hitherto most dependable troops, meaning the Southern Democrats."

It was an apt description of our predicament. Being so to the point, the quotation answered best the charge that Truman acted on civil rights as a political maneuver.

What so many people failed to understand was that the President rarely used circumlocution to gain his ends. He meant what he said. That is why so many pundits failed in trying to analyze the President's actions. They were always looking behind what he said or did, looking for an explanation other than the obvious. They preferred to use the old aphorism of the "lady" who when she said no meant maybe, and when she said maybe meant yes; and if she said yes, she was no lady!

The decision to send this far-reaching civil-rights message to the Congress for action—"We need only the will"—took courage. Truman had said in effect, "Damn the political torpedoes," and ordered full steam ahead. This fitted no pattern of political behavior and caused Republicans and Democrats alike difficulty in trying to make it fit a recognizable political formula.

Congressman Dorn of South Carolina was among the first to fire. He said the President was attempting to "out-Wallace Henry Wallace."

Senator John Overton of Louisiana stated angrily that the South should "vote Republican or for another Democratic Party on the national ticket and only regular Democrats locally."

Tom Abernethy, Congressman from Mississippi, demanded in a telegram to Mississippi Governor Fielding L. Wright that the "Southern Governors should get together for a showdown."

The Southern Governors Conference, meeting in Tallahassee,

133

Florida, departed from its agenda to consider calling an "all-South" political convention. Then, after hurried consultation, the Governors declared: "The President must cease attacks on white supremacy or face full-fledged revolt in the South." They passed unanimously a resolution offered by Governor Thurmond of South Carolina, calling for "joint and common action" by the Southern states to bolster their position with Congress, and with the leadership of the Democratic Party.

The resolution placed a forty-day time limit for this action and provided for another meeting of the Governors to consider what had happened in the interim. Governor M. E. Thompson of Georgia hoped this would provide a "cooling off" period for both sides.

Governor Thompson's more moderate attitude was also taken by Senators John Sparkman of Alabama, and Claude Pepper of Florida. The two Senators declared that "the problem will be worked out within the Democratic Party and President Truman will be elected with the vote of the entire South."

From Troy, New York, Senator McGrath said he would receive the special committee of Southern governors appointed by the Southern Governors Conference. He added, "The Democratic Party must continue to play its traditional role as the champion of human rights."

And the President? He grinned and seemed to be enjoying the uproar. On Sunday following delivery of his message to Congress, he attended religious services at the First Baptist Church of Washington. Purely by coincidence the pastor of the church, Dr. Edward Hughes Pruden had selected the matter of civil rights and the President's message as his subject.

Among other things, the Rev. Dr. Pruden said: "Some of those who oppose most vigorously social pioneering indicate by their very intentions that they are just a little afraid that there is some truth in the things they are opposing and they make up for their lack of logic by the volume of their protest."

The good minister was so right. Whether or not the protests were logical, they sure were loud.

134

Wilson Wyatt's Jefferson-Jackson Day Dinner was held on February 19. The turnout was so large the dinner had to be held in two sections with 1,200 people in the Mayflower Hotel and another 900 in the Statler, with the President appearing at both places. In his address, the President did not refer to the raging furor over his civil-rights program. But if any of the diners needed to be reminded, all they had to do was look at the empty table located conspicuously in the middle of each room directly in front of the speakers' table. They were tables reserved by Senator Olin Johnston of South Carolina. He had bought tickets but decided not to attend the dinner. He entertained his guests elsewhere, listening to the program on radio, no doubt expecting some reference to civil rights and to his pointed absence. He was disappointed.

On the following Monday the special committee of Southern Governors met with J. Howard McGrath. Present were Governor William Preston Lane, Jr., of Maryland, chairman of the Conference of Southern Governors; Governor J. Strom Thurmond of South Carolina, chairman of the special committee of Southern Governors; and three members of his committee: Governor R. Gregg Cherry of North Carolina, Governor Ben Laney of Arkansas, and Governor Beauford H. Jester of Texas. Governor Lane attended the meeting as an observer and was not a member of the special committee.

Prior to the meeting, Governor Lane had talked at length with Senator McGrath. It was his feeling that the problem was not so serious as the volume of protests would indicate. He would attend the meeting as a sort of "friend of the court," and if he could intervene or be of assistance, he would.

At two-thirty in the afternoon the special committee arrived and was ushered into McGrath's private office. Trailing the Southern Governors were battalions of the press.

The latter were bedded down in my office and in the conference room with a solemn promise that I would keep them advised as to when they might talk to the respective parties involved.

In McGrath's office, Governor Cherry took a relaxed attitude, joking in friendly fashion with Howard. Ben Laney of Arkansas also acted as if this were a meeting between reasonable men, who, although they might disagree, still could be friends.

Strom Thurmond was different. Vouchsafing no more than a formal greeting, he refused to be seated. He did not join in the pleasantries. He didn't smile, and he took a chill attitude of complete disapproval of the others who were not so partisan.

I sized up the meeting and decided, since Thurmond was the spokesman for the group, he was going to make a record. I suggested that a transcript of the proceedings be kept, to which all agreed. I organized a team of stenographers to take down the proceedings in relays.

As soon as a secretary filled up a sizable amount of space in her book, I'd replace her while she typed out her notes. In this way I hoped to keep nearly current with the conference.

Governor Thurmond refused several more invitations to be seated and was obviously anxious to dispense with idle talk and get down to business. Finally all was in readiness and Senator McGrath asked the Governors' committee, "Gentlemen, what is your pleasure?"

Governor Thurmond immediately began to read from a prepared list of questions. His manner was that of a prosecuting attorney. At first Senator McGrath answered at length the formal questions posed by Thurmond. In the general discussions which followed each question and its answer, the atmosphere was quiet and very serious.

The general opposition of the special committee to the President's civil-rights proposals was based on the theory of states' rights. Most of the questions were so phrased as to be unrealistic.

For instance, at one point Governor Thurmond asked: "Will you now, at a time when national unity is so vital to the solution of the problem of peace in the world, use your influence as Chairman of the Democratic National Committee, to have the highly controversial civil-rights legislation, which tends to divide our people, withdrawn from consideration by the Congress?"

McGrath's answer was a firm and simple "No."

136

As the conference went on, McGrath, who had been answering in detail in an effort to present a reasonable attitude, began to realize the hopelessness of the situation. His answers grew shorter and shorter. More and more often he would reply to Thurmond's sonorous questions a flat "No."

I was in and out of the room taking care of the preparation of the transcript, checking items for McGrath with which to refresh his memory on questions of law and other matters.

During a short rest period taken to allow the Governors to caucus, I said to Howard, "Senator, I think there's a chance to patch this thing up if you can compromise. With the exception of Thurmond, they seem to want to come to some sort of agreement."

"There'll be no compromise," said McGrath sharply. "No compromise. As Chairman, I'm not going to push this thing one spot further than the President's message. But neither will I withdraw one inch from the confines of that message."

The meeting lasted for about ninety minutes. It ended in no agreement. The press buttonholed each of the Governors as he emerged. Governor Cherry and Governor Jester agreed in saying that they were impressed by Senator McGrath's "cordiality." Governor Thurmond said there was only one recourse: to take direct action which would stop the threat to the South. All stated finally that they would study the transcript before giving a more detailed statement in regard to the meeting.

Senator McGrath guardedly discussed the meeting with the press and sent them on their way.

When we were alone in his office, he turned to me and shrugged. His face was grim as he said, "This was hopeless. These people don't realize the change in the times.

"They see in the present situation, with Wallace already an avowed third-party candidate and with the Palestine situation hurting us so deeply, an opportunity to make us bow to their will.

"What is going to happen will happen to them, not to us. President Truman will be nominated. And he will be elected, elected without the solid South and without New York!"

CHAPTER 14

THE MEETING with the Governors' committee was only the beginning of the uproar.

In Virginia, Governor Tuck initiated action in the legislature to ban the names of the nominees of the national Democratic Party from the ballot. The idea was to have the voters of the state vote Democratic, in effect on a blind ticket, and the electors would cast ballots for whomever they chose. In defense of this legislation, it was argued that the Constitution provided for an electoral college, not for a popular vote. Thus the Byrd political machine in Virginia sought to breathe life into the presumed dead and *pro forma* electoral college.

In Alabama, Governor James (Kissin' Jim) Folsom was loyal to the Democratic Party but the leadership in the state took action to prevent the President's name from appearing on the ballot.

In other Southern states, Mississippi, Louisiana, and South Carolina, special steps were taken to deny the national party its usual place on the ballot—under the cock. Candidates nominated by the state Democratic organization were to be placed there instead. The national party was given a heading of its own, as a sort of third party. In most Southern states, the cock is the symbol of the Democratic Party instead of the donkey that is more familiar to voters in the North and West. In some areas voting is done strictly on the basis of "voting the cock"; therefore losing the symbol of the Democratic Party was a severe blow.

Bill Primm, a North Carolinian, was engaged to bring legal action to try to protect the rights of the national party in the

138

Southern states. With the aid of local leaders who remained loyal, Primm was able to defeat the Virginia plan and to save the normal place on the ballot in most other states.

In Washington unnamed sources on Capitol Hill predicted that the President would water down his civil-rights proposals. This story was based on the "political" premise; and it was rumored that the President, having gained his political ends in the North by his delivery of the civil-rights message, would consent to gutting his proposals to make them acceptable to the South.

When I told Charlie Ross of this development he called a press conference of White House correspondents and informed them that this was emphatically not so. It turned out that the rumor was a Republican maneuver to force the Democrats into a tighter box. The reasoning apparently was that if Truman let the water-down propaganda stand, he would weaken the effect of the civil-rights message in the Northern cities; on the other hand, if he further denied it, he would further stir up the rebellion in the South. The latter effect was, of course, achieved.

At committee headquarters, we were looking for some stratagem to ease the situation. The Republicans themselves gave us the opening.

For several years there had been an effective coalition of conservative Southerners and reactionary Republicans in Congress. Much liberal legislation was defeated because the coalition held the balance of power in both houses of Congress. Now, erstwhile Republican members of this coalition approached their Southern counterparts on a deal. The reactionary Republican group would help the Southern Democrats kill civil-rights legislation in the Senate, if the Southerners would in turn bolt the Truman ticket in November. The exact identity of the group making the suggestion was not revealed to me by my informant, but there was no question as to the authenticity of the information. However, it wasn't hard to "G-2" that the authors of such a scheme could have but one thing in mind: to aid the candidacy of conservative Senator Taft.

On the basis of this information, Senator McGrath issued a

statement condemning the Republican Party for the offer. He pointed out that the GOP platform adopted in 1944 called for a civil-rights program and this deal constituted cynical trading of principle for political advantage.

Again the purpose was twofold: we knew the offer to kill civil-rights legislation would alienate the vote in the big Northern cities from the Republican candidate and it would make the rank-and-file Southern party member disgusted with Republican tactics. It was political maneuvering, of course; but I wish to emphasize again that the information on which our attack was based was accurate. Later such a coalition did appear in the Senate to do exactly what I have outlined.

It can be seen that the nature of the problem of the Negro in the South has changed little, if at all, since 1948. At that time the issue was triggered by a Supreme Court decision banning Jim Crow seating arrangements in interstate transportation. The President had called for a far-reaching program to outlaw poll-tax legislation, provide for anti-lynching laws, provide for a civil-rights division in the Department of Justice and protect both the economic and political rights of the Negro in the South.

Today, the same general issues inflame the South. But progress has been made in that Southerners in Congress in 1957 did help work out civil-rights legislation which touched on these same points. The explosion of trouble this time came from the Supreme Court ruling on segregated schools. Damned and double-damned in 1948, the Supreme Court has been thrice-damned in 1957. Many of the same names keep reappearing in the picture: Senator Byrd with his massive resistance program of 1957, Congressman Dorn of South Carolina, and J. Strom Thurmond, now United States Senator from South Carolina. As the French are credited with saying, "The more it changes, the more it remains the same."

It is true that General Eisenhower in 1952 and again in 1956 made inroads in the South, but these Republican gains were possible only for the President. With 1960 coming up and no Eisenhower to add luster to the Republican ticket, it was necessary, the Republican strategists thought, to demonstrate dramatically their position on civil rights. The purpose in 1957 was to gain voting strength in the Northern and Western big cities where the importance of the Negro vote had grown. The GOP was willing to junk its relatively unimportant gains in the South to accomplish this end. It was part of their strategy to tar the Northern Democrats thoroughly with the civil-rights brush so that there would be another Dixiecrat revolt against the Democratic Party.

Attorney General Brownell advised the use of troops in Little Rock. The President acceded. But there was actually no need to use soldiers for this purpose. The situation in Little Rock was not truly a serious one. As many observers pointed out, Governor Faubus in effect created the problem himself. But even as aggravated, the situation could reasonably have been handled by the appointment of a few deputy United States marshals by the federal court which had ruled on the integration of the Little Rock high school.

A relatively small force of deputies could have accomplished the end of protecting the persons of the few Negro students involved—nine. But such an action would not have created so dramatic a situation as the dispatch of troops accomplished. So in 1958 the Negro finds himself still a pawn in the game of politics, with the lives and minds of young people being warped and swayed in cynical fashion.

Fortunately the Little Rock incident has proved to be a sort of nine-day wonder, with the failures of the President and his Administration in the fields of national defense and scientific research overshadowing completely the shabby maneuvering in Arkansas.

In early 1948 other events were shaping the campaign. Jack Kroll, one of the Congress of Industrial Organization's most successful organizers, was appointed chairman of the Political Action Committee to do on behalf of the industrial unions what Joe Keenan was assigned to do for the American Federation of

Labor: to oppose re-election of members of Congress who had voted for the Taft-Hartley Act and to replace them with liberal Congressmen who would vote to repeal the law.

On the House side, Congressman Michael J. Kirwan of Ohio was elected chairman of the National Democratic Congressional Committee, the organization which is dedicated to the election of Democratic members of the House of Representatives. Congressman Kirwan succeeded Pat Drewry of Virginia, who had died. Assisting Kirwan was Victor Hunt Harding, known as "Cap" to all Democrats and renowned for his detailed knowledge of the 435 congressional districts in the United States. Congressman Drewry had been content to leave the operation of this important committee almost entirely in the competent hands of Cap Harding. Congressman Kirwan utilized Harding's abilities to the fullest, but also brought into play his own remarkable political sense and organizing genius.

From Kirwan the Democratic National Committee could expect hard-hitting aid at the grass-roots level, the level at which we were making our principal effort.

Meanwhile an amusing incident occurred. A Senate riding page delivered to my office a large and imposing envelope. It was addressed simply: "National Committee." Recognizing the envelope as coming from the Senate, I opened it. Inside I found a confidential run-down on all Republican National Committee members. I found this was a report done by Senator Taft's office to indicate what action was needed in each individual instance to produce for the Ohio Senator sufficient convention votes to secure the Republican presidential nomination. The description of the personal habits and voting peculiarities of the Republican committeemen was frank and to the point.

I very carefully thought over this windfall of information. Then I sent it out and had it photostated. This I did because I had the very definite feeling that neither Senator McGrath nor the President would sanction use of the report and would insist on its being returned to Senator Taft.

After the photostats had been made, I took the envelope in to

142

Howard. He was horrified that I had opened it. Senatorial courtesy was in the saddle.

I explained that I had opened the envelope all unsuspecting that the contents were part of Senator Taft's confidential files, which was true. I then suggested that this information could be very useful.

Senator McGrath wondered if perhaps the Senate riding page had been dishonest in bringing the envelope to the Democratic Committee. I pointed out that the envelope was addressed merely, "National Committee." Perhaps, I suggested, the page in the course of some fifteen years of Democratic administration, had forgotten there was a Republican National Committee.

Senator McGrath directed me to send the documents back to Senator Taft at once, and indicate carefully that the envelope had been misdelivered and opened by mistake. I did. But I fed the photostats to Drew Pearson, who had a field day with them.

However, to cover my tracks it was necessary to pay for the photostats out of my own pocket so that McGrath would not detect my fine hand in the project. I think he suspected what had happened but he never questioned me and I never mentioned the matter again.

There are, I know, those who will claim my action was not ethical; but here was one of the accidental breaks that come once in a while in politics. I had no intention of missing a boat which I held firmly by the painter.

Meanwhile Wallace was smarting as we pinned Red labels on him and his followers. Through every avenue we were pointing out that Wallace and his third party were following the Kremlin line slavishly. Finally in a speech in Ohio, Wallace issued a formal denial of the charge. He said the test of Communism was whether there was an intention to overthrow the government by force. Neither he nor any of his supporters, Wallace indignantly declared, had ever evidenced any such intent. He asked President Truman and all of the Republican presidential aspirants to sign a written pledge repudiating the support of any group which advocated the overthrow of the government of the United States

143

by force, of groups such as the National Association of Manufacturers and those elements within the Democratic Party which opposed civil rights.

This was a good sign. Wallace explaining that he was not a Communist meant that the iron of the Red charge was biting deep.

One of the methods which the Progressive Citizens of America used to build emotional acceptance for Wallace in his public appearance was, paradoxically, the very thing which strengthened the belief of many Americans that he was either a Communist or mixed up with some other foreign ideology. This was the very effective use of lighting to build suspense.

Jo Davidson, the sculptor, who headed the PCA, was undoubtedly the one who dictated the "chosen man" technique in the use of lights. It was very simple and very effective.

The preliminaries of a Wallace meeting were conducted noisily and brashly like any other political meeting. But when the time approached for the coming of the leader, the lights were turned low, the music was subdued with an undertone of suspense-building drums. One large spotlight played on the door. Suddenly the man appeared out of the darkness into the light— all very symbolic. Wallace would stride down the aisle, every step of the way emphasized by drums coming to a crescendo. And the crowd worked itself up to an emotional ecstasy unknown to most American political gatherings.

It was dramatic and effective, but it was foreign. It was the sort of thing the Nazis did for Hitler, what the Bund did for Fritz Kuhn in prewar days, what Communists did for Stalin. It didn't fit the American political scene and Americans felt it.

Some Democrats urged us to employ the same tactics, but we refused. Instead we played up the foreign aspect of this sort of theatricals. Most newspapermen covering Wallace's appearances pointed out the use of the stage-managed music and lights to create acceptance and excitement. People began talking about the "phony and un-American showmanship." It helped pin the label of Kremlin domination on Wallace.

Although we were having luck in combatting Wallace, there

was as yet no answer to the Thurmond group. And the effect of these two fringe revolts began to show up in the opinion polls.

One of the imponderables in any political poll is the side effects that follow such a revolt as that of Wallace or Thurmond. The fact that there is a revolt, even though it has no local application, is mirrored in what the polled individual answers.

With the South up in arms and Wallace seeking to make inroads in the industrial North, many voters the country over began to think of Truman's campaign as a hopeless one. This feeling, in turn, was reflected in the polls.

Thus, with revolt on both left and right, an opinion poll taken in Pennsylvania indicated severe loss to the President. It showed:

Truman	41%	Wallace	7%
Dewey	46%	No opinion	6%

Adjusted to eliminate the "no opinion" group, the standing was:

Truman	44%	Dewey	49%	Wallace	7%

In Chicago, where there was a strong Democratic organization, a poll showed:

Truman	42%	Wallace	12%
Dewey	41%	No opinion	5%

Again adjusted to account for the "no opinion" group, the standing was:

Truman	44%	Dewey	43%	Wallace	13%

This was bad enough, but for the entire state of Illinois, the figures were much worse. These showed:

Truman	37%	Wallace	7%
Dewey	48%	No opinion	8%

Corrected, the Illinois statewide figures read as follows:

Truman	40%	Dewey	52%	Wallace	8%

In New York the story was the same. We were on the downgrade. And the Democratic Party was beginning to feel the pinch in funds that follows automatically when a political cause looks like a losing one. Money which had come to the Democrats from the liberals of the far left was going to Wallace. Money from the South had dried up. What there was went to Thurmond and the Dixiecrat organizations which were supporting him.

The Palestine issue lost us campaign funds which would normally be contributed by the business community of the Jews. Due to minor squabbles with which any party is perpetually plagued, James Landis, the liberal head of the Civil Aeronautics Board was replaced, and Marriner Eccles, a well-known economist, was dropped as chairman of the Federal Reserve Board. Loss of these two and several others, darlings of the not-so-far-left-as-Wallace liberals, dried up still other sources of funds.

Big Business, which normally contributed some money to the Democratic Party as a hedge, believed the situation was such that hedge contributions were not necessary. Their sure-thing money went to the Republican Party.

There was open talk of ditching the President. Drew Pearson "revealed" that there was a boomlet in the making for Supreme Court Justice William O. Douglas. There were gossip-column items about a "draft Ike" movement within the Democratic Party. And if we needed anything further to prevent overconfidence, we got it from New York.

There, in a by-election for a vacant congressional seat, a Wallace-ite, Leo Isaacson, garnered enough votes to win.

To add insult to injury, the New York *Herald Tribune* found itself in the position of having it made both ways on one issue. In every edition they screamed about Communists in government, for which they blamed the Democrats. At the same time Bert Andrews, their able Washington Bureau chief, was writing indignant articles about the sufferings of innocent victims of President Truman's loyalty program. The final insult came when Andrews was given the Heywood Broun Award for fine reporting for his series on the loyalty program and later was the recipient of the Pulitzer Prize.

Sometimes you can't win.

146

CHAPTER 15

IN THE EARLY SPRING of '48, the Democrats began to
have Eisenhower troubles. The Palestine question
and the civil-rights problem combined to scare a number of Democratic leaders, particularly in the big cities. They were ignoring
all of the political facts of life in a frantic search for a candidate
with whom they might win.

Jack Arvey of Chicago was one of these. To some extent Arvey
had precedent for his actions. In the hectic days before the campaign for mayor of Chicago in 1947, he had, as chairman of
the Cook County Democratic committee, sought a new Democratic standard-bearer to supplant Edward J. Kelly, the incumbent mayor. Arvey brought in Martin H. Kennelly to be the
candidate and then broke the news to Kelly. Kennelly was
elected and promptly became "above" politics, to Arvey's chagrin.

Undaunted by this experience, Arvey was willing to try again.
He wanted Eisenhower and was willing to ignore Ike's withdrawal as a Republican candidate. Apparently Jack rationalized
Ike's refusal on the Republican side indicated the General was
a Democrat and would be available to replace President Truman
at the head of the Democratic ticket. No one knew whether Ike
was a Democrat or a Republican because he had never voted.

147

Joining Arvey was Mayor Bill O'Dwyer of New York City, chiefly influenced by the power of the Zionist movement in Democratic politics in New York. Noisiest of all the "Eisencrats" was Leon Henderson, former OPA administrator, who professed to have a solid assurance from General Eisenhower that he would take the nomination if it were proffered.

There were other rumblings in New York, enough to make us afraid that not only New York City but the whole state might be disaffected.

From the West Coast came alarming reports that Jimmie Roosevelt was flirting with Arvey in his movement to draft Eisenhower as a Democrat. In Detroit our national committeeman was an open advocate of ditching the President. And in Kansas, Carl Rice, the Democratic national committeeman for this arch-Republican state, was also in revolt.

It was a panic move for these otherwise smart politicians. They failed to realize that dumping the President would be a confession of failure of the Democratic Administration; and their only hope with the electorate would be, after confessing failure, to promise not to do it again. Actually, Arvey, Henderson and company were hoping that Eisenhower's personal popularity would overcome this obvious adverse point.

McGrath asked me to accompany him to the White House. He wanted the President to announce his candidacy and thus head off the Eisenhower movement before it became unstoppable.

Politically it's generally good strategy to delay formal announcement of one's candidacy simply because this heightens suspense and helps the political build-up. But a President doesn't need build-up. He is already famous.

The only drawback to announcing Truman's candidacy was the speculative one that we might have to pay for radio broadcasts sooner than usual on the basis that certain speeches usually broadcast free as a public service might be classed as political and therefore have to be paid for.

With us when we called at the White House was Gael Sullivan.

148

The President greeted us cordially and listened attentively as McGrath and Sullivan outlined the reasons for advising him to declare himself as a candidate for election.

"If you think this is the time," the President said, "you can tell them."

That settled, the discussion continued on the political problems arising out of the civil-rights message and the Palestine matter. On civil rights the President reiterated his determination to stand fast.

"We have the Zionist Jews in the office every day," I told the President, "and the pressure is building up a terrific head of steam."

"It's no use putting pressure on the committee," the President declared. "The Palestine issue will be handled here. And there'll be no politics involved."

I pointed out that Arvey, O'Dwyer and other defections resulted from Jewish political pressure in their areas.

On this the President was explicit. The Palestine issue was to be handled outside the field of political pressures. We should so state to anyone who tried to sway him through the committee. The issue was complex, involving not only the welfare of the Jews in Israel but the well-being of the United States and the peace of the world. There would be a decision when the time came and not before.

"Meanwhile," he emphasized again, "no politics!"

I went out of the room to sketch a few sentences for an announcement to be made by McGrath and while I was gone, the discussion continued. When we were coming out, we were waylaid by the White House correspondents in the west wing.

"The President has authorized me," McGrath told them, "to say that if nominated by the Democratic National Convention, he will accept and run."

These words gave the rank and file of the Democratic Party the assurance they needed, that President Truman would carry to the polls for a popular decision the fight he had been waging

149

for a stable, prosperous economy at home and peace and freedom in the world.

The announcement came while both reactionaries and friends of Communists were trying to persuade the country that the leader of the Democratic Party would not head the election fight for the things in which he believed. McGrath's announcement also covered two points of national policy which affected the political scene.

"I talked to the President with respect to his civil-rights message," McGrath reported to the press. "The President's position remains unchanged since he delivered his message.

"I might state that it is my view, which I explained to the President, that the substance of his message is as old as the Constitution of the United States itself and as new as the 1944 Democratic platform.

"I asked the President to explain the present status of the Palestine situation, which he did in considerable detail. The question is one which affects the security of the nation and probably of the world; and the President will continue to handle the problem without regard to its effect on politics."

McGrath's statement of the President's intentions cleared the air on the question of whether the President would be a candidate to succeed himself. But it spurred the draft-Eisenhower group to new efforts. It also stirred new vituperation against the President in the South.

I have cited the names of a few of the principals in the draft-Eisenhower movement but to say that this was the extent of the revolt would be wrong. Probably no one knows how deep the movement actually ran. And the press kept working the story, naturally enough, for it isn't every day that a political revolution seems in the making. In addition it looked like a chance to unseat the Democrats, a project in which most publishers were interested, so the headlines grew blacker and blacker.

Other solid issues were in the making. In the field of agriculture, Congressmen Walter Ploeser of St. Louis, and Harold Knutson of Minnesota, Republican chairman of the House Ways and Means Committee, were continuing their attacks on the farm co-operatives. Their latest line was that the co-ops were bankrupting small business. At the same moment that this new line of attack was launched, the Republican National Committee wrote formally to the farm co-operatives that it "was proud of the chance to support the co-ops."

This doubletalk naturally amazed the farmers and caused them to be even more suspicious of Republican promises. In the week following Taft's farm talk in Omaha in which he came out for a system of sliding parities, farm groups contributed more than two thousand dollars to the Democratic Party in Nebraska alone.

The cost of living continued to rise. Steel announced a five-dollar-a-ton increase just as Republicans were congratulating themselves that there were signs of the inflationary pressure leveling off. The steel price boost brought from Senator Kenneth Wherry, the Republican Whip, the remarkable statement, "I am more convinced than ever that high prices themselves are the surest cure for high prices."

And Senator Taft remarked that, with the prices of meat so high, the people in the lower income brackets could always adjust their diets.

"Beans," he said, "could be used to lower the cost of meals."

We compared Taft with Marie Antoinette of France and predicted that his "Let 'em eat beans" would become equally as famous as her remark. That one stung and the Republican press gibbered.

Following the President's announcement of his candidacy, several articles appeared by newspaper columnists revealing intimate details of our discussion in the meeting with Truman. McGrath was concerned about these stories for the accounts were remarkably accurate.

151

He came back to my office and sat down, a rare thing.

"Have you been seeing the stories about our session with the President?" he asked me.

"Yes." I hadn't given it much thought. "They hit awfully close to what happened."

"Awfully close." McGrath smiled sourly. "Word for word on some things." He threw his question at me, "You got any idea where the leak is?"

"No." I was still not particularly interested. "Why?"

"Well, for one reason," he said, "the President doesn't like it. And for another, neither do I."

It finally dawned on me that he was trying to locate the leak and he was looking at me.

"Look," I said and I was mad, "if you think I leaked the stuff, you're dead wrong. You'll have to find another candidate."

McGrath was abashed. "I didn't mean to offend you. I know you wouldn't leak it, but I thought there was a possibility you might have been putting it out as guidance and the newsmen themselves were guessing where it came from and so crediting it."

"I haven't had a word to say about the meeting at any time. You've been the only one as far as I know who has had anything to say and that was when we came out of the President's office."

McGrath looked at me meaningfully. "Do you know what you're saying? I haven't talked to any newsmen at all on this matter. You haven't talked to anyone. I'm damn sure the President hasn't been telling tales on himself." McGrath paused. "Think it over. There was only one other man in the room with us when these things were discussed. Sullivan."

"I don't believe it!" I was aghast. But Howard's logic was unanswerable.

"That's what's on my mind," said McGrath. "And I don't like it. More important, the President can put these things to- gether, too, and you know how he hates leaks!"

My thoughts were turning over rapidly. It was a thing that Gael often did—talk over matters with a few newsmen whom he liked. It was entirely possible he had made this mistake once more. If he had and the President learned of it, there would be fireworks. As a result of this line of thought, I almost missed McGrath's next remark, something about California.

"What? I didn't hear that, I'm sorry."

"I said," McGrath repeated, "that we're going to the West Coast again next week."

"The Coast? Where?"

"We'll go out with Maggie Magnuson. First, we'll go to Spokane, then to a Jefferson-Jackson Day Dinner in Seattle. We'll see Mon Wallgren [Governor of Washington] at Olympia, then go on to Portland. There'll be a Jefferson-Jackson Day Dinner there too. After Portland we'll go to San Francisco, then to Los Angeles for another dinner speech and finally to San Diego and back home. I'll need some ideas on the speeches. If you want to start making plans, you can start now. We'll leave Tuesday."

Back to California! And problems for Gael! I went into Sullivan's office and asked him, "Gael, have you been talking to the columnists?"

"What do you mean?"

Doggedly I went on, "I mean, Gael, that if you've been talking to columnists like Willard Shelton [of PM] and some of the others about our session with the Boss last week, there's hell to pay."

"Why, yes," he answered. "I talked to some of them. They see me and I let them know what's going on. What's up?"

"Just this, Gael. The Boss has seen the stuff in the papers and he's upset. I wouldn't bring it up straight with him but if you can manage to see him on something else and mention it in passing, it would be a good thing. Might take off the heat."

Gael thought for a moment. Then he said, "You remember some time ago you told me that a lot of times if you did something, it was all right; if Hannegan did something it was all right; but if I did the same thing, there'd be trouble?"

"I remember."

153

"That's what this is. They've got me pegged. Any time I'm out alone on a limb, the limb gets sawed off."

"I don't think it's that so much, Gael," I told him. "It's just that you get out on more limbs."

"Maybe. Maybe. Anyway I've just about had enough of it. In fact, I've had too much of it. I'm going to take off. I'm sick of playing it carefully. If they have no confidence in me, if they're worrying about what I'm saying to the press, about what I'm saying to everybody, then it's time I got out from under. That's what I'm going to do."

Sullivan was worth a great deal to the Democratic Party and his leaving the committee was bound to be harmful. Yet there was no question that his influence had definitely waned, despite the fact that McGrath had leaned over backward to give Sullivan his due. However, there was no doubt about it—Sullivan had reached the end of the line.

But my immediate problem was the upcoming trip to the Coast. Ken Fry and I talked over the possibilities of a nationwide broadcast from the West Coast. It seemed to me that such a program would help tell our story. McGrath would speak from a new dateline, and it would make the trip to the Coast worth while from a national standpoint.

Our first thought was to originate the broadcast from either Los Angeles or San Francisco; but we decided against both cities because they were too much like New York, Chicago or Washington. We wanted something a little different.

We finally chose Portland, Oregon. It was the heart of a Republican stronghold and would indicate that we were seeking votes wherever they might be. It would also cause the Republicans to take a look at their hole card in Oregon. Fry requested time and called the networks and got a half-hour sustaining period on Mutual to come from a downtown hall in Portland.

I called Lew Wallace, the Democratic National Committeeman in Oregon, and told him of our plans. He was pleased and promised a full house of three to four thousand people for the broad-

154

cast. To supplement McGrath's radio speech, Wallace would plan a supporting program which would have local candidates and other officials on it, making the occasion an important one to Oregon Democrats.

Brightman and I went into a huddle on speech copy. The Los Angeles dinner was being broadcast throughout Southern California and McGrath was to be on the air for fifteen minutes. That meant careful copy. In addition, I wanted advance releases for the appearances to be made in Spokane, Seattle, San Francisco, Olympia and San Diego.

First stop on our western swing was Spokane, generally regarded as a Republican stronghold. Here we had a good luncheon meeting. While Republicans were predominant in the area, Senator Magnuson had many friends and always ran well. I don't think we made many votes in the city, but we didn't lose any either.

The next day we went on to Seattle. As soon as we arrived I called Dave Beck, then executive vice president of the International Brotherhood of Teamsters, and asked for a meeting. He was glad to talk to us, he said, and we arranged to meet that afternoon in his office.

I briefed McGrath on Beck and on the position taken by Dan Tobin, aging president of the million-member Teamsters Union. Tobin had been close to President Roosevelt. In fact he was said to have had a key to the back door of the White House and could get in to see FDR whenever he wished. But Tobin didn't like President Truman. Always less than lukewarm toward the President, he had been downright cool in recent months. Only a few days before we left Washington I had been told of a remark made by Tobin in speaking to his executive board in Indianapolis.

"Truman? Truman, that squeaky-voiced tinhorn," he was reported to have said, "I want nothing to do with him."

This attitude sprang, I told McGrath, from the fact that Truman had done nothing to court Tobin, and the old man's vanity was injured.

155

"But," I added, "Tobin is no longer the power in the Teamsters. The real power is Beck. At the next election, he'll be elected president of the union. If we can talk to Beck and get him with us, Tobin will have to go along."

So we went to see Beck. But any hopes of support from him soon went glimmering. We had no more than got into his office when he started to talk. The gist of what he had to say was that he, Beck, was a Republican. Even though he had helped Democrats in the past, the Republicans were the party he would support this time.

Beck said, "I know that Truman vetoed the Taft-Hartley bill. I know he's done some other things for labor. But he can't win, and the time to make a deal is before an election, not afterward. I will support Governor Dewey. I think the union will follow my lead. You understand," he concluded, "I have no ill feeling toward the Democrats, but I think there's going to be a change and I'm personally a Republican so I'm in a good position as a labor leader to make the change without seeming to abandon my principles. It's been nice seeing you."

That was that. It had been short and sweet.

"Well," Howard said as we left, "we didn't have to waste any time on it, anyway."

The Jefferson-Jackson Day Dinner in Seattle was an unqualified success and Howard spoke brilliantly. The next day we drove down to Olympia, the state capital, where we stayed with Governor Mon Wallgren at the Governor's Mansion. It was a fine afternoon and evening. We spent practically the entire night in a basement billiard room eating Alaska king crab and watching the Governor demonstrate trick billiard shots. The next day we drove to Portland.

In Portland the first person we saw was the national committeewoman, Mrs. Nancy Robinson. Nancy, who was not the "battlewagon type" but a lovely young lady, was not enthusiastic about the possibility of carrying the state for Truman in November. There were problems, she said darkly.

Dick Neuberger, now Senator from Oregon, came to McGrath's suite at the Multnomah Hotel and the tale he told was one of disaster and defeat. It was revealing to listen to Neuberger for he was no crier of doom, yet he could see no hope for the Democrats in the state. His opinion, however, was conditioned to some extent on his lack of confidence in the state Democratic leadership.

Later Lew Wallace came in. He was cheerful and enthusiastic but it was obvious to me that McGrath was not impressed. He had the feeling, he told me later, that Wallace was whistling past a graveyard. Wallace briefed us on the dinner and the plans for the radio broadcast. Everything was in order, he assured us; we could relax.

That evening we went to the dinner at the Multnomah Hotel. It was well attended and McGrath made a short speech explaining that he was saving his principal effort for the radio broadcast later.

When we arrived at the hall where the broadcast was to take place, I realized what Neuberger was talking about. About thirty Democratic candidates were on the stage. Out front where there were some four thousand seats was a chummy audience of possibly one hundred people.

With the radio engineers and our own group, there was a total attendance of possibly two hundred. We rattled around like dice in a box. They didn't need an echo chamber for special effects on the air; McGrath sounded like the voice from the tomb. It was a depressing experience and Howard was indignant, but it was too late to do anything about it.

As we separated to go to our rooms afterward, Howard said to me, "Jack, remind me in the morning to cross Oregon off the list. We won't get enough votes out here to fill up a corporal's honor guard."

Before we left by train the next day for San Francisco, a serious young man named Monroe Sweetland came to see McGrath. He said he was going to be the next Democratic national com-

157

mitteeman in Oregon, succeeding Lew Wallace, who was going to run for Governor. Sweetland talked with Howard for nearly an hour. He was full of ideas, full of enthusiasm and sure that Oregon could be switched to the Democratic column if a proper effort was made.

"Senator McGrath," he concluded, "in ten years we'll have a complete changeover. We'll have Democratic Senators and a Democratic Governor, and the state will go Democratic in a presidential election."

Howard said, "I hope so."

Sweetland was a good prophet. He became national committeeman. At present writing, Oregon has two Democratic Senators, Wayne Morse and Richard Neuberger, there is a Democratic Governor, and three of the state's four Representatives are Democrats. In 1960 the new Democratic Party of Oregon will have its first opportunity to vote Democratic for a President.

In San Francisco, state chairman Bill Malone had given one of his assistants, Harold McGrath (no relative of the Senator) the job of setting up Senator McGrath's political conferences.

Harold McGrath worked his senatorial namesake as he had seldom worked before. One group followed another, each with its separate and special problems. They were ushered in on the very minute of their appointments and Harold McGrath chased them out the minute their allotted time was up. Most of the meetings were of a routine nature. However the labor delegation headed by Jack Shelley, then president of the California State Federation of Labor, reported exceptionally good progress.

McGrath was particularly impressed by Shelley, who later became Congressman from the San Francisco district and one of the leading powers in the House of Representatives.

Harold McGrath's grim efficiency brought one amusing incident. The day was drawing to a close and the Senator was weary. Finally he took up a newspaper and announced he was retiring to the "library." Harold consulted his watch and, as the Senator disappeared behind the bathroom door, said to me, "I've got another group coming in right away. I'll give him five minutes."

It didn't occur to me that he meant it. But four minutes and thirty seconds later he began banging on the door of the Senator's bathroom.

"Senator," he shouted, "you have only a half minute more. Then you'll have to be out to meet the group from the Sacramento area."

The Senator burst out in less than thirty seconds, and he was hot enough to explode. But by the time he singled out Harold, the Sacramento group was ushered into the room and he had to contain himself in peace. Me? I sneaked out, bursting with laughter.

In Los Angeles Jimmie Roosevelt met us at the station when we arrived. There were cars to take us to the hotel. Little men ran about in all directions, making arrangements for our well-being.

Despite all the attention, I sensed a strained atmosphere. I mentioned to Senator McGrath that there was something a little too hectic about the whole thing; but he laughed at me. At the hotel we couldn't have a minute alone; people were constantly in and out of the room.

That night there was a private party in McGrath's honor. With drinks flowing like water and good food in great abundance, I still sensed a strain. I had a feeling that whenever I joined a group to talk, the subject had just been changed.

The following day was more of the same. Meetings after meetings and then a press conference. Everything seemed a little artificial to me, but by this time I had convinced myself that I was seeing bogeymen under the bed.

A cocktail party for the guests at the head table preceded the dinner at the Biltmore. Here I saw the list of speakers for the first time. It staggered me. Senator Claude Pepper of Florida, Senator Joseph O'Mahoney of Wyoming, Congressman, later Senator, John Carroll of Denver, Governor Mon Wallgren of Washington, Senator Sheridan Downey of California, Governor

159

Herbert Maw of Utah, McGrath and Jimmie Roosevelt—all were scheduled to address the dinner guests.

Pat Brown, who is running for Governor in 1958 but was then San Francisco district attorney, caught me by the arm. "I have to talk to you," he said.

We stepped into a quiet corner. As he told me his story, I knew why I had been feeling something was up. Something *was* up!

"McGrath's going to be crucified here tonight," said Brown. "He seems like a good guy and I don't want it to happen without his having at least a little warning. Roosevelt's coming out for Eisenhower. And there's some sort of a demonstration set for McGrath. They'll let him start his speech, but the first time he mentions Truman, all hell's going to break loose. That's the signal for Roosevelt. He'll follow McGrath in speaking and he's going to pop Eisenhower on the place. And, believe me, it'll be popular too."

I thanked Pat for warning me and went off in search of McGrath. After some maneuvering, I got him out from under the suspicious gaze of Jimmie Roosevelt and alerted him to what was planned for us.

He frowned, then said, "Get the other speakers to meet in our suite right away, before dinner. It won't hurt to have a get-together on this."

A few minutes later we were all in McGrath's suite. He told them briefly that he had received some important information and asked me to outline the story. I did.

"What should I do!" McGrath asked the group.

Governor Maw of Utah burst out at once, "Hit back. Don't let them get away with it."

The others were more conservative. All were surprised and shocked that the dinner program seemed about to take this turn; but with the exception of Governor Maw, the counsel was for moderation.

McGrath listened attentively, then said, "Thank you, gentlemen, for your reactions. I appreciate your help but the fact is, of course, that I have to meet the problem myself. It's my job. Let's go!"

The group of honored guests returned in time to take their places in line to file into the dining room. I was sitting with the press directly in front of the speakers. A few feet behind me I saw Sy Bartlett, who invited me to sit with him for a drink.

As he poured out the champagne, he said, "I'm sorry for you tonight."

"Why?"

"They're going to take out after Truman tonight and your friend, Senator McGrath, is going to be roundly booed. It's all laid out."

I guess I didn't seem surprised, for Bartlett asked, "Did you know about it?"

"Yes. We know all about it."

"What are you going to do?"

"We'll have to sweat it out."

He was solicitous and poured out more champagne. "Better have more. You're going to need it."

Back at the press table I was unable to eat. I noticed some men from Roosevelt's press department sitting with packages which I deduced were copies of Roosevelt's speech. It amused me to walk over and start opening one of the packages. That almost started a riot. I was told the copy wouldn't be released until Roosevelt began to speak.

I looked innocent and said, "But I'm not press. I'm publicity from National Committee. See here, why can't I see a copy? You're not hiding anything, are you?"

That shook them. Nevertheless I got no advance copy.

Then McGrath began to speak. He worked along, speaking almost conversationally as he began, gradually building up toward a climax, as was his custom. He listed Truman's accomplishments: his veto of the Taft-Hartley Act, his statesman-like approach to the Palestine issue.

161

"What more can a man do?" McGrath demanded. "Would anyone ask more?"

With that, the house came down. "Yes . . . yes . . . yes . . . yes . . . boooo!"

With a visible effort McGrath maintained his composure at the microphone, his face reddening, yet containing his rage. As I watched him, I sensed the activity of Roosevelt's publicity people distributing advances on Roosevelt's speech upcoming next. One of the men shoved a copy of the speech into my hand, saying jubilantly, "You wanted one. Now take it!"

McGrath waited until the booing died down; then he picked up and finished his speech as though nothing had happened. Roosevelt followed and declared for Eisenhower. The crowd was in ecstasies.

If this had been the grand finale it might have started an avalanche. But speakers droned on until two in the morning and the crowd's excitement died with the evening. By the time the dinner broke up, there was no spark left. Roosevelt had timed his bombshell badly. The excitement turned into ennui.

McGrath and I found ourselves alone. No little men were hovering over us; there were no good wishes. Roosevelt didn't make an appearance. We went to Governor Wallgren's suite and had a drink. Then we went to bed.

The next morning the telephone, which had been jumping for two days, was completely quiet. McGrath thought perhaps the management was protecting us from calls, but a question to the operator proved this to be wrong. The plain fact of the matter was that we were lepers. No one wanted to be seen with us. No one wanted to talk.

We took a cab to the station to catch a train for Rancho Santa Fe near Del Mar in Southern California. We were still alone. McGrath stood in the station at trainside and looked at me.

He smiled and said, "Well, we're getting out of town under our own steam anyway. I thought maybe we'd get tar and feathers and a ride on a rail."

162

Before leaving the hotel, I talked to my office and filled in Brightman on what had happened. I also talked to Ross at the White House and told him what had happened. He didn't seem surprised.

Sullivan told Brightman to pass on to me the following message: "See, it could have happened to me a year ago."

On the train to Del Mar, McGrath sat thoughtfully by the window. As we neared our stop, he said, "No politics here. We'll take a rest. And I think we need it."

CHAPTER 16

It was a time of meetings. The staff members met
daily to discuss current problems, though as time
went on, these meetings degenerated into a business of staring at
the dwindling committee bank balances. No contributions were
coming in. Everything was going out.

Meetings were held at the White House at least once a week,
sometimes three or four times a week. At each of these there was
a recurring recognition of the financial plight of the Democratic
Party.

In an effort to cut expenses, Gael Sullivan launched a project
to buy a headquarters for the Democratic Committee in New
York City. He figured that would cost less than renting quarters
in the Biltmore Hotel, which had been the traditional home of
the committee in campaign years. At Sullivan's meetings we
considered the suitability of various locations.

Sullivan, McGrath and I went to New York to look over the
old Lotus Club building on 57th Street. A huge old structure,
it had long been in disuse. Asked if the publicity division could
operate from there, I agreed it could if the place were cleaned
up. There was room for the rest of the committee operation with
the same qualification.

It was decided to purchase the building, but when estimates
were secured for refurbishing the place to make it usable, we had

to take another look. Meanwhile the manager of the Biltmore, hearing that we were contemplating a change, revised his rental fee. We ultimately settled back in the Biltmore at a much reduced cost.

Shortly after the Lotus Club purchase was turned down, Sullivan left the committee. Being passed over for the national chairmanship had disappointed him greatly and he had never fully recovered from it. He left to become executive director of the Theater Owners of America at a much larger salary, and was given a fine send-off from the committee.

The White House meetings were concerned with campaign strategy. First and foremost was the upcoming "nonpolitical" cross-country train trip the President planned. The recommendation we had made a year before was to be tried. The main questions concerned itinerary, the major problem of setting up meetings for the President to address, and adequate preparation locally to insure an audience. Almost equal to the President's trip in importance were the closing of the congressional session and the upcoming Democratic National Convention in Philadelphia. Present at most meetings were McGrath, Oscar Ewing, Charlie Ross, Matt Connelly, Clark Clifford, Steve Early (Roosevelt's press secretary and then a vice president of the Pullman Company), congressional leaders Sam Rayburn and John McCormack, Senator Francis Myers of Pennsylvania, Senator Barkley, and others.

Occasionally Secretary of State Marshall would attend but only when the discussion was likely to touch on foreign policy. He consistently stayed outside the political field except as it touched on State Department operations.

When a discussion of the party platform was held, I was asked to draft a paper which would be used as a guide by the convention platform committee. Secretary Marshall immediately told me that he would be delighted to discuss this with me at length, "before you start to write!" I agreed.

I was always a little in awe of Secretary Marshall because I had known him first as a regular army instructor for the Illinois National Guard, in which I served. When he was commander of the first United States Armored Force during the 1936 army maneuvers at Allegan, Michigan, I served under him again. Later I was, for a short time, a very junior first lieutenant in Washington while Marshall was Army Chief of Staff. So when Marshall spoke, all the years of his military rank fell on me, and I usually answered, "Yes, sir."

George Allen, getting a touch of fame or at least notoriety from Drew Pearson as President Truman's White House jester, attended these meetings quite frequently. He was bird-dogging General Eisenhower's day-to-day vacillation of whether he would or would not actively seek the Democratic nomination for the Presidency.

Time after time, when asked what the General was going to do, Allen would spread his hands and his answer would be a deprecating, "Well, I don't think he'll run. But then you know how the General is. He can't make up his mind."

I was worried at the tone of some of these meetings. There seemed to be little appreciation of the impact civil rights and Palestine might have on the total body of delegates to the national convention. I pointed out at one meeting that if everything coalesced against the President, he might conceivably be defeated in his fight for the nomination. Oscar Ewing snorted at this.

My rejoinder was, "You're right. It can't happen if someone, anyone, will get off his duff and do something, particularly in New York State where O'Dwyer is causing trouble." Ewing claimed New York as his home.

He didn't like my remark and said so. McGrath intervened before the discussion went any further, saying, "Redding's looking at things as they might be if we fail to do what is necessary."

As that meeting closed, President Truman stopped me for a moment and said, "Always look at the problem in the light of what is the worst that could happen. Then we can guard against it. Good work, Redding."

At another meeting I told the President that there would be an article in the *Saturday Evening Post* on his candidacy. "I've managed to get the *Post* to use a full-length article by Senator McGrath," I told him.

He laughed. "They won't use it!"

I had had positive assurances from Ben Hibbs, publisher of the *Post,* that the article would be used. I told the President that I was sure it would be in the *Post* soon.

"Tell you what I'll do, Redding. If that article appears in the *Saturday Evening Post*, I'll give you a bottle of the best bourbon there is in the White House."

"That's a promise, Mr. President."

The article did appear. But I have never reminded the President of the fact he owed me a bottle of bourbon until now.

One meeting was held on the presidential yacht, the *Williamsburg*. It was one of the pleasantest evenings I've ever experienced. McGrath and I were among a small group of about twelve. The President was at his charming best.

All the guests were congenial, the dinner was excellent and, as the President was in a mood for relaxation rather than work, problem talk was at a minimum. After spending five hours cruising down the Potomac from the dock at the naval gun factory, we finally put back to shore.

As we came off the boat, McGrath was thoughtful. "The President won't use his office for political purposes," he said, "but think what we could do if he'd only let us invite a few contributors along for a trip like this one. We'd have no finance problem at all."

A finance committee meeting called by Senator McGrath in June was held in the Mayflower Hotel. Only a handful showed up. Louis Johnson was there, so was Jim Bruce, one-time Ambassador to France and presently a senatorial aspirant

167

in Maryland. Jacob B. Blaustein of the American Oil Company in Baltimore was present, and a few others.

Charles Sawyer, Secretary of Commerce, was unable to come to the meeting. "Business," he explained, saying that he couldn't free the time. "I have an urgent appointment which I cannot break."

Senator McGrath was disappointed. Sawyer, a former Governor of Ohio, a political power in his home state and a wealthy man in his own right, was exactly the type of man McGrath wanted on the finance committee.

Later as the meeting convened, Stuart Symington, then Secretary of the Air Force, arrived and sought out McGrath.

"I can only stay a short time," Stu said. "I have a date out at Burning Tree Country Club that I've got to keep, but I didn't want to miss this meeting. I want you to know that I'll subscribe to whatever you want me to do on this committee. I have every confidence in you and you have my proxy.

"I'd like to stay longer," he added, "but Charlie Sawyer is threatening to take my hide on the links and I couldn't get out of the game!"

McGrath stared but said nothing.

Principal problem facing this meeting was the selection of a finance committee chairman.

Joe Blythe, national committeeman from North Carolina, had been appointed treasurer of the National Committee, replacing George Killion who had left to become president of the American President Steamship Lines, a position he still holds.

But Treasurer Blythe was not the man to bring in money. His chief function was to lend stature to the committee and demonstrate that it still had roots in the South. Of course, he supervised expenditures and did his job very well. In fact, after the campaign, President Truman gave public thanks to Joe Blythe at a victory celebration meeting the day before Blythe died.

McGrath asked each man present at the meeting if he would

168

take on the job of running the financial campaign for the party. There were no takers. Louis Johnson demurred, too; but finally he asked for the meeting to recess for half an hour while he went to the White House to see the President. When he returned, he announced that he would accept the appointment from McGrath.

From that moment Johnson swung his fighting talents into the business of financing the campaign. Nothing was too much for him, nothing daunted him. Sometimes his single-minded approach to the problem caused trouble, for Johnson was arrogant in manner and his attitude sometimes offended. The fact is that he did the job when no one else was willing to take it on.

McGrath's first meeting with Louis Johnson was a stormy one. Howard had met Johnson only casually until one morning in May when his secretary announced Colonel Louis Johnson. McGrath was on the telephone making a periodic check of leaders around the country. He was talking to Jake More in Iowa and still had a call coming in from Ed Kelly in Chicago. He finished his talk with More and took the Kelly call. The two calls lasted some fifteen minutes.

Meanwhile Louis Johnson sat waiting in the outer office seemingly content. The calls completed, McGrath went to the door and asked Johnson to come in.

Johnson stepped in, came to a smart military halt in front of McGrath's desk, and exploded. "Young man," he bellowed, "I didn't come here to cool my heels waiting for you. I have more important things to do. I came here to help the Democratic Party. I have nothing further to say to you. Good-by!"

McGrath listened to this, his mouth agape. As Johnson pivoted and started for the door, he caught his breath.

"Come back!" he got up and followed Johnson who, by this time, had his hand on the doorknob. "Come back here!"

Johnson hesitated.

McGrath was talking a little loud now, too. "I don't know what you're shouting about, Colonel, but if you think I insulted you, let me tell you something. I had Jake More, the state chairman of Iowa, on the telephone when you were announced. Ed Kelly of Chicago was waiting for me on another line.

"I don't know what you think, but in my opinion I could not fail to complete those calls. I want you to know I'm working for the Democratic Party, too; and I'm not getting a salary to do it.

"Now, you want to help the Democratic Party and I want to help the Democratic Party; so come back here and sit down and let's figure out how we both can do what we want to do."

Johnson hesitated, let go of the doorknob and sat down, the whole issue forgotten. From there on the conversation was a friendly one with the relationship between the two men progressing to a point of mutual respect and esteem.

Johnson worked like a dog at his new job. He sidetracked Acey Carraway, former chief fund-raiser for the committee, and replaced him with Nathan Lichtblau, a New York businessman, as his principal assistant. On several occasions when the treasury of the committee was empty, Johnson personally picked up the cost of operating the committee and meeting its payroll. He was repaid but this was not a measure of what he did in insuring continuity of operations.

Johnson had a tremendous impact on the campaign. If it had not been for his truly Gargantuan fund-raising efforts, the whole thing would have collapsed. There would have been no money with which to pay for the President's campaign train; there'd have been no money for radio, no money for printing, no money for any of the multitude of items which require cash to be transformed into action.

In the political field there had been talk of a boom for Supreme Court Justice William O. Douglas to supplant Truman at the head of the ticket. Nothing came of this simply because Justice Douglas would have nothing to do with it. The President had a very high regard for the Justice and Douglas was Truman's first choice as a running mate.

The question of a candidate for Vice President had been lost

170

to a considerable extent in the maneuverings at the top; but Truman's regard for Justice Douglas was no secret.

Truman had not stated his preference outright, since that would have shut off any competition for the job and offended others who wanted the nomination such as O'Mahoney of Wyoming, McCormack of Massachusetts, and Barkley.

Ten days before the convention was to open in Philadelphia, Tommy (the Cork) Corcoran, Roosevelt's old brain-truster and a close friend of Justice Douglas, came to McGrath with an urgent message.

"Howard," said Tommy, "I beg you to persuade the President not to use pressure on Justice Douglas to be his running mate. The Justice does not wish the nomination, won't take it. And if the President insists, it may mean that the Justice will hurt the feelings of a man whom he respects and likes. Give me your word, Howard, that no pressure will be used, for it can only hurt the friendship which exists between the Justice and the President; and it won't help the Democratic Party to have such a thing happen."

Howard's response was simple. "I can't answer for what the President will do. But, Tommy, I will promise to deliver your message and stress that the message was an earnest attempt by the Justice to evade any necessity for turning down a request by the President."

"Understand me," said Corcoran, "the Justice is not unwilling to be a candidate for the Vice Presidency. It just happens that he prefers to remain as a Justice of the Supreme Court. This is what he wants to do."

McGrath nodded. He delivered the message but it did not divert the President in his effort to place Douglas' name on the Democratic ticket.

Another problem which was current was the necessity for an advertising agency to represent the committee in the upcoming campaign. The President had a warm personal friendship for Milton Biow, head of the Biow advertising agency in New

171

York, one of the biggest ad firms in the business. Knowing the President's feelings, I went to New York and discussed with John Hamm, vice president of Biow and one of the smart young men along Madison Avenue, the matter of the Biow agency representing the committee.

Hamm was reluctant to make any commitments, saying that the matter was really a question for Milton Biow himself to handle. I did manage to arrange a meeting between McGrath and Biow.

Howard went to New York especially for this purpose. In Biow's office, he found himself forced to make a personal plea in the name of the President before the adman would agree to take our business. He finally consented and John Hamm was designated as our contact man. This arrangement suited me, for the Biow agency was an excellent one and John Hamm a good practitioner.

I was commuting to Philadelphia for meetings with the convention director, Neale Roach. We were splitting costs with the Republicans and it was necessary for plans to be carefully dovetailed with our Republican counterparts so that costs could be held to a minimum while providing the facilities which would be suitable for our differing requirements.

Television was coming along to a position where it was of importance as a medium. Earlier we had recognized TV's impact and, with Ken Fry, worked out a program which originated in New York, switched to Baltimore and then to Washington, all on the network. The network managers had said it was impossible to make instantaneous switches on TV, but the engineers took on the problem and worked out a good show.

Now TV planned top-flight coverage of the two conventions. Technical coverage of the convention was relatively simple, but reception was limited by the existing distribution of television sets. There were plenty of receivers in the big eastern cities but the problem of intercity transmission was still largely unsolved.

172

Cities in the rectangle extending from the Potomac River to New York, westward to Chicago and south to St. Louis could be covered by use of expensive coaxial cable, feeding the programs live from the convention hall. Boston and points north of New York could be fed programs during limited hours by means of a series of radio ultra-high-frequency repeater stations. Elsewhere, it was impossible to receive signals from the convention hall, and film would have to be used.

Clashes developed between the newsreel companies and television on the manner of lighting the convention. The reels needed high-power carbon lamps; TV could use the lower-powered fluorescent lamps. The difference was considerable in candle power and heat. We spent thousands of dollars solving this difficulty. In addition we built special TV and newsreel balconies on each side of the hall to allow good pictures for both.

In contrast to the TV and newsreel problems, the difficulty of taking care of the newspapermen and magazine writers was minor. The problem was how much space was needed. Seats at a national political convention are always at a premium and each allotment made to the standing gallery of newspaper correspondents meant one less seat for participants and guests.

The combination of political meetings, financial meetings, technical meetings, commuting time, planning for the departure of the presidential nonpolitical train all added up to some twenty-eight hours of work a day. One day the breaking point was reached.

I had a meeting arranged with Milton Kronheim of Washington in connection with the convention. As I prepared to leave the committee office for the appointment, I suddenly felt so tired that I was sure I'd go to sleep standing up. The feeling was so strong that I lay down on the floor to keep from falling. I could have stayed there for days; but I dragged myself up and crossed the street to a doctor. He took a cursory look at me and shoved me in the hospital.

173

I was in a hospital bed when I met with Kronheim the next day. I asked him for two cases of liquor, one scotch and one bourbon. He was a little surprised.

"Send it to Dewey Long at the White House," I told him. "He's putting the President's train together for the western trip. The liquor is for the newsmen on the train. Send it with my compliments if you will."

Kronheim, a really nice guy, agreed. The next day, only an hour before the train was to leave, Charlie Ross and Matt Connelly, the President's appointment secretary, came over to see me. They had the liquor and would ration it to the White House correspondents at strategic intervals.

"The Boss said you better get up out of that bed damn fast," Connelly told me. "We miss you!"

CHAPTER 17

THE PRESIDENT had one goal in making his cross-country trip: to drive home to the plain people of the country the true story of the Republican record in the Eightieth Congress. This was not a record the Republican Party wanted to see set forth in plain, simple, clear language.

Those of us who were more interested in the political aspects of the trip wanted to see if our judgment of how the people of the United States would react to Harry S Truman, the man, was correct.

While the President was on his trip, I spent the time in the hospital, sleeping. The doctor called it resting. He did let me read the papers and there was no question, from the newspaper accounts, about the President's success. He drew large crowds. The crowds listened and they cheered. His attacks on Congress were not only cheered by the people but covered by the press.

Brightman wrote an account of the reaction of the country to the President's backfire on Congress that summed it up very well. It read, in part:

The Republicans prefer to distribute the record in sugar-coated form as prepared by their congressional press agent (paid with federal funds) or by Senate Boss Taft's personal press agent, or by the slick high-priced publicists of such Republican adjuncts as the National Association of Manufacturers.

175

Through the rose-colored glasses of these propagandists, the Republican record appears in considerable distortion.

The Taft-Hartley Act is dressed up as a bill to "help" working people.

The help-the-rich tax cut is prettied up to look like a great "boon" to the low-salaried worker.

The failure to act to halt inflation is described as a "great victory" over regimentation and bureaucracy.

Police state "thought control" legislation is camouflaged as a "constructive" program against Communism.

Failure to act on housing, health and education programs, on a long-range farm program, on programs to curb floods, build up power resources and develop the West—all these are glossed over by the Republican propagandists.

When the President cuts through this morass of fancy words and doubletalk to carry the plain unvarnished facts directly to the people, he jolts the back-room boys of the Republican old guard and gives their congressional errand boys a severe case of pre-election jitters.

Typical of the President's effective speeches was the one he delivered in Los Angeles, where crowds estimated from 750,000 to one million turned out to cheer him. The size of the crowds must have given pause to Jimmie Roosevelt who was so actively trying to replace the President at the head of the ticket with General Eisenhower.

The President told his Los Angeles audience that he had the "right and duty" to talk to the people of America about the issues before the nation; and that he had taken his trip before Congress adjourned so that its members could learn "what the people think of those things that they have not done."

He listed the things left undone by the Eightieth Congress:

First, action to curb high prices and stop the inflationary spiral.

In this connection the President remarked, "This Eightieth Congress has said that prices would adjust themselves. Well, the prices have adjusted themselves and are adjusting themselves and have almost flown off the graph adjusting themselves in favor of the man who controls the goods. And the consumer pays through the nose."

Second, a federal low-cost rental housing program.

Third, rebuild the damage Congress itself has done to the Department of Labor.

Fourth, broaden the base of social security.

On this point the President inquired, "Do you know how Congress has broadened the base of Social Security? They've just taken 750,000 people *off* Social Security."

Fifth, adopt a federal health-insurance program.

The President pointed out that "there are only two classes of people who get the proper medical care nowadays; they are the very rich and the indigent."

Sixth, adopt a program of federal aid to education.

Seventh, expand reclamation, public power and irrigation development.

The President concluded his Los Angeles speech by praising members of Congress as individuals.

"When I speak of the Eightieth Congress and its accomplishments," he continued, "I say that Congress has not done very much for the benefit of the people. They passed a rich man's tax law. They've passed a lot of special legislation that helps special classes. I'm against class legislation and I've tried to show that in numerous vetoes. And I've made this trip so I could lay before you personally my views on this subject. If I'm wrong, you'll have a chance to tend to me later on, but if I'm not wrong, you ought to attend to somebody else."

This was the President's challenge. It was to constitute the burden of his theme throughout his campaign—later dubbed his "give 'em hell" campaign.

Taft undertook to defend Congress and, as he did so, he lost his temper. He accused the President of being soft on Communists. At the same time, in almost the succeeding sentence, he accused the President of being friendly to the "Fascist groups."

177

How Truman could be both at the same time was not explained. Then Taft said Congress should quit right now and settle the issue at the polls in November. This was a mistake because ordinary people understood it as a threat to "take my ball and go home" as a child does when the game goes badly, and considered it poor sportsmanship.

In the course of his speech Taft declared, "The President is blackguarding the Congress at every whistle stop in the country. . . ."

It was an opening too good to miss. The Democratic committee announced with sober face: "Mayors and Chambers of Commerce of thriving, patriotic, modern, civic-minded attractive and prosperous American municipalities recently described by Senator Robert A. Taft (Rep. Ohio) as 'whistle stops' are being polled to determine whether they agree with Taft's unflattering description of their homes.

"The poll is the result of inquiries to the Democratic National Committee as to whether whistle stops would be a factor in the forthcoming campaign.

"The poll is being conducted on a nonpartisan basis. Mayors and Chambers of Commerce were sent this telegram:

" 'Please wire the Democratic National Committee whether you agree with Senator Taft's description of your city as a quote whistle stop unquote.' "

Thirty-five cities were polled.

Most of these cities replied, by telegram, that they disagreed violently. Seventy-three per cent of the replies received set forth in no uncertain terms just how wrong these towns considered the Senator's description.

The following were characteristic answers:

"Must have wrong city. As the lumber capital of the world and important industrial center of the Pacific Northwest, our whistles never stop blowing. Mayor Earl L. McNutt, Eugene, Oregon."

"Characteristically Senator Taft is confused, this time on

178

whistles. President, Laramie (Wyoming) Chamber of Commerce."

"Seattle is not a whistle stop, but everyone who sees her stops and whistles, including Presidents and Senators. Mayor W. F. Devin of Seattle, Washington."

"If Idaho Falls is a whistle stop, it is the biggest and best whistle stop in the United States; population 22,000. According to *Life* Magazine a few years back, Idaho Falls was (and still is) the fastest growing city for its size in the nation. Bonneville county families average income of $4,400, and Idaho Falls is the hub city of the russet realm, producers of the potato without peer. P.S. We have the best trout fishing anywhere. Aden Hyde, President, Idaho Falls [Idaho] Chamber of Commerce."

"If Senator Taft referred to Pocatello as 'whistle stop' it is apparent that he has not visited progressing Pocatello since time of his father's 1908 campaign for President. C. Ed Flandro, Pocatello [Idaho] Chamber of Commerce."

"Grand Island was never a whistle stop. Third largest city in Nebraska with 25,000 of the finest people in the Midwest; first sugar factory in the United States here; largest livestock auction market in the world. Mayor B. J. Cunningham of Grand Island, Nebraska."

"As the central campus of the largest university in the world, the site of the cyclotron where the atom was split and atomic bomb conceived and the home of 110,000 people of culture, achievement and wealth, we find it hard to think of our city as a quote whistle stop unquote unless the whistle be one of admiration which our soldier boys give to a girl of breath-taking beauty exclamation point. Mayor Laurence L. Cross of Berkeley, California."

"Senator Taft in very poor taste to refer to Gary as quote whistle stop unquote. 135,000 citizens of America's greatest steel city resent this slur. Mayor of Gary, Indiana."

"... The term hardly applies to the Los Angeles metropolitan area in which presently live one-thirty-fifth of all the people in

179

the United States, considerably more than half of the population of Ohio. The number of new permanent residents within the city limits of Los Angeles since 1940 approximates the total population of Taft's home city, Cincinnati. I feel quite confident that anyone who could have been in Los Angeles last Monday, a perfect day in June with Southern California sunshine and blue skies, and witnessed nearly one million good American citizens lining the streets to welcome their President, would have both whistled and stopped. Mayor Fletcher Bowron, of Los Angeles, California."

Mayor Bowron, incidentally, is a Republican.

"Senator Taft's description of our town as a whistle stop is rather misleading in view of the fact that Crestline, Ohio, a town of 5,000 population, is served by two of the world's greatest transportation systems, Pennsylvania Railroad Company and the New York Central. Forty-two passenger trains make regular scheduled stops here daily. Suggest Senator Taft consult time tables of the above referred to transportation systems for a proper classification, proper description of a 'whistle stop.' Mayor A. P. Soner of Crestline, Ohio."

Seven per cent of the total group of cities answered merely that it had not occurred to them that Senator Taft's statement could be interpreted as applying to their town. The remaining twenty per cent of the replies took no position, contenting themselves with asking more details of Senator Taft's statement. Most of these indicated, however, that official disagreement with the Senator would be forthcoming since the towns requested that the specific information be telegraphed immediately.

There was only one dissident note. The president of a Chamber of Commerce in a small Dakota town wired irately, "This Democratic plot against Senator Taft. Should be law preventing such scandalous and libelous treatment great American patriot and law maker. Bet you ten to one anything you want Senator Taft next President. Wire answer collect."

I wired him two words: "Tsk! Tsk!"

The poll made Taft look ridiculous, emphasizing that he had lost his temper. We got regional stories in every town and city polled. In addition the rest of the country had a hearty belly laugh at Taft's expense.

I went to Minneapolis, Minnesota, to consult with Charlie Ward, head of Brown & Bigelow, on some materials to use at the Democratic convention to keep the delegates' minds on their President. Before I went Howard McGrath said, "Go all out. Don't stint on money! We want this thing done up right."

I did a double take. But I carried out my instructions fully. I picked up pencils, badges, nomination balloting score cards, notebooks, pins, thimbles and other knickknacks, all with Harry S Truman's name, picture or both all over them. Several thousand big pictures were ordered of the President to be plastered all over Philadelphia on the day the nominee of the convention would be selected. I ordered thousands of stickers with the words: Harry S Truman, President of the United States. These were stuck on every hotel bathroom mirror the day the convention opened.

The cost was about seven thousand dollars. When I returned to Washington, I gave the bill to McGrath. He handed it right back to me.

"Tell Steve Harrington to send the bill to John Nangle, Democratic national committeeman for Missouri," he said. "That's Missouri's contribution to the President's campaign for nomination."

Meanwhile Congress was driving toward adjournment in preparation for the Republican National Convention. They were delayed in their adjournment plans by the attempt to obtain some concrete action on housing and on a farm program.

Nothing was done on housing; but the Republicans in their convention cynically ignored this and put a big housing plank in their platform anyway.

The Aiken sliding parity plan could not be put over as the farm program. With time running out on adjournment, the Republicans in desperation agreed to extend the existing Democratic farm program for another year while they "investigated" further. This helped our campaign with the farmers.

Within the party we were being plagued by Eisenhower problems. But so were the Republicans, and for the moment the spotlight was on the GOP.

On the Sunday preceding opening of the Republican convention the president of the Pennsylvania Railroad, Martin W. Clement, threw a garden party on his modest six- or seven-hundred-acre estate, rumored to be all lawn, for the principal Republican candidates. I arranged for a photographer, who was assigned to cover the party for one of the wire services, to see what he could make for the Democrats in the way of pictures which might be of special value.

He got a shot of the president of the Pennsylvania Railroad, one of the two or three biggest corporations in America, with one arm around Republican candidate Taft and the other around Republican candidate Dewey. All three were beaming and Clement was the object of the adoring gaze of both candidates. We had the picture printed all over the country, and labor picked it up in every union publication. The shot cost the Democratic committee ten dollars.

Brightman and I wangled two of the very best seats at the Republican convention and went up to see how they were running things. We were unsuspected as we drank GOP whisky and watched while the Republicans nominated their presidential candidate.

One thing which struck both of us was the "spontaneous" demonstrations which accompanied each nomination. The banners, placards, state signs, et cetera, were all carried in each demonstration by the same people. This was Republican efficiency.

182

A bearer of Taft signs merely hung up his Taft banner, took up a Stassen banner, and then after the Stassen demonstration, carried banners for Dewey and Warren. I discussed this phenomenon with a few newsmen. They agreed it was a good feature story, but didn't bother to do anything about it.

"Paper wouldn't print it," they explained.

When we returned to Washington I recommended at a White House meeting that we guard against such "spontaneity."

"The tame fat cats of the press who covered the Republican convention will be raging tigers when they cover us Democrats," I told the meeting. "We'll get the full treatment if we leave ourselves open to it."

Brightman and I were in the Pennsylvania Railroad lounge, operated at the GOP convention as a "watering" place for elephants. Suddenly I was enveloped in a bear hug by Al Whitney of the Railway Trainmen. With him was Carroll Cone of Pan American. Whitney explained he was in town to see the convention and to raise some money for Truman.

We were joined by one of the most prominent society matrons of Washington who asked me, "Do you think Senator Vandenberg would be a strong candidate?"

"Don't mention his name," I said. "It might get him nominated." He was the one candidate who worried us most.

"Oh, no." She smiled sweetly. "The Senator is all through. I thought he'd be a dangerous candidate too. All week I've been telling the delegates stories about him. Everyone in Washington knows. I've filled in all the society reporters and the story has been in the gossip columns. They won't dare nominate him now."

She was right. Vandenberg's destruction as a candidate was complete.

The moral of that story is, in Kipling's words, "The female of the species is more deadly than the male."

There were a number of ballots, but the result was foregone.

183

It was Dewey. Taft was second, with Stassen and Warren gathering a few scattered votes. If the stop-Dewey boys could have concentrated their forces around one candidate, they could have won. But each of the other candidates held out stubbornly and Dewey licked them individually.

The issue was clear. It would be Dewey running on Taft's congressional record. The course of action which we had followed for more than a year now was justified.

CHAPTER 18

THE SENATOR couldn't read his script. He had left his glasses in his hotel room. Colonel Charles Baron of Chicago, an assistant sergeant at arms of the Democratic National Convention assigned as an aide to Senator Barkley, hurried back to the Bellevue-Stratford Hotel and rummaged the Senator's suite for his glasses.

Having found them, he hurried back to the convention hall. The newsreel men once more got ready to roll their cameras to do an advance of Senator Barkley's keynote speech.

But the glasses didn't help. The lights glared so that the speech couldn't be read. Colonel Baron took the four-minute excerpt from the keynote speech to convention headquarters at the Bellevue-Stratford where it was retyped on a speech typewriter with extra-large letters.

Baron sped back to the convention hall only to find the type was still too dim to be seen in the glaring lights.

Senator Barkley put his hand on Baron's shoulder and said, "I'm just getting old, I guess. My eyes aren't as good as they were." Then he stood up like the trouper he was and gave his lines from memory.

Baron was exhausted. Heat, worry and the feeling of urgency had worn him out. He came back to the hotel with the Senator

185

and told me, "I don't know how you do it. I can't. I'm going back to Chicago." Baron, who was a gay, café-society bachelor and owner of one of the biggest Ford agencies in Chicago, decided he had "had enough"—at least of campaigning.

When Barkley was appointed keynote speaker by Chairman McGrath, he had asked me to draft portions of a speech for him. After he read the draft, he asked for research material which we supplied. Then he threw the draft away.

"I'll take this down to Paducah and write it while I sit out under the apple tree," he said.

He sent me a copy for duplication for release to the press. It read wonderfully but we timed it at an hour and forty-five minutes. Ken Fry was in a quandary.

"I promised the nets the speech wouldn't go more than forty-five minutes," he said.

Trying to limit a keynote speech at a convention seemed futile and I told him so. But we did try some cutting in an effort to bring the speech closer to the time Fry had agreed to. It was then that I first realized that it was a great speech. It couldn't be cut without losing in every instance some important portions. So we let it alone.

But, with the lighting problem, how would the Senator carry on with a speech almost two hours in length? We tried to devise a stronger rostrum lamp that would highlight the page without blinding the speaker. But the rostrum lights simply were not effective when the camera lights were on. In addition the great overhead lights in the convention hall produced strange contrasts in light and shadow.

Senator Barkley was not worried. He'd work it out all right, he said. Tuesday night he went to the rostrum for his speech before some twelve hundred apathetic delegates. But they were not apathetic long, for after a few short sentences Barkley had their attention. His rendition was masterful. With never a flaw, never a hesitation, emphasis came where emphasis was needed.

186

The Senator was a great orator. On this evening he gave one of the greatest keynote speeches ever delivered to the Democratic conventions over the years.

His pitiless dissection of Republican failure and his vibrant recital of the articles of faith for true Democrats brought on a wild and tumultuous thirty-minute floor demonstration for the veteran Kentucky legislator at the close of his speech.

The Senator told the Democrats:

We have assembled here for a great purpose.

We have a solemn commission from millions of American men and women.

We are here to give them an accounting of our stewardship in the administration of their affairs for sixteen outstanding and eventful years, for not one of which we make apology.

At every convention since 1932 and on every political rostrum, Republican politicians have hurled their anathemas at this "New Deal" as if it were some blight or plague that had poisoned the lives and consumed the liberties of the people and kept them chained and helpless.

In determining the validity of these diatribes, let us inquire what is this cankering, corroding fungus growth, which every Republican orator at their recent convention denounced with accustomed rancor; then, in their platform, hugged to their political bosom as if it were the child of their own loins?

In the first place it was recovery.

The new Administration of Franklin D. Roosevelt breathed into the nostrils of every worthy American enterprise, large or small, a breath of new life, new hope and new determination. What, therefore, is this New Deal which Republican orators denounce and their platform seeks to imitate?

Then Senator Barkley gave the convention the answers. He gave the convention chapter and verse on the accomplishments of the Roosevelt and Truman eras. After checking off the long

187

list of Democratic accomplishments, Senator Barkley turned to the reactionary record of the Eightieth Congress.

First, the Senator pointed to the attempts of the Republican Party to destroy the basic rights of labor.

"While lacking in courage to repeal the Labor Relations Act and the Fair Labor Standards Act," Barkley said, "the Republicans have sought . . . to destroy . . . the rights enjoyed by labor in the collective bargaining process."

From labor, Senator Barkley turned his guns on the record on housing.

"Where is that housing legislation? It is not on the statutes! It furnishes no roof over the veterans, workers or farmers. It is just another gone goose!"

Barkley went down the list of Republican failures, then turned his attention to the 1948 GOP convention. The Senator paid tribute to the leadership of "Old High Tariffs" Joe Grundy in the Republican convention. He recited:

All hail the power of Grundy's name,
Let candidates prostrate fall,
Bring forth Republican diadem,
And crown him boss of all.

As he neared the close of his speech, the Senator commented on Republican plans for a housecleaning in Washington.

The Senator declared:

The Republican candidate for President announced he would inaugurate the greatest housecleaning ever seen in Washington if he should be elected.

The Republican nominee has also announced, with characteristic finality, that he proposes to clean the cobwebs from the government at Washington.

I am not an expert on cobwebs, but if my memory does not betray me, when the Democratic Party took over the government of the United States sixteen years ago, even the spiders were so weak from starvation that they could not weave a cobweb in any department of the government in Washington.

He concluded his oration with a moving plea:

Behold, civilization knocks at the door!
Behold, the assembly of unnamed and unnumbered men and women who yearn for peace knocks at the door!
Shall we hear the voices and open the door? Or shall we slam it in the face of an appealing world, turn our backs upon a divine obligation and refuse to lead the children of men out of the bondage of fear and slavery into a free world and a free life?

As Barkley concluded, the convention hall became bedlam. And for more than a half hour the crowd continued to cheer the Senator from Kentucky. He took a convention that was sick to its political belly from an overdose of intraparty strife, Gallup polls and the gloomy forecasts of an unfriendly press, and breathed life into it. Barkley's speech made him the leading candidate for Vice President.

After the tumult died and Senator Barkley turned away, I went to the rostrum for his speech copy; I had noticed he was not carrying it as he left. I found the copy still in perfect order.

He had given the entire speech from memory!

The candidate for Vice President on the Truman ticket had been getting a great deal of attention. Leading all the rest in the advance calculations in the press was Justice Douglas, followed by McCormack, O'Mahoney and a number of others. Back in the ruck was Barkley's name. There was a question whether Barkley himself wanted the nomination; there was also the question of whether President Truman wanted him.

Barkley had one asset which was of great value: Les Biffle, then secretary to the minority in the Senate, was managing his campaign backstage. There was never a smarter operator than Les Biffle and his position of sergeant at arms of the convention gave him an ideal place from which to maneuver.

189

I was in Senator McGrath's office in the Bellevue-Stratford when a call came in from the White House. It was from Truman. The President had called Douglas in Oregon, where the Supreme Court Justice was vacationing, and asked him to accept the nomination for Vice President. Douglas refused and the President was disappointed.

I went to our press room and announced: "Justice Douglas has authorized me to say that he will not be a candidate for the office of Vice President on the Democratic ticket in 1948."

Merriman Smith, whose job it was at the White House press conferences to say, "Thank you, Mr. President!" at the end, didn't give me a sign-off. He took off for the nearest telephone.

A political convention is like nothing else in the world, particularly for those who wait on it and tend to its wants and needs. The task of putting on the quadrennial party gatherings is monumental; but there is the additional job of handling tickets, of ensuring that those who have tickets use them so that the convention hall is not deserted while the committees work. Everyone wants tickets to the sessions of the convention, but unless there is something spectacular or dramatic in the wind, the majority of the tickets go unused.

Everyone wants a badge. There are press badges, officials' badges, delegates' badges, badges for the staff of the sergeant at arms, workers' badges, and then a lot of meaningless badges which are designed to take the pressure off the people handing out badges.

This convention was little different from others that had gone before. Perhaps there was more excitement because of the strife within the party and the general desire on the part of everyone to be present if and when the roof blew off.

Early on the first day we held press conferences for Senator McGrath and Leon Henderson, who was there to make his pitch to draft General Eisenhower. It may seem strange that we held the press conference for Henderson, but theoretically the National Committee is neutral and it supplies meeting rooms and facilities for all groups within the party.

190

Henderson was bombastic. He got a good play in the press, for he represented one phase of the opposition to the President. Senator McGrath was more restrained. His statements had more to do with arrangements at the convention at this stage.

The platform committee, under the chairmanship of Senator Francis Myers, had been working for days on testimony from which they would draft the final version of the official party platform. When they finally settled to the writing of it, a real fight developed within the committee. It was the same fight that platform committees have had at every convention since—civil rights! Some of the names ring a familiar note to those who have watched the party conventions on television in 1952 and 1956.

Hubert Humphrey, then a candidate for Senator from Minnesota, was one of the leading exponents of a civil-rights stand with teeth in it. Jimmie Roosevelt, Franklin D. Roosevelt, Jr., and a little-known young man named G. Mennen Williams, destined to become five times Governor of Michigan, were also in the forefront.

Opposing was Strom Thurmond of South Carolina and his entire phalanx of followers, including Fielding Wright of Mississippi, and the Louisiana contingent.

The platform committee was meeting in a top-floor ballroom at the Bellevue-Stratford. As the time approached for the report to be made to the convention, we had to begin making duplicate copies of it. Our security arrangements were simple but, I thought, adequate. The platform was transported page by page, either by me or by another trusted committee member, to our locked mailing room where it was mimeographed and then assembled to await completion and distribution. During each of my journeys from one room to another I was practically swarmed over by newsmen trying to see the papers or asking questions which they hoped might draw an unguarded answer. But all was going smoothly.

Suddenly Mary Clynes, a librarian for the committee, called me. Word for word, the platform was coming across the United Press ticker. Meanwhile UP's competitors had been notified that

191

UP had a beat. Claiming foul, they descended on Myers and Scott Lucas. The Senators turned on me.

The session with the two Senators was short and sharp. It was late at night and tempers were hot. The problem was to avoid a quarrel and concentrate on finding the leak.

I hurried to the mimeograph room and seized all copies of the platform. Then we conducted a hurried investigation. It was disclosed that a UP official had given one of the mailing-room boys a case of whisky.

To protect the other newsmen and discredit the UP version of the platform, I suggested making some changes in the final platform copy. This was done.

As I recall this incident now, I realize that as a result of that leak we received a great deal more publicity on our platform than we would have had otherwise. If it hadn't happened, we should have planned it!

Our civil-rights plank was very similar to that of the 1944 platform, but Dixiecrats now insisted on complete rejection of the entire issue or they would bolt the convention. There was, of course, no possibility of weakening the stand taken by the President.

It was obvious there would be a walkout of three, perhaps four states. To dramatize the departure of bolting delegates, it was suggested that we mount a photographic enlargement of the Bill of Rights over the main entrance of the convention hall. This would etch deeply the Southern rejection of the President's position on civil rights. I argued against the plan and was backed up by McGrath. Pointing up the symbolism in this manner would only make the return of the Southern delegates more difficult.

On the second day the break came, as expected. After a floor fight the convention adopted the civil-rights plank; and the Dixiecrats departed, calling for an all-South convention of what they termed the "true Democratic party." However, the bulk of the South held firm, backing the nomination of Senator Richard Russell of Georgia, who took the more moderate position that the issue should be settled within the party.

there were no flowers, there were no decorations, the importance of the Greek-American committee was not understood. He said that Redding was trying to sabotage the Greek-American committee because "Redding hates me."

After his outburst, he concluded, "I'm going to see that the White House hears of this. The President won't stand for it. General Vaughan will see to it that Redding is taken care of."

Cieplinski didn't understand what was happening. He didn't realize two things: first, that Maragon was trying to impress Helis with his White House connections; and, second, I felt he was hoping to embarrass me for having denied him access to my office. However, Cieplinski finally exploded, told Maragon off and was promptly seconded by Helis. That subdued Maragon and the meeting went amicably on its way.

But Maragon wasn't through. He called General Vaughan and gave him a highly colored version of the entire incident. Vaughan called McGrath and Louis Johnson and both of these gentlemen called me. I offered to quit. It was my contention that the meeting was a good one; that it had been adequately staffed and housed and that if Maragon could carry his malicious gossip to the White House and get away with it, I wanted no part of the campaign.

It was a silly tempest in a teapot. All of us had been working under a forced head of steam and it was a relief to blow off. Like most tempests of this nature, it was resolved by cool heads, and forgotten. But it was very evident that Maragon didn't forget it.

Helis and Scopas initiated a campaign among their countrymen to help finance the National Democratic Committee so that the President would be able to carry his message to the country. They did a yeoman job, especially in one instance at the end of the campaign.

The lack of money was always hanging over our heads. We were meeting bills by virtue of Louis Johnson's heroic efforts; but each bill was a separate and difficult problem.

225

On Thursday, October 28, a meeting was held in Johnson's office with Paul Fitzpatrick and Senator McGrath. Fitzpatrick reported that New York was teetering between Dewey and Truman. This was great news, for the attitude of most New York leaders up to this time was that the state was irretrievably lost.

"It's close," Fitzpatrick said. "Dewey is still ahead and the Wallace group is taking votes from us. But it's now so close that if we could drop fifty thousand dollars into the campaign over the week end, I think we can carry the state for the President."

McGrath was delighted. But fifty thousand dollars? He looked at Johnson and raised his eyebrows. Johnson nodded. McGrath told Fitzpatrick that putting fifty thousand dollars into New York meant that the money would have to be raised in some special manner because it wasn't either in the treasury or in sight.

Johnson, picking it up, then assured Fitzpatrick that the money would be raised and made available. They settled down to talking details.

Fitzpatrick stressed the importance at this stage of Mrs. Eleanor Roosevelt's influence in New York. An atmosphere of coolness had come between President Truman and Mrs. Roosevelt—nothing serious but a coolness nevertheless. Up to this point, she had refused to take part in the campaign, saying that as a delegate to the United Nations, she didn't feel that she should be active politically. (Mrs. Roosevelt had, in a letter to Madame Perkins, former Secretary of Labor, stated that she was for Truman.) I said that Mrs. Roosevelt would give the whole country a lift if she could be persuaded to make her support of the President known.

In addition Fitzpatrick wanted to place advertisements in New York papers outlining the facts of Dewey's record as Governor. "The true story," said Fitzpatrick, "will explode the myth of Dewey as a great administrator."

This was a proposal that I had previously made but I had

226

been turned down for lack of funds. Now Fitzpatrick was making the recommendation on a "must" basis.

McGrath and Johnson agreed on both the advertisements and a nationwide broadcast for Mrs. Roosevelt, subject, of course, to Mrs. Roosevelt's agreeing to talk. The rest of the fifty thousand would be used by Fitzpatrick on election day to man the polls with watchers. As the meeting closed, I was asked to produce Mrs. Roosevelt.

That was a dilly. I didn't know Mrs. Roosevelt well. I knew that she had been approached on the subject previously and had refused. Besides, she was in Paris attending United Nations sessions.

How then to "produce" her for the broadcast? I got Ed Flynn, former Democratic National Chairman from New York and at that time a national committeeman. Fitzpatrick agreed that Flynn was probably the one person who could influence Mrs. Roosevelt because of their long-time friendship.

But when I talked to Flynn, he expressed serious doubts. "I've discussed this with the lady," he said. "I don't think she'll budge. She feels strongly on the matter of not taking part in politics as long as she's with the United Nations."

However, Flynn agreed to get Mrs. Roosevelt on the telephone in Paris.

"But you'll have to do the talking," he told me. "I've already tried and been told no. If I try to talk to her on this subject, I'll just be cut off."

The call was placed. Flynn spoke to Mrs. Roosevelt and briefly stated our problem. Then he said, "I won't try to influence you, Mrs. Roosevelt. But I wish you'd talk to Jack Redding, publicity director of the committee." He handed me the phone.

My conversation was brief. After polite greetings, I outlined quickly the fact that New York was in the balance, that the whole election was close, that despite the Dewey claims and the polls and the strong pro-Dewey press, Truman was close to winning. Then I concluded, "I think, Mrs. Roosevelt, that you are the key to the situation. I think your influence in America could elect President Truman. Without you . . . well, we may fail."

This grand lady didn't hesitate. "I have been reluctant to be part of this campaign because of my United Nations responsibilities. You know that?"

"Yes, ma'am."

"But if it's as close as you say, and if you think I can help, I'll do it. But how?"

I told her that I would have a radio-network representative contact her in Paris; that she should prepare a six-minute speech and that we'd have it short-waved to New York for re-broadcast in the United States.

"It may be," I told her, "that you'll have to do the actual broadcast late at night because of the problem of getting your voice here with broadcast quality. Short wave at this time of year is best at night."

That didn't bother her. "Have them get in touch with me and I'll have a six-minute speech ready. What do you want me to stress?"

"Mrs. Roosevelt, stress the thing for which everyone in this country loves you—your fight for peace."

"All right," she agreed.

Then came the decision as to when we should air the broadcast and over what network. I consulted with Lester Malitz of Warwick & Legler, our radio-time buyer. Sunday night, October 31, was when I wanted to stage the broadcast. This would give forty-eight hours for the effect of Mrs. Roosevelt's speech to make itself felt.

Malitz advised that the top program on Sunday was "Stop the Music" on the American Broadcasting Company network between eight and nine o'clock.

"That's Bert Parks's show," he said, "and it peaks in the last

228

fifteen minutes. But I don't know whether ABC will clear the time for you."

I informed Fitzpatrick that I was going to use this particular time for the broadcast. Also, I requested that he ask former Governor Herbert Lehman of New York to speak on the same program because his voice was a potent one in Jewish circles in New York. Fitzpatrick agreed.

Then, with Malitz, I called on the ABC network to buy our time. Because Malitz had expressed doubt as to ABC's willingness to clear the time we wanted, I did not request them to do so. I informed them that the Democratic Party was pre-empting the time from 8:45 to 9:00 P.M. EST in the public interest under the provisions of the Federal Communications Act. ABC didn't like it. This was their top show and they didn't want it interrupted for politics, not even for Mrs. Roosevelt.

Malitz and I were discussing this with several of their executives. Suddenly their faces lit up and I got a cold chill. Obviously they had thought of an out. They had.

"I'm sorry, we won't be able to clear this time for you simply because neither Mrs. Roosevelt nor Governor Lehman is a candidate. The FCC will not require us to clear time for you under the circumstances."

This was an angle I hadn't thought about.

"You confuse me," I said with my fingers crossed. "You say there's no candidate? I thought I had made it clear that the broadcast would include Senator Barkley, broadcasting from Louisville. He most certainly is a candidate."

That did it. With reluctance they agreed to clear the time. But they insisted payment for the time would have to be made no later than noon on Saturday. And the cost would be $25,721.

They agreed to have their Paris man arrange for a short-wave broadcast of Mrs. Roosevelt's speech. He would contact Mrs. Roosevelt that afternoon.

Now it was up to me. I had to produce Senator Barkley and

229

I found the Senator had a problem. He was to address a meeting in Paducah that evening and the time of the broadcast would find him remote from a radio station, actually on the rostrum at his meeting. There was no easy solution so we accepted the additional cost of running lines from the Paducah radio station to the hall where the meeting was to be held. He would do his broadcast from backstage. Incidentally, ABC was upset because it was Paducah instead of Louisville as I had originally told them.

The program was set. Barkley would open the show for four minutes from Kentucky and introduce Mrs. Roosevelt. When Mrs. Roosevelt finished, Governor Lehman would take over. He would speak for three minutes, leaving time for a political disclaimer by the network. Everything was in order. Fitzpatrick was organizing listening parties all over the state of New York. I informed the party leaders in the other states, giving them the times when the program would be broadcast in the various time zones.

Next we got some static, and not from the radio. A prominent Democrat in New York went to Fitzpatrick in the interest of the cigarette company which sponsored the last fifteen minutes of "Stop the Music." Would Fitzpatrick intervene to keep us from pre-empting the time? Paul referred him to me. I said no.

"Then," he said, "I'll not be responsible for what Bert Parks will do on the air when he signs off."

It sounded suspiciously like a threat.

"I don't know what you mean," I told him. "But if anybody, anywhere, sabotages that show, I'll ruin him between Sunday night and election time Tuesday. I'll make any sabotage scheme roar back like nothing has ever roared back before in history."

Then I rang for my secretary and in my caller's presence dictated to her the request he had made which I suspected was a threat. He left my office a mortal enemy, I'm sure.

Of course nothing happened. I'm convinced Bert Parks had

230

never indicated that he would be a party to such a threat, even implied. But I could not afford to take chances.

We weren't out of the woods yet.

By ten o'clock on Saturday morning, the cash—$25,721—had not been produced to pay for the show. With a noon deadline for payment and with ABC positively anxious not to have to put on the program in place of their top show, this was a real worry. I called Louis Johnson.

"Where is the money?"

"Haven't you got it?"

"No."

"Call William Helis at the Plaza Hotel. He's there now. He told me you'd have the money this morning."

I called Helis. He hadn't known about the noon deadline.

"But," he said, "I think the committee has finished collecting it. It'll be in your office by eleven-thirty."

I chewed my nails, fidgeted, worried. Then right on the dot of eleven-thirty, the money arrived in my office. A little man brought it in a paper shopping bag. It made a solid thump when it was dropped on my desk.

Leyshon, Malitz, and Brightman were with me when I opened the bag. There it was, $25,721 in one-dollar bills, fives, tens, a roll of fifties, and nearly two hundred dollars in change. Obviously the Greek committee, spurred by Helis, had collected offerings from every Greek restaurant and business in the New York area.

I picked up the bag and carried it up to Paul Fitzpatrick's office on the floor above ours in the Biltmore.

"There," I said, dropping the bag on his desk. "I hope you weren't worrying as much as I was. But there it is, every penny of it. Get it up to ABC right away. Don't give them any excuse to cancel!"

Delighted, Fitzpatrick hurried off to make the payment.

On Sunday evening the broadcast went on the air without a

hitch. The short-wave recording of Mrs. Roosevelt was of top quality. There were no side noises from Paducah where Barkley was speaking backstage in an impromptu studio. Governor Lehman was eloquent in his brief talk. The program went so smoothly that for us it was anticlimactic.

How effective was the show? There's no yardstick by which it could be judged. It didn't save New York for us, but all over the country Democratic Party leaders were jubilant. They had earnestly wanted Mrs. Roosevelt to express support for the Truman-Barkley ticket. Now she had done so!

CHAPTER 22

CHAIRMAN MCGRATH accepted an invitation to appear on "Meet the Press." I had staved off participation in the show for months, but McGrath, finally cornered, was unable to refuse. On the day of the show, McGrath, Brightman, Fry and I conferred for several hours, so the Senator would be prepared as much as possible for the nasty questions like "Have you stopped beating your wife?"

"Never be at a loss," Fry warned him. "If you don't have an immediate answer to a question, ask one back and make it wordy just to slow things down so you can get a chance to reflect on your answer."

And I threw in, "There's one gimmick to watch. During the last minute on the air, you'll be asked a real mean question. The idea is to have the program go off the air with the victim gasping like a fish out of water. So watch for that last question right at the end and be ready to hit back."

Show time came. McGrath answered all legitimate questions thoughtfully and parried those that were meant to be needles. With about a minute to go, Bert Andrews of the New York *Herald Tribune* asked, "Senator, why did the President pardon Jim Curley?"

Curley, long a controversial figure in Massachusetts politics, had been in jail for nearly a year on a charge of using the mails to defraud. He was in poor health and this had brought a presidential pardon.

McGrath didn't hesitate. "To get him out of jail," he said. It was Andrews who was left gasping as the show signed off.

There was a great deal of maneuvering by both parties to obtain the best radio time for their candidates. The Republicans were able to proceed with more confidence for they had money available. On the other hand, I often contracted for radio time, knowing there was no money in the bank to cover the commitment. Each time this was done, we went ahead only after a meeting with Louis Johnson, Joe Blythe and Mrs. Mary Zirkle, comptroller of the committee.

In June the four radio networks had submitted proposed contracts to the national committees of both parties, covering credit arrangements for the purchase of radio time during the campaign.

The agreement called for payment on the fifteenth of the current month for any broadcasts between the first and fifteenth, and for payment on the first of the succeeding month for broadcasts between the fifteenth and the first. This seemed fair to me and I told McGrath so. We signed the contracts and returned them to the networks.

But after the convention, when it became evident that the Democrats were hard pressed for cash, there was a change. NBC and CBS submitted revised contracts on an "or else" basis. These new contracts, drawn to supersede the ones we had already signed, called for payment seventy-two hours in advance of any scheduled broadcast. It was a unilateral action seemingly aimed directly at the Democrats.

When I discussed the new contracts with McGrath, he was furious.

"The hell with them," he said. "We'll get along without them."

There was nothing I would have liked better but this attitude was not realistic.

"We've got to have the two major nets to reach the country,"

234

I told him. "If we could get along with Mutual and ABC, I'd say let NBC and CBS go. But it isn't in the cards. We'll have to go along."

McGrath reluctantly signed the contracts. But on the NBC paper he made a little line drawing of a man with his fingers to his nose under it. The contracts were duly delivered to the networks, but no one made reference to McGrath's artistic addition.

The new arrangement complicated the entire problem of radio for the Democrats. On one occasion Louis Johnson called me about a scheduled $100,000 broadcast to say, "We don't have the money in the bank to meet this bill by the due time, Saturday morning. But we'll have the money on Monday. What can we do to stretch our credit?"

Warwick & Legler were handling the details of payment. We arranged to give them a check on Saturday morning too late to be deposited and cleared in that day's business. They, in turn, gave their own check to the network for the hundred thousand. On Monday they agreed to hold up the deposit of the committee check until late in the day, although Louis Johnson had more than enough money deposited in the bank by 10:00 A.M.

We were very grateful to Warwick & Legler for helping us over a bad bump but what the ad agency never knew was that at the time they received our check and delivered theirs to the network, the committee bank account was down to something like five hundred dollars.

About this time the Chicago *Tribune* searched its isolationist soul and declared itself for Dewey as "the least worst" candidate.

The newspapers were outdoing themselves each day in their predictions that Dewey would win. When Secretary of State Marshall announced at the United Nations session in Paris that the United States would support the provisions of the Bernadotte Report on Palestine, the New York *Herald Tribune* indignantly reported that the President had not cleared this with Governor Dewey and John Foster Dulles. The entire tone of the *Herald Tribune's* story from Paris was scolding for this lapse.

In the New York *Times* two political pundits, Bill Lawrence and Jim Hagerty, father of Eisenhower's White House press secretary, ponderously predicted state after state going Republican. In the last two weeks of the campaign Lawrence weakened to the extent of expressing some doubts as to results on the congressional level in Pennsylvania. For the rest it was all Dewey and why was the campaign being dragged out?

About mid-October four of the top reporters covering the political campaigns decided to call on those strange people at the Biltmore who continued to see Truman as the victor. Pulitzer Prize winner Ed Folliard of the Washington *Post*, the Associated Press congressional reporter Jack Bell, Jim Hagerty and Merriman Smith came to me to arrange for an interview with McGrath.

Howard talked with the reporters for an hour, going down the list of states and analyzing each briefly. His conclusion was: "The worst that can happen would be for the election to be thrown into the House of Representatives for lack of a majority of electoral college votes for either major candidate."

Four pairs of eyebrows were raised. There were polite questions. But it was obvious that McGrath's analysis was not taken seriously. Looking at a map which had the status of each state, as we saw it, charted, Hagerty asked if he could print it. We agreed and the *Times* a few days later carried the map and Hagerty's story on the McGrath interview. He played the story straight but took great care to handle all predictions in quotes so that no one would think such fantastic predictions were his own. In fairness to Hagerty, he handled very well an assignment made difficult by fact that his son was then Dewey's press secretary.

The tone was objective too in the other three stories written concerning the interview.

But when registrations closed in New York City with a disappointing total of 3,321,000 on the rolls, Warren Moscow of the New York *Times* saw this as an indication of lack of enthusiasm in the Democratic organization in New York.

Financial difficulties continued to plague us at national headquarters. A pictorial history of the President, a publicity project which the opposition insisted on calling a comic book, had been initiated in the early spring. Malcolm Ator had sold me the idea of bringing out a popularized pictorial story of President Truman. Brightman and I wrote Truman's life story as a guide for this project. The White House approved every word of this copy, and later the final script for the picture book was carefully checked by Ross.

We had planned a first printing of three million books for distribution across the country. But this project, like everything else, ran into money problems. Each week saw another postponement of the delivery date. In vain I tried to persuade Ator to run the books and bill us as was usual with other printers. But he wouldn't turn a press until the money was on the barrelhead. And he wouldn't run off more books than were covered by the money he had on hand.

In October Louis Johnson called a meeting to discuss the project. He wanted to determine whether to allot money for printing the book or to abandon the whole project. It seemed that I was being second-guessed by some of the money-raisers who had told Johnson the "very idea of a comic book about the President is undignified."

My answer to that was twofold. First I asked about the critics. "Who are they? Where'd they get reputations either as judges of good taste or as judges of publicity values?"

Finally I said, "No matter what happens to this project, it's going to cost money because we're committed for the artwork, plates and composition which has already been done. The additional cost of printing and distribution is not too large. It wouldn't be economical to waste the investment already made by failing to spend a little additional."

This argument reached Johnson and the money was forthcoming but it came in bits and pieces. Ator's policy of only printing what he had cash in hand for ran up the costs and delayed deliveries. The last batches of the book came so late that shipments

237

to the field had to be made by air express. It was an example of money waste resulting from delays.

The book itself received a good deal of publicity. *Time* ran a full-page spread concerning it, saying it was well done and effective with "some groups." *Time* was not sure, however, it was dignified for a presidential candidate to have his career pictorialized in "comic book" fashion.

Some of the White House stalwarts who hadn't been in on preparation of the volume thought it should have been cleared with the President. They were crestfallen to learn that he had approved it some months before. Whatever the critics had to say concerning the book, the real test was in its reception by the public. This was tremendous. Workers at the precinct level reported it as the most effective piece of campaign material they had.

Distributors of these books in city after city reported that "they always take them home. You never see them lying around the street after you pass them out." In Massachusetts many schools permitted distribution to students; and in this instance we found the books were being taken home to be read by parents as well as by the school children. The demand for the booklets was so great that we could have used ten million copies instead of the three million available.

The most heartfelt approbation came in the form of criticism voiced by local organizations nationwide. "Why did we get them so late? It's a shame we didn't have them earlier, for the book is effective. People want them."

Largest shipments went to California, Illinois, New York and Ohio. In southern California, Helen Gahagan Douglas, the liberal Congresswoman from Los Angeles, found the books particularly effective. She was constantly on the telephone seeking additional shipments. Cieplinski and the nationalities division alone could have used them all.

There were other innovations. In 1947 I had read about a proposal made to the Republican National Committee for a soap-opera type radio program aimed at the women's vote. It seemed like a good idea and it had the virtue of never having been tried. India Edwards and I discussed the matter. When plans were being drawn for the campaign, I insisted that provision be made for a women's daytime program in the radio budget.

In September, I assigned Don Gibbs of the Warwick & Legler staff to work out a women's program that could be financed for approximately $50,000. Gibbs had gone to work with Mrs. Edwards and Ken Fry to produce a show which would reach women voters in their homes. I went to the studio to hear the first show recorded. After the first one, it was to be a live disc-jockey-type show. After listening to it, I immediately okayed scheduling the program for 3:45 P.M. EST, nationwide on the ABC network, three times a week from October 12 until November 1. Then I arranged for a press review of the recorded premier.

The show was an immediate hit. Gibbs had done a superlative job of combining several gimmicks with biting humor to achieve a program that had real political impact. Following the preview, *Variety*, the bible of show business, reported, "The 'Democratic Record' show is the best election pitch ever made on radio."

The program opened and closed to the strains of "The Missouri Waltz." After a few words by Galen Drake, who revealed the program to be a political show for the entertainment of women, he spun the first platter, a recording of Eddie Cantor singing "Now's the Time to Fall in Love." As Cantor's voice came to the line, "Tomatoes are cheaper, potatoes are cheaper," the announcer shouted, "Stop the Music," the title of the top radio show on the air. Then followed a brief recital that the song was wrong, that all prices were higher due to Republican inflation. Mrs. Josephine Fusco of New York City came on the air to say bitterly that she couldn't make ends meet for her family of six, despite the fact that there were three wage-earners in the family. "Prices are too high as a result of knocking out price controls by the Republicans."

Following this, a telephone bell rang. This was a request for the Democratic record. Galen Drake filled the request, playing "Every Day I Love You a Little Bit More." Noting the popularity of giveaway shows on radio, Drake announced the "Democratic Record" show would have a booby prize to give away too. The first award was made to Senator Kenneth Wherry for being an outstanding headache to housewives, based on his statement, "I'm the fellow that knocked out meat controls." The prize was a personally conducted tour with Senator Taft through the nearest butcher shop.

Next on the program was a contest to identify the "hidden melody." It was, "Why Was I Born?" Helen Morgan's hit from "Sweet Adeline." This title, said Galen Drake acidly, illustrated a question asked by many Americans during the Republican depression. Then he announced the guest star for the day, Mrs. India Edwards, who spoke for three minutes. First she said that Mrs. Truman and daughter, Margaret, were the kind of family "you'd like for next door neighbors." She credited the President with goodness and understanding. In a folksy manner she continued, "Goodness may be mocked at these days, but women like it in a leader." She concluded by urging women to vote for the return of President Truman to the White House as the man able to "maintain Peace in the World."

After more music, the Ghost of the Eightieth Congress complained in a plaintive voice that he couldn't sleep because the wails of the hungry and homeless abandoned by the Republican Congress kept him awake. The Ghost then begged the audience to vote Democratic so that the cries would cease and he could rest.

"Where are you going?" Drake asked the Ghost as he was leaving.

"To haunt Governor Dewey."

"Good haunting!" was the tag line as the show went off the air.

In each show, the contest varied. In a contest to identify the hidden candidate, the clue was an interval of absolute silence. The solution telephoned in on the show was: "Governor Dewey, the man in the rubber-soled shoes, who says nothing on any issue."

On another occasion the Ghost of the Eightieth Congress said he had to go eat. Asked what a ghost ate, his answer was, "Ghosted cheese sandwiches and ghost toasties."

Entertaining and filled with laughs and sharp barbs, the show had an enthusiastic reception. ABC network stations began to receive mail pro and con the day following the first show, mail which grew in volume as the series progressed. I was not impressed too much by the mail that came in from Democrats, for if they were interested enough to write we had their votes anyway. But the letters from those who identified themselves as Republicans were of great interest. The Republican mail totaled something like two to three hundred letters per day. It was about evenly divided between those who bitterly resented the show and its attacks on Dewey and the Republican Party; and people who signed themselves "Disgusted Republican," "Independent Republican," "Former Republican" and the like. We were getting home to women voters, literally getting home to them.

One other factor underlined the response to the show and indicated acceptance. On most radio programs, we urged local party organizations to run advertisements in their newspapers, giving the time and station over which specific programs could be heard. We found the "Democratic Record" show was being advertised by local organizations bigger than anything we had ever suggested. This was done all over the country and illustrated the approval of our own rank-and-file organization.

On one occasion it was decided at the last moment that the President should be on the air from a meeting in Pittsburgh where he was to speak on the very important issue of national defense and foreign policy. The meeting was on a Saturday night and the top radio show was "Your Hit Parade," an extremely high-cost show coming in the middle of the most expensive "A" time.

One of the tricks of buying political radio time was to come up with a spot either during or right after a top show. On the

Saturday night in question, the Republicans undertook to dodge part of the high-cost show by taking the last fifteen minutes of "Your Hit Parade" and the fifteen minutes following. It looked like good radio time buying.

Les Malitz and Ken Fry put their heads together and came up with the time including the first portion of "Your Hit Parade," directly preceding the Republican broadcast on the same network. Thus the Republicans were in the sad position of following half an hour of political radio with another half hour of political radio.

In addition to the pictorial history of the President and the "Democratic Record" show, our efforts to give a different flavor to political publicity and avoid stodginess included a book on the party position. This was started in June with a publisher, Julian Messner, ready and waiting for copy.

The writing was entrusted to a committee employee outside the publicity division. Only three weeks before the publisher's deadline, we found that nothing had actually been written. There was only one solution: write it ourselves. So Brightman and I sat down and hammered out a campaign book entitled, *The Power of the People* for Senator McGrath's by-line. When India Edwards, a real trouper, heard about our problem, she promptly took over the task of doing a fine chapter on the role of women in the Democratic Party.

Usually we were hard put to find the money to float our publicity projects, but there was one time when we were offered payment and had difficulty handling it. I had written an article for the *Saturday Evening Post* to be run under Senator McGrath's by-line. The *Post* insisted on paying us its regular price, $1,500, for the piece. The question arose of how to make out the check. The committee was willing to waive payment but the *Post* insisted. We finally agreed to accept the check because the committee was in such financial straits that fifteen hundred dollars looked like big money.

It amused me to play with the thought of allowing the *Post*

242

to make out its check directly to the Democratic National Committee. A check so written would by law have had to be accounted for to Congress by the committee comptroller as a "contribution." I imagined the gnashing of teeth if the *Saturday Evening Post*, prime Republican magazine that it is, should suddenly appear in a congressional report as, first, a contributor to the Democratic National Committee and, second, as a violator of the Corrupt Practices Act, which prohibits corporations from contributing to a political campaign. It was an amusing thought, but not a charitable one, nor a grateful one. I advised the *Post* to make out the check to J. Howard McGrath to defray the expenses of preparing the article. If there is some shock at my even considering allowing the *Post* to get in such an unwarranted position, I can only plead that I was so conditioned to "hitting at anything that moved" that it was necessary sometimes to slow down and assess each thought as it came.

CHAPTER 23

Editor & Publisher, the professional journal of the newspaper field, reported that a survey of 771 daily newspapers in the United States showed 65 per cent of the papers, with 78.5 per cent of the total circulation, supporting Dewey. The President was supported, they said, by 15 per cent of the total number of papers, representing 10 per cent of the national daily circulation. The rest were split between Wallace and Thurmond, mostly the latter, with a few not committed. This came as no surprise. I would have thought the percentage higher. In the New York area alone, the Democrats received support from but one paper, the starveling New York *Star*, successor to the defunct *PM* and itself on its last tottering pins. Even the New York *Post*, normally liberal in its outlook, embraced the bandwagon school of thought and declared for Dewey.

We had hoped that the New York *Times* would stay uncommitted; but, reversing its 1944 stand when it editorially supported Roosevelt against Dewey, it took Dewey over Truman. The editors must have had some doubts about this policy for they took nearly four columns to rationalize their stand. I was concerned by the *Times's* position and wrote a note to the publisher commenting on the editorial, saying I thought a newspaper which prided itself on its reputation for fairness should give the Democratic Party an opportunity to answer. Almost immediately a young lady called me to offer space in the *Times's* "Letters to the Editor" column for such an answer.

"How much space?" I asked.

"Half a column."

"You betray a lack of faith in your cause," I told her, "if you feel the case which your editors built up in four columns can be answered in half a column. We will not try to answer with a space limitation. We feel the *Times* has the complete right to give us some space to answer, adequate space to answer or no space to answer. But we feel that in the New York *Times's* choosing against the Democratic Party and its candidates, there is a larger issue. We will not answer in a half column!"

That afternoon Arthur Hays Sulzberger, the publisher of the *Times,* called. After the usual courtesies, he reopened the discussion.

"Do I understand," he asked politely, "that you were threatening the *Times?*"

I said, "No. I wasn't threatening the *Times.* If I did it would be an empty threat, for I haven't the power to carry out a threat against the *Times.* There's been a misunderstanding. I merely said I could not see answering a four-column editorial in half a column. I did say that I thought a newspaper with the reputation of the *Times* would be expected by the millions in the Democratic Party to permit an adequate answer. I don't feel that half a column is space for an adequate answer."

"I agree. You send me your answer to whatever length you see fit to write and we'll print it."

"I'll measure the copy line by line and inch by inch and balance your editorial to the last em," I told him. "I'm delighted by your fairness."

It was a real and generous concession, but in the larger sense it meant little, for we were balancing only one editorial, and this by virtue of the *Times's* feeling for fair play. The tide of unfavorable editorial opinion was disheartening for there is a weightiness to printer's ink that gets you down.

About this time I called in the publicity staff and issued instructions that no one must ever agree with anyone—even privately—that Truman was beaten. I got some raised eyebrows on that one.

"This isn't thought-control," I explained. "But people give a great deal of credence to what is told them by someone they may know at headquarters. I don't want us creating talk that 'a fellow I know at Democratic headquarters was telling me that Truman is sunk.' That's using the word-of-mouth technique right back at us. The thing to do is to say that we have positive information that Truman will win. If you don't believe it and don't want to start gossip in the right direction, okay. But in that case, keep your mouth shut!"

Brightman thought I was being arbitrary.

"That's right," I told him. "Arbitrary as hell!"

A telephone call from a friend brought us information concerning a short feature film the Republican National Committee was readying for release.

"It's good," I was told. "Technically perfect. Louis de Rochemont—he made the *March of Time* films—made it for them and it's costing a fortune. It'll be released through the newsreel outlets and it'll hit every movie house in the country."

That news disturbed me. In May I had recommended that a movie be made of the President for campaign purposes. But there were delays and when it was finally agreed a film would be needed, there were no funds. There were still no funds. We were finding it hard to pay running expenses and radio time for our candidates. Any substantial expenditure for a film was out of the question. Nevertheless, I pleaded with McGrath for a special allotment, even though I realized it was a hopeless cause. Howard was sympathetic but—no money. I talked to Jim Sauter, who was director of our stage, screen and radio division, but he had nothing to offer. I came to the conclusion that if the Demo-

246

crats could not have a film, the thing for me to do was to prevent the effective use of the Republican film.

There were a couple of leaks in the Democratic Committee, leaks to the Republican Committee. I made sure that it was well known that I was conferring with labor leaders, like Whitney, on the matter. Then I called Gael Sullivan's office at Theater Owners of America. Gael was delighted to hear from me and full of questions about the campaign. He tended to believe that Truman was beaten.

"Gael," I asked him, "do you know about the Dewey film? Is it going to be released to the regular movie houses?"

"Yes," said Gael, "I've seen the film. It's good. It'll be released about two weeks before November second so as to cover the country. They've bought 900 prints for distribution, at thirty-five dollars a print."

"How much did the reel cost them to produce?"

"I'm told thirty-five thousand."

"Well!" I was impressed. "Here it is. Gael, we don't have a film on Truman."

"I know. It's too bad!"

"That's what I think. I feel that if we don't have one, the theaters should not show the Dewey film."

"You'll never get them to agree. They'll say, 'Hard luck!' "

"I don't expect them to agree; but," I said, "I can make it difficult. If the movie houses show a Dewey film without a balancing Truman film, I'll have them picketed as unfair!"

Gael took a sharp breath. "You can't do it."

"You know better, Gael."

"All over the country? Impossible."

"The hell with all over the country. I'll hit the big cities where the big audiences are. I can do it and you know it!"

Sullivan was arguing now. "You'll make the biggest stink that ever happened. Every paper in the country will be down on you. The movie producers will buy ads denouncing you. It will beat you sure as the devil."

247

"So what've we got to lose? You read the papers. What difference do you think a few more bad stories will make? We've got nothing to lose."

Gael was quiet. Then he said, "Jack, what are you trying to do to me? What do you want me to do?"

"Gael, I don't want you to do anything. All I want is for you to tell your people what I've just said. Then they'll ask you whether you think I can make it stick. I don't know what you think about that; but you know me and you can give them an answer." I hung up.

I sat tight and let the thing work. Something would happen. Maybe the movie people would get me fired or they'd do something else. But I was sure of one thing—they wouldn't ignore it.

I was right. The next day my telephone rang. It was Les Biffle in Washington. Some of the movie people were worrying about the fact that Truman had no film, he said, and they wanted to talk to me about it.

"Sure," I said. "I'll be glad to talk any time."

Next Jim Sauter, who didn't know about my talk with Gael, came in. "Jack," he said, "I'm supposed to talk to Spyros Skouras about the Dewey film. Maybe we can get our foot in the door."

"Did he call you, Jim?"

"No, some of his people suggested we get together."

"By all means."

Sauter talked to Skouras and he used the soft approach. His line went something like this: "Why don't you people give Truman a film? Everyone says he hasn't got a chance, so what difference does it make?"

Skouras asked, "What you mean, Jim, is that we help Truman lose?"

"What's the difference? Besides, there's still going to be a Democratic Party and you'll have to deal with them. The industry will be much better off to have a reputation for being fair."

Skouras seemed interested, Sauter reported to me.

248

Sullivan called to tell me he had delivered my message.

"What did they say?"

"Well," said Gael, "first they said, 'He'll just have to picket!' "

I shuddered. I didn't want war!

"Then they asked me if I thought you could do it. I told them not nationwide. 'But he can make it stick in some of the big cities, maybe most of the big cities.' " Sullivan added, "You may get away with this, Jack. I don't know. But I have a notion that you may make it."

Sauter went to another meeting with the movie moguls and reported there was the possibility of our getting a film made by the motion-picture industry. He wanted to join the President's train to find out if the President wanted a film.

I could have told him, "Of course the President wants a film." But I knew what the score was. The movie producers wanted the message delivered directly to Harry that they would do this for him. So I urged Sauter to go to Texas and see the President. Sauter caught a plane that burst into flames near Memphis but he finally arrived safely in Fort Worth. He saw the President on the campaign train and was told that the President would be delighted to have a film made for use in the campaign.

While he was in Texas, Sauter helped set up a television broadcast on Amon Carter's new TV station. Carter, a colorful old raider who published the Fort Worth *Star Telegram,* had waited to go on the air until the President arrived. It was a historic occasion. The only flaw was that there were no TV sets in the Fort Worth-Dallas area, except for about fifty sets Carter brought in to be put in hotel lobbies, bars and other public places for the opening.

Sauter returned to New York full of enthusiasm. The President wanted the film. Now maybe we could get to work and have it done.

The next day I was invited to a meeting of the heads of the four major newsreel companies and Robert Rubin, general counsel for Loew's, Inc. I took Sauter with me.

In Rubin's office we discussed problems affecting the campaign in general terms. Finally, "You know that Governor Dewey has a film to be released before election?"

Yes, I knew.

"We think," said Mr. Rubin, "that the President should have a film, too. Have you given this any thought?"

"Yes," I admitted, "I have given it a good deal of thought but we have no money for this purpose."

"No money at all?"

"None."

There was a chorus of well-bred astonishment at this. After all, the silver screen was the most important medium of expression of all. Didn't we realize that?

I explained that a lack of money, a complete lack, was an even more important expression. At least it governed. With that, a general discussion began which culminated in the offer of the facilities of the newsreel studios to make a film about the President for campaign use.

"I understand from this, gentlemen," I said, "that you mean to accept the costs of production of this film in your studios?"

They agreed.

"Thank you, gentlemen," I said. "This is a real contribution. I know the President will be extremely grateful personally; and the Democratic Party—I know I can speak for Chairman McGrath—appreciates your generosity. This is a real demonstration of faith in the two-party system of government in this nation. And although I don't know your personal sentiments as to who will win this election, I must say this action speaks well for your patriotism."

We shook hands all around. Everyone stood up. I sat down.

"There is one other thing, gentlemen, which I think we must discuss," I said.

"Yes?"

"Yes. The matter of distribution."

"We'll distribute it through the newsreel outlets just as we are doing for the Dewey film."

250

"That's where the rub comes," I told them. "I understand that Governor Dewey's group has purchased 900 prints of his film at thirty-five dollars a print."

"That's so."

"Much as I appreciate your willingness to make a film for our use, it would be of no help to us unless we also had enough prints to provide for release."

There was a gasp. Outraged, one of the newsreel men said, "You mean after we offered to make you a film, and offered to distribute it, you want us to buy prints too?"

"No," I said, "I'm not asking you to make prints and pay for them. I'm merely pointing out that without prints, the film is of no use to us. None whatsoever! We have no money at all, gentlemen. And 900 prints would be about thirty thousand dollars more than we have."

There was considerably more discussion but the outcome was certain. We would get the prints as well as the film. And so it proved. I thanked the group again and I was completely sincere for, to my mind, the motion-picture project would round out the President's campaign.

Actually, I felt distribution was by far the most important phase of the contribution. There were approximately twenty thousand theaters in the United States and the weekly audience which we would reach through a release made by the four news-reel companies would total upwards of sixty-five million people. Furthermore, these millions of people constituted a "captive" audience, for they paid to sit in the theater and were not going to get up and leave when our film came on the screen. Nearly as important was the fact that we'd be reaching people of all political persuasions, not just Democrats.

There was one more point to be settled. Who would make the film? It was decided to flip a coin for it. Coins were produced and flipped and Universal Newsreels "lost," as they put it. They would produce the Truman film.

Before ending the meeting, we also settled the release date for both the Dewey film and the Truman film. Because the Truman film still had to be produced, it was decided that it would be released last. The Democratic film would be released to primary theaters on the Tuesday before election and would be shown over the country in all theaters through the day of election.

Although this timing was the result of the production problem —our film would not be ready earlier—I could not have been happier. This gave us the superior time of release.

When I returned to my office in the Biltmore, a phone call was waiting for me from Sullivan. He wanted to tell me that the newsreels had agreed to make a film for the Democrats.

"You got away with it, Jack. I wouldn't have believed it possible, but the thing's in the bag."

"Thanks, Gael, I'm delighted," I told him. "Maybe they did it simply because they feel it'll do no harm to Dewey's chances, anyway. And why have a fight?"

That afternoon Sam Brightman and I moved to the Universal Newsreel studios at 106th street. Thomas Meade, the managing director, had everything in readiness for the project. Ed Bartsch, the chief film-cutter, was on hand to discuss a script. Brightman had brought along a copy of the "Life of Truman," which we had written as a basis for our projected "Truman Pictorial History," and this provided guidance for preliminary film scanning.

Because Bartsch admired and believed in the President, a personal interest in doing a good job was added to his great professional skill.

"I've seen the Dewey film," he told us, "and it has a very serious weakness. It doesn't have any guts. That guy has never done anything. The film clips in the library are practically barren on him. So de Rochemont had to go out and shoot film on everything. The new film is all staged. It doesn't have a real life thing in it. Now our guy has been 'on stage' for years. There's unlimited material in the library on him so we can make a film that'll be right out of the history books."

He proved to be right. Bartsch, using our Truman history as a guide, worked out a basic 2,500 feet of film which would be cut back to a two-reel, ten-minute special feature length of about 1,000 feet.

He dug up World War I film which showed American troops embarking for France, and even a few battle scenes. He tied these shots to a 1918 snapshot of Captain Harry S Truman, field artillery, AEF. The film proceeded with clips on Senator Truman's contribution to the war effort in World War II when his Senate Investigating Committee saved the government billions in money and years in time.

From the newsreel library we picked shots of Truman. In one particularly effective clip, the cameraman had caught the President saying, "I would rather bring peace to the world than be President of the United States." Other shots showed him as a farmer; as a humanitarian—we found a sentimental clip of the President with a child stricken with polio; as a leader in world events; addressing Congress; meeting Chaim Weizmann, grand old man of Zionism; inspecting national defense troops and installations; and facing up to leaders in world affairs both in the United States and abroad. We closed showing him as President at his desk in the White House.

After final cutting of the preliminary film, it was necessary to time each sequence and write script for it timed to fit exactly. Most of this writing was done by Brightman.

On the last day of script-writing we were baffled in our efforts to find a suitable ending. There was a reluctance on the part of the newsreel employees to suggest how far we could go in appealing for votes.

Sauter was sitting in on this session and finally he suggested: "Soldier . . . statesman . . . farmer . . . humanitarian . . . Harry S Truman . . . the President of the United States!" As the band played "The Star-Spangled Banner," the shot of the President faded into the streaming folds of the American flag. It was terrific.

Tom Meade, looking at the finished product, laughed as I've seldom seen anyone laugh.

"It's fantastic," he explained his laughter. "I was told that this film would be a flop because there'd be no time to do any shooting. But this thing is the best I've ever seen.

"Did you know," he asked, "that in Bartsch you've got probably the best film-cutter in the business? Actually, Democrats from all the studios have been helping on this. I've never seen anything like it."

The Dewey film was duly shown with its 900 prints. This meant that motion-picture houses would be serviced piecemeal. I was resigned to the same treatment for the Truman film.

But the technical perfection and the interest of the subject matter in our film changed that. Instead, each studio put together its regular order of prints to service its separate theater clients. Instead of 900 prints a total of more than 2,000 prints were made.

Thus, during the last six days of the campaign no one could go to the movies anywhere in the United States without seeing the story of the President. It was probably the most important and most successful publicity break in the entire campaign.

The motion-picture industry to this day is convinced that their film elected Harry S Truman, President.

There is an interesting sequel to this story. Only recently when I was discussing the Truman file with Universal's Meade, he told me, "We, in the industry, think that the Truman film elected Harry. But there were others who thought the same. One of them was Prime Minister St. Laurent of Canada. When he was running for election shortly after the 1948 election here in the United States, he had us make a film for him. It was done on the basis of the Truman film. St. Laurent won. A few years later when he was up for election again, he again had a film made by Universal on the Truman pattern. He won again. But in 1957 they didn't think it was necessary to have another film made. And this time St. Laurent and the Liberals lost. I think it proves something."

254

CHAPTER 24

FITZPATRICK's last-minute drive to place New York State in the Democratic column was in full swing. Additional workers were functioning in every precinct in New York City. It was necessary to produce a tremendous Truman majority in the city if he was to overcome Dewey's upstate advantage. The problem was heightened by the American Labor Party's endorsement of Wallace but Fitzpatrick felt confident of victory.

Louis Johnson had produced money not only for additional workers and the radio broadcast featuring Mrs. Roosevelt, but for a series of paid advertisements as well. Don Gibbs of Warwick & Legler, who had been doing such excellent work on the women's radio show, was given the task of writing the copy for the advertisement. This was the same material we had vainly tried to utilize in an advertisement earlier. At that time no money was available and we had to be satisfied with digesting the copy for use in *The Democrat*.

Gibbs produced a full-page ad which was devastating. It took the financial statement of the state of New York and factually blasted Dewey's reputation of being a super administrator and prudent with money.

With the copy and layout approved, mats were ordered and dispatched to party leaders across the country. We couldn't

255

finance a nationwide space-buying campaign but we reasoned that if the ad was available in mat form, many state and local Democratic organizations would buy the newspaper space themselves. This proved true and nearly half a hundred major newspapers carried the advertisement in the last few days of the campaign.

We made our main effort in New York City. Warwick & Legler were authorized to buy a back page in the New York *Times,* and in the New York *World-Telegram.*

The selection of these two newspapers was carefully thought out. The *Times* was most widely read, not only in New York City, but also around the country; therefore we would get a plus out of our ad appearing in it. The *World-Telegram* had consistently ignored Democratic publicity copy; and when it did print something about Truman, it was done with an approach we felt was slanted. In addition, the readership of the *World-Telegram* was largely Republican and we wanted to reach independent Republican voters with the true story of Dewey's record as Governor of New York.

To my amazement the New York *World-Telegram* turned down the advertisement. They claimed the copy in it was "not true and factual."

Pleased as Punch, I told Sam Brightman, "Now if the *Times* will only turn us down, we'll have our case against the Republican one-party press proved beyond all doubt. Keep your fingers crossed and let's start thinking how we'll use this. It's a real break!"

While we waited for the *Times's* decision, the New York *Sun* called. It wanted the copy. This was a little surprising because the *Sun* had the reputation of being even more Republican than the *World-Telegram.* Even the arch-Republican *Herald Tribune* solicited our copy, claiming they were even more influential than the *Times.* But the *World-Telegram* stuck by its guns.

This was taking place October 29 on the eve of Harry Truman's New York City appearance in the final week end of the

256

campaign. We decided to print the advertisement ourselves, about 500,000 of them, full newspaper-page size, and distribute them throughout New York City. The heading was to be: "The advertisement the press refused to print."

Then the New York *Times* crossed us up. They accepted the ad. I showed their salesman the refusal given to us by the *World-Telegram* and advised him to consult with his newspaper.

"They may not want to accept the ad," I suggested. "We wouldn't want you to be penalized because you made a mistake concerning your paper's policy."

But the *Times* was of a different mold from the *World-Telegram*. The man with whom I discussed the matter didn't have to refer his decision to higher authority. He had read the copy, he said, and it was in good political taste and certainly seemed acceptable.

"It shakes me," he added. "I've been figuring on voting for Dewey, but maybe he isn't such a hotshot after all."

Now we knew the face of our enemy. We fired our first shot in a publicity release, saying in part:

Senator J. Howard McGrath, Chairman of the Democratic National Committee, reported today that the New York *World-Telegram* has refused to publish a paid advertisement setting out the facts of Governor Thomas E. Dewey's record as Governor of New York State.

The advertisement was offered under the usual procedures. It was to be paid for at the usual political advertising rates. The Democratic Party found it necessary to resort to paid newspaper advertisements throughout the nation to present to the American people the facts of Governor Dewey's record.

The advertisement reported that the cost of administering the New York State government under Governor Dewey is twice what it was under his predecessor, Herbert H. Lehman; an increase from $112 million a year to $280 million.

The *World-Telegram* refused to print these figures, which are taken from the New York state budget. The advertisement stated the entire New York state budget had doubled under Governor Dewey. That statement was not plucked out of the air by the Democratic party; it was taken right out of the budget.

Of course, the facts about Governor Dewey's administration do not square with the claims made for the Governor in the editorial and news columns of the *World-Telegram*.

There was more about Dewey's army of press agents and the fact that his New York State Department of Commerce had spent $826,000 of state funds in the 1948 fiscal year to publicize Governor Dewey and his administration.

The press release damning the *World-Telegram* was bitter and it was answered bitterly if not logically. The incident became a *cause célèbre*, with editorial comment, both pro and con, throughout the country. Actually the *World-Telegram* couldn't have figured out a better way to help us, although that was not their intention.

We changed the headline on our reprint to read, "The ad the *World-Telegram* refused to print." And when the President toured New York City with millions of people packing the streets for a glimpse of the Missouri fighter, our precinct captains acted as newsboys, hawking the reprints throughout the crowd. At the mammoth Brooklyn rally, every person who was able to jam into the hall got a copy.

We had ordered 500,000 reprints from Jerry Weinstein of International Printing. But Jerry did us a favor. He ran an additional 200,000 and donated the cost as a campaign contribution. We could have used another 500,000.

On the Saturday before election, Truman stopped at the Biltmore Hotel to visit campaign headquarters. All up and down the two floors of campaign offices, secretaries and campaign workers were out in the halls to greet the President. He went down the line, smiling, shaking hands and giving each person a few words of thanks for their work and loyalty.

Weinstein was out in the hall with a copy of a cartoon, pre-

258

pared at Congressman Kirwan's direction, which showed the difference in the contents of a housewife's shopping bag in 1946 under price controls and in 1948 as a result of inflation. I had ordered a million of these to be distributed by air express to states east of the Mississippi. It was too late in the campaign to reach the West.

As the President came down the hall, Weinstein started to duck into an office to be "out of the way." I wouldn't hear of it. He had just told me about running the 200,000 extra ad reprints and I was grateful.

When the President came toward us, I pulled Jerry forward saying, "Mr. President, I want you to meet Jerry Weinstein, our printer, and a damn good Democrat."

Truman reacted as only Truman would. He grasped Weinstein's hand, shook it firmly and then put his arm around his shoulder.

"Jerry was trying to get away," I said. "He was afraid he would bother you when you were busy with the staff."

Truman, still holding Weinstein's shoulder, said, "I'm never too busy to talk to a good Democrat. Remember that, Jerry. And we're going to win on Tuesday with the help of a lot of good Democrats like you!" Then the President went on his way.

Weinstein, who had been gloomy about the chances of a Democratic victory, was jubilant.

He turned to me. "Jack, he can win! He can win! He's going to win!" Suddenly he became aware of the copy still in his hand. "Why," he said, "you don't want a stinking million of these things. You want two million and I'll pay for it!"

To return to our campaign among the foreign-language groups, we had decided that the Germans and Scandinavians were possibly the two groups which would be hardest to sway. Among the Scandinavians, we fought nothing more than a containing operation.

With the Germans, we made more progress but not without

259

effort. Governor Stassen was the biggest ace the Republicans had to hold their German support: Governor Stassen and the publisher, Victor Ridder. But we found that the President's program appealed strongly to the citizens of German descent.

President Wilson and President Roosevelt were not the great heroes to the Germanic peoples in the United States that they were to other groups. Loyal as they were to America, many of them still had strong connections through relatives and friends, with the Fatherland. The fact that we had fought two major wars against Germany influenced them and this is no reflection on their patriotism, for there was no great love for either the Kaiser or Hitler among German-Americans. But they did have a natural and deep sympathy for their countrymen who bore the brunt of the war.

However, the President had made a record for which the Germans were particularly grateful. His strong stand against Russia, taken in the case of the Berlin Airlift, gained him tremendous support. These German-Americans were anti-Red and Truman's strong reaction to the Russian attempts to starve Berlin into submission was of cardinal importance.

In addition, the President had caused postal relations to be resumed between the United States and Germany and specifically permitted the flow of food and medicine to the suffering population. This, too, brought widespread approbation in the United States.

Finally, the President's firm stand in aiding the economic recovery of West Germany had endeared him to Americans of German origin.

Based on these three points, a strong appeal was made to the German-American population.

Cieplinski's special knowledge once more paid off. One of his close friends was Dr. Gerhart Seger, editor and publisher of the *Deutsche Volk-Zeitung* printed in New York. Dr. Seger strongly supported Truman in the columns of his paper but this was only part of his contribution.

Seger, a full professor of economics as well as a physician, had been a member of the German Reichstag, the prewar German parliament. He had vigorously opposed Hitler from 1933, when the paper hanger came to power, until the very day when Hitler dissolved the Reichstag and the Gestapo arrived to throw Seger into a concentration camp where he languished for three long years.

In the summer of 1948, Dr. Seger returned to Germany on a visit. He saw the tremendous progress made in West Germany under the President's program of economic rehabilitation. He talked to the people of Berlin concerning their experiences during the time of the Russian blockade and the American-British Airlift. Seger came back to America convinced of President Truman's greatness.

Then he took the lecture trail, telling the story of American aid to Germany and of American resistance to Communism in Europe. And he gave the credit where credit was due, to President Harry S Truman. Seger made seventy-two lectures in the main centers of German-American population in the United States during the late summer and fall of 1948. His influence was enormous, for he had no direct connection with the political fortunes of any candidate. He paid his own way and told his own story. And that story was of incalculable value to the Democratic Party.

And Seger, because of his personal fame among Germans, was always the subject of stories in the local German language paper wherever he went. He reached not only the ears of those to whom he talked, but also the minds of those who read the German-language papers.

Among Czechs and Slovaks, Colonel Joseph Triner of Chicago, later Chairman of the Illinois Athletic Commission, and Andrew Valushek, editor and publisher of two of the most important Czechoslovakian newspapers in the country, worked hard and long for President Truman.

Space does not permit adding up all the tremendous efforts of twenty different nationality groups; but let me paraphrase briefly from the *Saturday Evening Post* article by pollster Sam Lubell, assessing the campaign after the Truman victory. The vast majority of Americans of foreign descent, Mr. Lubell said, voted Democratic in the 1948 election. Cities like Buffalo, Boston, Chicago, Cleveland, Detroit, Milwaukee and St. Louis gave even greater support to President Truman than it gave to the Democratic ticket in 1944. In Massachusetts, President Truman got a larger popular vote than President Roosevelt. Italian precincts in this state went two or three to one for President Roosevelt, but six to one for President Truman. In Buffalo, Poles gave President Truman nearly one-fourth of his total city vote. Polish wards in Cleveland, Detroit, Milwaukee, Pittsburgh and Chicago went Democratic three or four to one. In St. Louis German precincts, which Dewey carried against President Roosevelt in 1944, fell to President Truman. President Truman won German wards in Wisconsin and other Midwestern states which were Republican until this election.

As Lubell recognized, the campaign of the nationalities division was successful, phenomenally so. And the success was, in the final analysis, due to the fusion of political unities to which I alluded earlier. President Truman's record supplied the basis of the campaign. The vast approval for President Truman's policies, particularly those affecting the homelands of 11,000,000 voting Americans of foreign descent, was transformed by a powerful and imaginative political campaign into Democratic ballots.

It was a classic example of great political returns rewarding competent leadership and strenuous effort, all at small financial expense.

As the final returns were brought in on the day after election, there was an isolated item which gave me great satisfaction, the defeat in a German district in St. Louis of Congressman Walter Ploeser, who had survived four Roosevelt-era congressional campaigns. He had plagued our friends in Congress and his defeat was an extra dividend.

CHAPTER 25

TREMENDOUSLY INTERESTING was the President's hegira by train across the country. Such a rear platform campaign was at the heart of our plans and to highlight this portion of the campaign it is necessary to go back in time to late summer, 1948.

The President was seated in the East Room of the White House discussing with his advisers the formal campaign which would begin on Labor Day in Detroit. There had been general talk of finance, politics and the outlook for November. The atmosphere wasn't gloomy, but it certainly wasn't gay.

"The situation isn't as bad as the newspapers make it look," the President said. "It is my intention to go into every county in the United States if possible. I want to see the people. This is the only way to answer the Republicans."

That was to be the theme of the President's personal campaign: "I want to see the people." His certitude was that if he could see the people, explain things to them himself, the people would give the Democratic Party a vote of confidence. It was this faith in the people which always buoyed Truman's faith in himself.

As the meeting broke up, I walked out with Secretary of the Interior Oscar Chapman. He was going on leave of absence from his Cabinet job to be advance man for the President's trip into Michigan for Labor Day.

"I'm going to Michigan, too," I told Chapman. "I have a date to talk to the Republican Attorney General of the State, a man named Black, who has some serious charges against Republican money-raising techniques. If you want, I'll join you in Detroit and work with you on setting up the train. I can do both."

Chapman agreed and the following day I went to Detroit.

Before leaving Washington, I made arrangements for *Capital Comment* to be incorporated into *The Democrat*, a four-page campaign newspaper and clip sheet edited by Joe Evans. We had planned to eliminate *Capital Comment* entirely but learned that some six hundred newspapers were carrying all or part of it as a political column. *The Democrat*, which furnished mat service on all cartoons and pictures, was printed by the American Newspaper Union under the direction of Walter Shead, and was sent out to a mailing list of sixty-five thousand.

In Detroit, Attorney General Black had specific charges against money-raising tactics practiced by Republicans in auto manufacturing circles. Cars were still difficult to get. The method was to assign a quota to an auto dealer to contribute to the Republican Party. If the quota was not met, the delinquent auto dealer had his supply of new cars shut off the following month. The dealers got the point very quickly and the money rolled in.

In addition, Attorney General Black charged that the Republican Administration of the state had in effect excused these "loyal" dealers from paying state sales taxes on their used car sales. Attorney General Black contended that this practice had cost the state nearly thirty million dollars. Black was an honest man who was convinced he had run into a corrupt situation and proposed to do something about it. His activity had already cost him renomination on the Republican ticket.

He was working with the United States district attorney, he said, and they had found positive evidence of violation of the Corrupt Practices Act. The sales tax evasion charges were violations of state law.

264

I took copious notes and promised to help him all I could. Then I met with Chapman who had set up headquarters at the Book-Cadillac Hotel. I was delegated to cover the other cities in Michigan which the President would visit and see what I could do toward making the trip a success. The schedule included Grand Rapids, Lansing, Detroit, Flint and Pontiac.

In each city I contacted Democratic Party officials and leaders in the labor movement. In some instances, I was present while the Secret Service, who were making advance security arrangements, looked over plans. They were good enough to defer to me on a few variations within the limits of security. Mostly, however, I sought local details of interest which I could prepare for inclusion in the President's speeches.

The enthusiasm was high. If there was an antidote for political depression in 1948, it was to go out where people were. Ordinary people were willing to concede that Truman couldn't win but they, personally, liked him and, win or lose, they were going to vote for him. After talking to a few people who felt like that, and they seemed to be everywhere, I just couldn't stay depressed.

In Detroit, Oscar Chapman was busy with labor leaders while George Fitzgerald, the Democratic national committeeman, made arrangements for the big show in Cadillac Square. Mennen Williams, the Democratic candidate for Governor, co-operated fully. Although he was given little chance of being elected, Williams was carrying on a vigorous campaign.

He had the all-out support of the CIO. Fitzgerald was attorney for Jim Hoffa of the Teamsters Union. Normally in Michigan, having the CIO on one side automatically lines up the Teamsters on the other. But in this instance we had a happy marriage of interests and both big unions were co-operating to get their membership out for the meeting.

On the morning of the big day, at 5:30 A.M., I was in Grand Rapids to meet the presidential party. Even at that hour the town was stirring and early arrivals were on hand to get front row positions in the main square of the town to see and hear the

President. I milled around talking to these people and found they were mostly Republicans, but they wanted to see Harry Truman.

"He seems like a good man," they said.

By seven when the train was due, a substantial crowd of about twenty-five thousand was on hand. The train came in, the autos were ready with the Secret Service men, to transport the President to the town's main square. I gave my speech notes to Clark Clifford and I was on my own.

The townspeople, mostly Republicans, were warm in their applause of the President's speech. When the train pulled out, I was aboard in the President's car, the last one on the train.

As we rode along, I marked something which was to become familiar to those on the train. Hundreds of people stood along the right-of-way, curious to see the President's train and hoping for a glimpse of the President himself. And Truman, who understood people so well, time and again went to the back platform to wave as the train thundered past knots of people.

In Lansing he made a scheduled platform appearance which lasted perhaps ten minutes. The crush was intense with the crowd here almost as large as the earlier meeting in Grand Rapids and more enthusiastic. There were cheers as the President discussed the issues briefly; there were more cheers when he spoke out against the Republican Eightieth Congress; and there were still louder cheers when he referred to the housing shortage at Michigan State University located at Lansing.

The train made several short stops on the way into Detroit where we arrived about noon. Detroit was aflame with enthusiasm. The route of the President's party to Cadillac Square was packed with people standing six and ten deep along the streets.

In the great square there were more than 250,000 people, packed solid. The Detroit chief of police estimated the crowd at 300,000; and the Detroit papers, stanchly Republican, estimated 175,000. Whichever figure was right, the crowd was big.

266

The President's Labor Day speech, which was broadcast nationally, was well received by the crowd. They cheered in thunderous approval as he told them of his personal efforts to defeat the Taft-Hartley Act and condemned Republicans for their attempts to "destroy labor rights at the bargaining table."

Present at the Detroit rally was Sam Youngheart, who was anxious to see politics in action. He saw crowds, and was trampled by crowds, shoved by crowds, laughed at by crowds. After the speech he told me, "I never saw so many people before in my life, even in New York."

From Detroit, the President motored to Hamtramck through aisles six and ten deep of cheering people. The masses who greeted him at Hamtramck itself rivaled the crowd in downtown Detroit. Then we set out for Pontiac.

This ride of about twenty-four miles was through solid lines of parked cars, loaded with people, cheering and waiting for a glimpse of Harry Truman. State police estimated the crowd along the roadside at three thousand per mile. It was impressive and heart warming to see such enthusiasm.

In Pontiac the meeting was a solid success. The park where a speakers' stand had been set up was filled to overflowing. The crowds were orderly but packed so densely that it was almost impossible to pass through.

Then on to Flint, after reboarding the train outside Pontiac. The route from the Flint station to the ball park where the meeting was to be held in the very late afternoon, was flanked by another large crowd. I was gratified to see that even the most cynical White House newsmen were impressed by the size and sincerity of the throngs.

After it was over, I was tired to the bone, dirty, sweaty, but happy. I settled down in the club car with Merriman Smith of UP and Bob Nixon of INS for a drink.

Charlie Ross came through the train. "I'm looking for you," he told me. "The President wants you."

I followed him to find that I was being summoned for dinner.

Margaret Truman was hostess and Attorney General Tom Clark and I were the guests. It was a simple dinner but both the President and his daughter were radiant. The day's success had made them gay.

But me? I couldn't relax. I seized this opportunity to tell the President and Attorney General Clark of the need for cracking down on the Republican method of raising money in Michigan. It wound up with Clark promising to look into the matter personally. When the dinner broke up, I had won my point and I, too, was happy.

An hour or so later we arrived in Toledo where I was to get off the train to go to Chicago. It was eleven o'clock at night but a mass of people were in the station waiting to see the President. Truman, who had been ready to go to bed, was up and out on the platform talking vigorously as I left.

This was my sole trip on the campaign train. My job was in New York. Ken Fry proceeded ahead of the train to handle production arrangements where nationwide broadcasts were being made. Bill Boyle, later chairman of the Democratic National Committee succeeding Senator McGrath, was set up in Washington to direct a central operating headquarters for the train. Here all details of dispatching, scheduling and day-to-day detail with the railroads were handled. Clark Clifford was the chief of staff on the train itself, directing the operations of the presidential staff.

The next trip was scheduled for early September with the first big speech in the Ak-sar-ben auditorium outside Omaha. Ed McKim, the President's former administrative assistant, was in charge of arrangements on the spot. Secretary of Interior Chapman was again acting as advance man. There were high hopes of a great meeting.

It was a disastrous flop.

Somehow the impression got about that the meeting was for members of the President's old World War I outfit, Battery D, only. Then that night a tremendous thunderstorm hit the city.

The combination held the crowd down to a few hundred people in an auditorium which holds 12,000.

The Republican press, bell-wethered by *Time* and *Life*, played the flop to the limit. Explanations were ignored. The press preferred to spread the story that the "flop" was the result of no interest in Truman. Actually, the newsmen couldn't be blamed; explanations always follow a failure and no matter how emphatic and truthful the explanations, they don't change the facts.

But this trip seemed fated for bad luck. At one place, the President dedicated an airport to the wrong man. The caravan got lost on a cross-country motor trip and delayed meetings in the next towns. *Life* Magazine had photographers assigned to make pictures to stress a "lack of crowds" theme. In a picture taken at Cheyenne, Wyoming, they posed a lone man in front of a host of empty seats and indicated that he was the only person on hand for Truman's meeting there. Actually, the meeting on the steps of the Capitol was quite successful.

However, in Los Angeles where Truman had drawn a million people only a few weeks before, another meeting failed to draw capacity crowds. The President was alarmed and upset. Everything seemed to be going badly and if ever Truman was close to admitting defeat, it was at this time.

From California the train was due to return east through Texas where Truman was to appear at a giant rally in Dallas; then proceed northward to Oklahoma City, back through Ohio and then to Washington for a brief rest.

In Washington, Boyle was frantic at the lack of crowds. He called Don Dawson, the President's assistant for personnel, and pulled him out of bed at midnight to catch a plane for Texas.

"I want you to take over advance arrangements in Texas," he told Dawson. "Get going."

Dawson protested that he knew little about such things, but his protests were overruled. Advance arrangements for the fast-moving train had become too big a job for one man; from then on, it was a split between Chapman and Dawson.

The next day in Dallas, Dawson was initiated into Texas politics at its worst. There were two Democratic factions in Texas, the so-called Texas "regulars" and the Truman liberals. Wright Morrow, Democratic national committeeman for Texas, was a member of the regular faction. In preparing for Truman's arrival in the state he had appointed a number of chairmen to handle details, all of whom were from his own faction. Many loyal Truman supporters had been ignored. The situation was bad although there was no suspicion that Morrow had been anything but impolitic in his arrangements.

Dawson changed everything. Recruiting Harry Seay, a Dallas insurance man, and Bill Kittrell, a local public-relations man, he threw himself into organizing an enthusiastic meeting. Later in the day he talked to Matt Connelly on the train.

"Don," said Connelly, "we've had a fizzle all the way through the northern tier of states. Los Angeles was rough. I'm scared of the rally in Dallas. Let's not try to do anything ambitious. Just hold a back-platform meeting at the station. There's no risk in that."

Dawson tried to argue but got nowhere. At two in the morning with the Secret Service men making security arrangements, Seay, Dawson and Kittrell looked over the railroad station.

"It was hopeless," Dawson told me later. "The station was being rebuilt and there were construction materials and machinery all around. We thought perhaps we could take the President to a sort of sunken garden in front of the depot proper. But this had sloping sides and I was certain we'd have broken legs and damage suits if we tried to hold a meeting there."

Dawson told his little staff, "We'll just go ahead and schedule a major meeting and not tell the train. It will be a surprise." Then he added, "It better be a good surprise!"

The meeting was planned for Rebel Stadium, a short distance outside the main area of Dallas. Dawson and Kittrell hired every sound truck in Dallas to start boosting attendance. Newspaper publicity, advertisements, arrangements with groups to attend en masse, every possible means to produce a crowd were worked out.

Meanwhile similar measures were being taken at El Paso and at the towns at both ends of Big Spring National Park, which the President was scheduled to dedicate. Dawson met the train as it neared El Paso.

Sound trucks were blaring as the train pulled in. "There were crowds blocks long lining the streets," Dawson recalled later. "I was never so relieved in my life."

From El Paso, the train proceeded toward Big Spring, stopping at every small town and hamlet.

"I remember at one little town," Dawson told me, "there were two cowhands on horseback on the fringe of a crowd of possibly three hundred people gathered about the rear platform. One of the cowboys, a youngster maybe twenty years old, was showing off on his horse, rearing and generally exhibiting his horsemanship. Well, he may have been a good rider but he was a menace to the safety of the crowd. He maneuvered his mount right up to the rear platform of the train. The President had been watching the boy. He came down off the platform, took the horse by the bridle to keep him from rearing. I was petrified. It was an explosive situation. Every one of the newsmen was out there taking notes. Anything could have happened. But I should have known the Boss could handle it. He reached up, opened the horse's mouth and studied his teeth. 'Not a bad horse you got here, son. Eight years old.' Handing the bridle to another man, he suggested it would be safer to have the horse back from the crowd, then went back to his place on the train. The kid on the horse? He was surprised. He kept muttering, 'Who'd of thought the President of the United States would know about horses?' "

At Big Spring the work of building interest had fared so well that the new park was dedicated at both ends by the President, each time before mammoth crowds. At Fort Worth, Amon Carter's TV station was opened and a meeting held that was very satisfactory.

Earlier a breakfast was arranged at Uvalde with Jack Garner, the 1933-37 Vice President of the United States. It was 5:00 A.M. when the train pulled in but a crowd was on hand anyway. The President was up, he was always up early, and he went out and talked to the crowd before taking off for a seven o'clock breakfast with Garner.

At Garner's home, the President produced from a small satchel a bottle of whisky which he gave Garner as protection against "snake bite." Garner was very pleased at the President's gift.

"This bottle isn't company whisky," Cactus Jack said. "This is for private drinking." In his library was a movable ladder to allow books to be secured from the top shelves. Garner mounted this ladder with the bottle and tucked it behind the books on the highest shelf.

"I'll bet it's still there," said Dawson recently, almost ten years later.

The run from Fort Worth to Dallas in the presidential motorcade was hair-raising. The distance is only about twenty-five miles but it was a solid line of cars, all proceeding at sixty miles an hour. Rebel Stadium was filled to overflowing. And those who had been in the parade from Fort Worth found it impossible in many instances to get in.

Besides being successful and a surprise to the presidential party, the meeting at Rebel Stadium had one other point of distinction. It was the first nonsegregated political meeting ever held in the state of Texas. The experiment worked without a bit of friction, so smoothly that Negro reporters traveling with the presidential party had to be told what was happening.

Biggest hit of the program at Dallas was Tom Clark. In introducing the President, Attorney General Clark said, "I sat with this man when he knocked out Joe Louis." He meant John L. Lewis, but the misnomer hit the crowd's funny bone and the laugh could be heard for miles.

While passing an orphanage in Dallas, the President called for a surprise stop and went in to talk briefly to the children.

This evidence of profound interest in children, especially orphans, was typical of the President. And the kids were very pleased.

When the train pulled into Bonham, Texas, Speaker Sam Rayburn's home town, General Bedell Smith was on hand to give the President a report on conditions in Europe. Everything was interrupted while the President went over Smith's report. Then he went to a political rally held in the high school football stadium where again the President was warmly greeted by an overflow crowd. After the rally, he spent several hours at Speaker Rayburn's home.

As the train rolled on toward Oklahoma City, the weather was good and the President in fine fettle. He spent most of his time on the back platform waving at people as the train passed. The phenomenon which I had noticed in Michigan was marked here in Texas and Oklahoma.

The rally at Oklahoma City was a big success but in the middle of success, problems arose. Cash for the train had run out. It was an ignominious position for the President of the United States and for the Democratic Party. It seemed possible the entire party might have to alight and get back to Washington the best way they could.

But this couldn't happen to Harry S Truman, not in Oklahoma. Governor Turner and W. Elmer Harber of Shawnee, Oklahoma, held a collection party in the President's private car and raised enough cash to finance the rest of the current trip and, also, another cross-country trip.

Greatly pleased and heartened by the crowds during the remainder of the trip, the President arrived in Washington. The back-platform trip which had started with disaster and bogged down in bad luck, had been snatched back to success. In the aggregate the crowds had measured up to expectations. Comparisons were being made between the numbers greeting the President and the numbers at Dewey's meetings. The comparison was such that the official Republican explanation became, "They

273

[the crowds] are just curiosity seekers. They came to look, that's all."

Trip followed trip; almost as fast as one ended, another began. Dawson was firmly ensconced as advance man, although Chapman still worked on it on occasions.

Toward the end of the campaign the train was due to stop in Akron, Ohio. Frank Lausche, a former Governor at the time and now a United States Senator, was the Democratic candidate for Governor. Always a lone wolf, Lausche was conducting his own campaign. He and Taft had joined forces to split the gubernatorial ticket from the presidential ticket. It was a political maneuver that happened to fit both men's strategy. At the time the split was made, Senator Taft had fond expectations of being the Republican presidential nominee. He felt Lausche would help the Democratic presidential nominee if he were on the same ticket. So Taft wanted the ballot separated. Lausche, for his part, thought that Truman would be the Democratic nominee and that he couldn't win. Lausche wanted no part of being third man on a losing ticket, so he was willing to deal to split the ballot.

Although Lausche ran his own campaign, he was impressed by the manner in which the President drew crowds, and the way he handled the crowds when he spoke.

"Golly," said Lausche once, "how the man can handle people!"

In Akron, Clarence Mott, the Summit County Democratic chairman, a political enemy of Lausche, plotted to force Lausche to declare himself for the President for the first time. In introducing Lausche to the President's rally, Mott said: "Governor Lausche has come here especially to perform one deed, to introduce to you the President of the United States and to declare his support for the President in this great fight."

Seated in my office in New York, Congressman Kirwan of Ohio, a keen political observer, read about Lausche's endorsement of the President. He looked up thoughtfully. "I've been getting good reports from Ohio, but now it's official. The President will carry the state. If he wasn't going to, Lausche would never have come out for him."

Shortly thereafter Dawson was in New Jersey making arrangements there for the President's visit. In Jersey City, he looked at the narrow streets and, like the showman he is, decided that here was an opportunity to stage a good scene that would make headlines. Without the knowledge of Jim Rowley, chief of the White House Secret Service detail, Dawson arranged to have the wooden saw horses, which were supposed to keep the crowd back, removed by the local police.

He prevailed on the police chief to strengthen his lines near Carpenter's Hall where the President's first stop would be. This meant a weakening of details on the approach streets. Then Dawson sat back to await results.

He got them, too.

Frank Hague had laid on a fantastic display of fireworks, spending all the available money on that and neglecting to schedule radio broadcasts. It had been agreed that the state organization would handle these details in New Jersey so the committee had not arranged for a nationwide broadcast either.

As the President's party hit the city limits, a giant cannon was fired as a salute. Then bombs, rockets and waterfalls of fireworks marked the progress of the presidential party. But the crowds lining the streets were so dense that the cars moved too slowly. Fire from a waterfall display singed Mrs. Truman's mink coat. But this was only the beginning.

When the procession reached the narrow streets where Dawson had planned for the crowd to break out of control, the resulting crush was more than even Dawson had expected.

The procession was completely broken up. The only car to reach Carpenter's Hall in addition to the President's car was that containing Mrs. Truman. Most of the other cars never did catch up with the show. Reunion was made at the railroad station when Charlie Ross and the newsmen, puffing and complaining, barely made the train.

The President didn't know of Dawson's perfidy but he approved highly of the excitement.

"That," said Truman, "was wonderful. I've never been so warmly greeted in my life. You need excitement to keep life in the campaign."

While the President was on a New England trip, I received a call from Senator Brien McMahon who was masterminding the campaign in Connecticut.

He said, "Jack, you've got to get a message to the President for me."

I agreed to do it.

"I want you to tell the President that when he gets in Connecticut tomorrow, he shouldn't use the 'give-'em-hell' technique. That's all right for the sticks but it won't go here. Dress it up, you know, make it sound good. That's the way it has to be here; otherwise, his visit will backfire on us."

"Brien, I'll deliver your message but the President isn't going to change his plans now."

"He'll do it," McMahon was confident. "He'll do it if you make sure he knows that I want him to."

I got in touch with Matt Connelly at Pittsfield, Massachusetts.

"I've got a message for the President from Brien McMahon," I told him. "It has to do with speaking in Connecticut tomorrow. Before I tell you what it is, let me say this—pay no attention to it!" Then I passed on McMahon's message.

In Boston, the President was invited to call upon Archbishop Cushing. Although the Catholic Church does not play politics, this was a major political boon, for Archbishop Cushing was probably the most beloved prelate in Massachusetts history.

Coming down into Rhode Island by car, the President was met at the state line by Howard McGrath. As they rode toward Providence, making frequent stops to greet the crowds, the President, in answer to a query by McGrath, said, "It's been going well, very well. But it's a strain."

He was silent for a moment, then added, "But it's worth it,

Howard. Even if we should fail, we're building a better Democratic Party for the future."

It was the closest thing to admitting the possibility of defeat that anyone ever heard from Truman.

And in Connecticut, Truman gave 'em hell, as usual, and despite McMahon's predictions, the crowds loved it.

One of the greatest demonstrations of the campaign was in Chicago only a week before election. Plans had started modestly for a rally in the Chicago stadium which could accommodate about 29,000. But Jack Arvey, all out for Truman since the convention, sensed victory in the state. To get that victory he needed a tremendous vote in Cook County. So the plans were expanded and the effort intensified.

I was in Chicago for the rally. Tip-off on what was to happen came in the afternoon as the President arrived and proceeded by car to the Blackstone Hotel on Michigan Avenue. Crowds estimated at nearly three hundred thousand were on the street pushing and shoving good-naturedly to get a glimpse of Truman.

Arvey told me then, "This wasn't planned. It's fantastic."

But if this seemed big, the mob that surrounded the Blackstone during dinner was bigger. I had dinner with a group of newsmen from the train: Jack Bell of the AP, Tony Vaccaro, also AP, Merriman Smith, UP, Bill Lawrence of the *Times*, Ed Folliard of the Washington *Post*, and several others. They were all needling me about my job security.

"What," they asked, "will you do for a job after November second, Election Day?"

This went on and on. Finally, exasperated, I threw money on the table and offered to cover any bets up to five hundred dollars even money that Truman would win. There were no takers. It wasn't that I had convinced them; they were nice guys and didn't want to take my money on what they thought was a sure thing.

We went to the Chicago stadium on the west side by bus, following behind the President's car. I had supplied the Illinois organization with five thousand large pictures of Truman and the same number of Barkley. Every store front along the route had at least one such picture and most had the glass solidly lined. The crowds were stupendous. Up State Street, the people were massed fifty deep on each side of the street. The mob at the world's busiest corner State and Madison, defied description. Westward on Madison for the twenty-four blocks to the stadium, you could have walked on the crowd and never stepped down, so closely were they packed.

Alderman Sonnenschein, of the twenty-fourth ward, Arvey's close friend, said to me, "Nice crowd we turned out."

"Sonney," I told him, "you didn't turn out this crowd. The Chicago organization never saw the day it could turn out a crowd like this. Truman brought them out."

He didn't like it and, actually, I was probably only partly right. The massive crowds did come out for Truman but they were triggered by Arvey's efforts.

At the stadium, the press was terrific. At least fifty thousand people outside listened to the speeches by loudspeaker. Inside you couldn't move, it was so densely packed.

It was a noisy, enthusiastic crowd that cheered anything that moved. When the President was introduced, there was bedlam. The introduction was made by Mayor Kennelly. Oddly enough, Kennelly had been reluctant to introduce the President for he was convinced Truman would be defeated. It was only when Arvey put on the screws that Kennelly agreed to do the job.

The President's radio speech was interrupted so often by spirited applause that it became apparent he would run over our allotted time. The rule, thrust down our throats by the networks, was that if a political program ran as much as two minutes over, we had to pay for the entire next period. If it happened, as on this night, that the succeeding period was a half-hour show, we would have to pay the entire half-hour time cost. We didn't have that kind of money.

Ken Fry, who was producing the show, leaned to me, copy of

278

the President's speech in his hand, and said, "He's going over."

"How much?"

"At least five minutes, maybe more."

I checked the CBS producer. "Can we go over?"

"I have no choice," he said. "If you do, you've got to pay."

I went back to Fry and told him, "Cut him off on a high note." Thinking that over for a second, I added in loud tones, "The networks won't let the President of the United States finish his speech."

Immediately I was surrounded by newsmen. They had heard my statement.

"What goes?" one asked.

Fry gave the signal and the President was off the air even though he was still speaking.

I shrugged. "The network has a rule that the President cannot run over more than two minutes without paying for a full half hour additional time."

That brought a story in the morning papers. It brought a flood of indignant letters to editors. It brought into the Democratic National Committee a number of small contributions from thousands of people around the country. The money went to insure the President's being allowed to finish his next speech on the air. This technique is known as making a virtue of a necessity.

Meanwhile Dawson was in New York smoothing details for the final swing into the big city. The Democratic state committee had relinquished its hold on Madison Square Garden for the traditional pre-election rally. No money! David Dubinsky, a strong Truman supporter, president of the International Ladies Garment Workers' Union and head of the Liberal Party of New York, had taken up the vacated site and date.

Dubinsky was selling tickets for the rally, each seat costing ten dollars. He was doing all right with his sales but Dawson was interested in making sure the seats were filled. That was more difficult.

After some discussion, Dubinsky agreed to allow the Garden

to be filled, tickets or no tickets. But the Garden management vetoed that.

"When you buy a seat in the Garden," they said, "you get the seat you bought."

It was agreed to set a time limit on claiming the seats called for by the tickets. If any seats were empty, the doors would be opened and it would be first come first served for the unoccupied seats. The Garden didn't like the arrangement but they finally acceded.

Then came the question of the amusement tax which had to be paid on every seat because tickets were being sold. Dubinsky agreed to pay a blanket tax on the entire seating capacity.

Arrangements seemed to be completed. The President arrived and made his swing first through the garment district and then down to Union Square and City Hall, up to the Grand Concourse at 125th Street and on to Harlem. Everywhere the crowds were immense.

As the day neared its close, the President sat down to an early dinner. Dawson was at the table but he was too worried to eat. At seven he went to the Garden. It was empty.

The President and his party were due at the head of the parade at nine. Surely the place should have people in it by seven. At 7:30 the hall was still a morgue. Dawson had the lights in the balcony turned down so no one could see whether the balconies were filled or not. This seemed all right until flash bulbs began to go off. Dawson investigated and found *Life* photographers were making pictures of the empty seats, just in case.

It was crawling up on eight o'clock and a trickle of people arrived. The time limit on the tickets that had been sold had not yet expired but Dawson got Dubinsky to open the gates and people began to move into the Garden in considerable numbers. Still it looked doubtful on filling the balconies.

Dawson had an inspiration. The parade! Gathering some of Dubinsky's assistants, he posted men on each gate. The parade could be heard approaching in the distance. The gates were

280

swung open for the Legion drill teams, for the bands, for all the other units of the parade. As each unit neared a gate, it was waved right on in. When they were all in, Dawson gave the signal and the gates were closed.

Ushers directed the units to seats in the balconies, and lo! the balconies were filled. The crowd completely filled the Garden.

The program began and there was noise and music and the President made a splendid speech. There was one minor difficulty: here where the Palestine issue was all-important, he couldn't say the word. For some reason every time he mentioned Palestine in his address, the word came out "Palesteen." But few noticed and the rally was a great success. Tallulah Bankhead, stimulated by the excitement and her role as mistress of ceremonies, climaxed it by kissing the President's hand in thanks for his leadership of the country.

The following night was the big Brooklyn rally in the Music Hall, then on to Kansas City and the election.

The day after election, Dawson rejoined the President's train in Boonville, Indiana, on its return trip to Washington. Don had with him a copy of the Chicago *Tribune's* Election Day early edition with the screaming banner headline: "Dewey Defeats Truman."

The President looked at the paper and smiled. "You know, Don," he said, "I'm going to have a lot of fun with this."

And he did. In Washington the next morning a photographer snapped Truman's smiling face behind the paper as he displayed it to the thousands who thronged Union Station to hail his return.

The result was the picture of the year.

CHAPTER 26

EARLY IN OCTOBER, Major Jim Mackin came to my office. He was a Justice Department political appointee and thus outside the jurisdiction of the Hatch Act, which forbids political activity by a civil service employe of the federal government. He had what he thought was the basis for an attack on Dewey. I was glad to listen.

Mackin had been a member of the legislative committee of the Veterans of Foreign Wars in New York State. As a member of this committee he participated in the annual conference with Governor Dewey in advance of the 1948 legislative session.

"In a fit of rage," Mackin said, "Governor Thomas E. Dewey, the Republican candidate for the presidency, told a Veteran of Foreign Wars legislative committee that all civil service employes were mediocre." Dewey had angrily gone on to say a great deal against the civil service.

This was important news indeed, for there are more than two million civil service employes in federal jobs alone, plus more millions in state and local civil service jobs all over the nation. The details were important.

The VFW committee had presented a twelve-point program covering such items as Communists in government, provisions for off-track betting in the state and the controversial civil service recommendations. When the item concerning civil service was reached, Governor Dewey stated heatedly that he was very much opposed to automatic promotion for civil service employes after ten years' service. Turning to Harold J. Burke, chairman of the group, the Governor said: "Burke, you know as well as I do that all civil service employes are mediocre at their best. If I had my way the present civil service system in force in national, state and local governments would not exist!"

Then he said, his voice rising, that he felt that government employes should be subject to removal like any private employe. He added: "If he isn't smart enough to get another job he should get out!"

Governor Dewey continued his tirade despite the shocked attitude of the VFW legislative committee. He said, "Anyone who cannot advance himself in ten years should be fired. If they can't get promoted through an examination, they should get out, but the trouble is, they couldn't make a living in private industry and now they want a promotion without taking an examination. I will veto such a bill if it reaches my desk."

Someone muttered that this attitude was contrary to the spirit of the civil service system. Dewey declared loudly: "You'd have me paying these sons of sea cooks for just breathing and it will not happen, not while I'm Governor. If I had my way I'd abolish civil service!"

The meeting broke up. As the group left the Governor's office, Paul Lockwood, Dewey's assistant who later became his campaign manager, said in a worried tone, "It is my feeling that this conversation should be off the record."

This choice item we made available as a general press release and published it in *The Democrat*, the Democratic Party's official newspaper.

Before I released the story I checked Mackin's facts carefully. I talked with nearly every one of the men who had been present. Some of them were too cautious to say more than "no comment." Burke confirmed the conversation in detail but asked me not to quote him for he had to deal with the state government and couldn't stand heat.

After it was printed, the Republicans denied the story. Jim Hagerty, at that time Dewey's press secretary, said flatly, "It didn't happen." Then, asked if he was denying the story for the record, said, "Don't be silly. We're not going to pay any attention to the pipe dreams of McGrath and Redding."

We countered by reprinting the official, authenticated report of the meeting with Governor Dewey made by Major Mackin to the Brooklyn County VFW council.

By this time all of the publications which are printed for the special field of civil service employes had picked up the story. Employes of the federal government, traditionally against the party in power as a group, began to change their minds. Civil service employes at state and local levels showed evidence of a build-up of resentment against Dewey's slurs.

The Republicans obtained specific denials from every member of the VFW's legislative committee except Mackin. This was countered by revealing what each one of them had said to the Democratic committee in the presence of witnesses. The story we told had the advantage of being documented.

The Republicans next charged Mackin's report was a forgery, that his original had been destroyed. We offered to submit the original to expert examination to determine its authenticity.

But the Republicans finally decided to drop the issue. We were left in possession of the field. We added one last turn of the knife by placing the whole story in the President's hands; and when he visited New York in the final days of the campaign he prodded the issue vigorously both at Madison Square Garden and in Brooklyn.

We raised Republican ire on another item. This concerned the dedication of Idlewild Airport. The President was requested to be the honored guest. Governor Dewey was also invited.

On the morning of the dedication Dewey was in New York City. The President flew from Washington into Idlewild in the *Inde-*

pendence. Dewey couldn't stand his role as a groundling. He motored to LaGuardia Field, chartered a plane there and flew the eight miles from LaGuardia to Idlewild so that he too could arrive by plane.

We learned of the incident and bandied it about the country as evidence of Dewey's pettiness. Republican Party papers and the one-party press all over the country denounced the Democrats for indulging in "personalities."

Then we got a good break. In Russia Stalin announced he would prefer Dewey as the President of the United States. Stalin in his statement did not impugn Dewey's patriotism, merely indicated that he felt he could get along better with the New York Governor than with Truman.

We were afraid someone might miss this one, so we issued a statement to the effect that Stalin should stop trying to influence the American election by selecting Dewey as the man he'd prefer as an adversary to Communism in its westward march.

We got another unexpected break. During the Governor's final swing through New England the Dewey train stopped at North Attleboro, Massachusetts, where it was boarded by Speaker of the House Joseph Martin. Martin held an immediate conference with Governor Dewey, at which time it was reported by press correspondents on the train that sharp words were exchanged. The story, which was promptly denied, was that Dewey was critical of Martin's lack of support for the Republican ticket. Martin, in turn, was reported to have voiced his feelings concerning the manner in which the campaign was being carried out by the presidential candidate.

As the train was readied to leave Boston for New York following this incident, Albert Martin, the Speaker's brother, made strenuous efforts to delay the train to permit loading aboard copies of the final pre-election issue of Speaker Martin's newspaper, the North Attleboro *Chronicle*. The papers arrived in time, however, and it was unnecessary to delay the train.

This anxiety to have the papers on board the train underlined

285

the importance of an editorial in the paper which was sharply critical of Governor Dewey's campaign.

It read in part: "Dewey's speeches are designed for tonal effect. His addresses are filled with maxims old and new, such as: 'We need a rudder to our ship of state and a firm hand at the tiller.' Sounds good and brings the applause. But promises nothing. 'Our country is at the crossroads of its history' is another Dewey phrase, old and a bit trite. Dewey also still uses 'profound' and 'profoundly,' although he wore both phrases (words) threadbare in 1944. . . ."

The same editorial was critical of Truman. But most observers saw significance in the timing of the editorial coming so soon after the reported difference between Speaker Martin and Dewey, right after the visit to North Attleboro.

When this flash came in from the Dewey train we reacted quickly. It was Saturday, October 30, and there was little time remaining.

"I can't believe this was deliberate," I told McGrath, "but it looks deliberate. We've got to treat it that way. It's my guess that the newspapers will downhold on the play in the belief that it is a mixup of some sort. They won't want to hurt Dewey. That'll be right up our alley. We have to get it out for our people to use. When it draws a denial it'll be too late."

McGrath agreed. We spent hundreds of almost nonexistent dollars to telegraph the portions of the Martin editorial which were critical of Governor Dewey to our state and big city organizations, urging them to "get it around" to every precinct captain; to print it as a flyer for distribution before the polls opened on Tuesday.

The Republicans reacted slowly. Their explanation was to the effect that Speaker Martin's newspaper bought an "editorial service" which supplied "canned" editorials, which in this case had gone into the paper without knowledge of what was in it. As we had guessed, newspapers across the country played the story down. At the very same time the Democratic local organizations were playing it up. By the time the Republicans realized what was happening it was Election Day and too late to limit the damage.

During the few days before the campaign ended, Walter Winchell, who made a complete turn from being a strong supporter of Roosevelt to being an ardent enemy of Truman, said in a radio broadcast that the official betting odds were 15 to 1 against Truman.

This hurt. It fostered a bandwagon concept which we had been combatting all through the campaign. But it was a difficult statement to counter.

But Governor Turner and Elmer Harber of Oklahoma got into the act. Turner called and asked if there was any truth in Winchell's report on the odds. I answered: "I don't think so but I can't prove it."

"I'm sending you a certified check," said Turner. "Get it down! If you can!"

The next day the check arrived, signed by Harber, for $20,000.

I contacted a betting commissioner in St. Louis and offered part or all of the $20,000 at the quoted odds of 15 to 1. He promptly lowered the odds to 8 to 1 and said they'd be lower the next day, he thought.

A betting commissioner in Pittsburgh, said to be one of the biggest, offered five to one. In Chicago I was offered 3 to 1. A Wall Street commissioner in New York offered 2 to 1. Finally we got the money covered at an average of 4 to 1.

Then I organized a group to call Winchell's office and demand where the 15 to 1 odds he had talked about could be had. At first such queries were answered generally, with references to "any" betting commissioner. That of course opened the door for an argument and my people would argue that the betting commissioners would offer no such odds.

Finally, Winchell's office changed their story to "betting's illegal."

All through the campaign the public opinion polls had been

a negative and annoying factor for the Democrats. Consistently the polltakers reported Truman hopelessly beaten. Elmo Roper had ceased taking his samplings in September, saying the results of further polls would merely serve to confirm what he had already reported, Truman's defeat.

Now in the last moments of the campaign the Gallup poll and the Crossley poll released their final figures. The Crossley poll gave a final national figure of 49.9 per cent for Dewey and 44.8 per cent for Truman, with the remainder credited to Thurmond and Wallace: The Gallup poll credited Dewey with 46 per cent of the popular vote and Truman with 40 per cent. The allotment to Wallace was 6 per cent.

Chairman McGrath sent telegrams to Archibald Crossley, director of the Crossley poll, and Dr. George Gallup, director of the American Institute of Public Opinion, in which he declared: "The figures in your poll when properly evaluated and corrected by an ever present historical error reveal the advantage to be with Truman and not with Dewey as your conclusion states."

To Dr. Gallup he stated: "These are not my opinions I am expressing but your own figures properly adjusted and correctly interpreted." He added that a state-by-state increase for President Truman of 4.1 percentage points would result in a Truman landslide with the President carrying 43 states and with 438 electoral votes out of a total of 511. This was important because Dr. Gallup said errors ranging up to five per cent were possible.

The telegram stated that the Gallup poll made errors favoring the Republican Party by 2.4 percentage points in 1940 and 2.8 percentage points in 1944. Senator McGrath stated:

This historical error in favor of Republicans mirrors the reluctance of some polltakers to go into factory and poor areas. It is the same sort of error which tripped up the *Literary Digest* poll in 1936. This failure to analyze and assess correctly the broad base of the population at the bottom of the economic scale

288

has always been a bugaboo for polltakers. It means that small errors become great ones when magnified from cross section sampling to the total of our population.

On the acceptance of food products or on fairly noncontroversial subjects, polls are generally accurate, but on genuine issues on which the mass of the people are deeply concerned, it is very difficult for polltakers to weight their figures properly.

In view of the historical errors and these contributing factors, it is my belief that the historical error shown in the Gallup figures for 1940-44 should be taken as a constant and for that reason your figures should be corrected.

When we realize that your allotment of 6 percentage points to Wallace and Thurmond on a national basis is probably far too high (a large newspaper poll for example shows today 6.3 per cent for Wallace in New York State as against the 12 per cent shown in your poll for New York State), when we also realize that the greater part of the so-called undecided vote will probably go to President Truman, and when we realize the fact that your final sampling was taken at least a month before the election; then these factors add up to the conclusion that the advantage is with Truman and not with Dewey.

I do not have to tell you that the Republican Party is striving desperately to keep people from voting by its propaganda that the election will be a walkover for Governor Dewey, and is using alleged polls to bolster its claims. For that reason, I call upon you to make public your final figures with the proper adjustments so that the voters may know the truth.

The telegram included a rundown of the states with Gallup's figures corrected by the "historical error constant." This corrected, the Gallup poll figures showed a result of 47.2 per cent for Dewey and 46.2 per cent for Truman—a virtual tie.

The telegram to Crossley was almost identical, varying only in the differences in figures. Crossley had shown final figures of 49.9 per cent for Dewey and 44.8 per cent for Truman. When corrected by the "historical error" found in his 1940 and 1944 polls the result showed 47.5 for Dewey and 47.2 for Truman.

289

With the dispatch of these telegrams we waited replies from the polltakers. Crossley called up the next day to talk to Senator McGrath but the Chairman was out. Instead Crossley talked to me. He was very polite, found our statement concerning the problems of polltakers "interesting" and said he hoped, "We can sometime discuss these matters fully."

We did not hear from Gallup, so I prodded several newsmen to question him on the McGrath telegram and his thoughts concerning it.

Meanwhile McGrath and I sat down in the Senator's Biltmore Hotel suite. It was late Sunday afternoon, October 31, two days before the election. We called every responsible Democratic leader at the state level across the country to get his final opinion on the President's chances.

One after another gave the same general reply: "He's coming. If we only had another week. But in the time left he can't make it!"

We'd ask concerning state candidates. The answer was usually: "We'll carry the state for the Senator [or the Governor]. We'll take the majority [or all] of the congressional districts. But the President? He can't make it."

When we finished, McGrath reviewed our notes. He looked at me and said: "They don't know what they're saying. You can't win all the things they say they're going to win and not elect a President too. After all, he's at the top of the ticket. We're either going to lose everything—every senatorial race, every congressional race, every governor's race, every courthouse—or we'll elect a President. I think we elect Truman."

We ran down the list of states and divided them into four columns: Dewey, Truman, Thurmond and "undecided." We knew Wallace could win no state.

In the last column—undecided—we placed the five big states: New York, California, Ohio, Pennsylvania and Illinois. In these states the issue was so close we didn't feel a prediction could safely be made.

290

Then we went down the Dewey states, totaled the Truman states and conceded the Thurmond states. In the latter instance we credited Thurmond with the four states he ultimately carried: South Carolina, Mississippi, Louisiana and Alabama. When we added the electoral votes represented by these columns of states we had Truman with a minimum of 252 electoral votes without counting any one of the five big states.

McGrath studied the figures, then said, "If we're right, the worst Truman can get is an inconclusive vote in the Electoral College. In that case the election will be thrown into the House of Representatives But if we carry any one of the five big states, we're in!"

We issued a last-minute press release for afternoon papers of Monday, November 1, 1948, in which we claimed the Senate by from three to five seats, the House of Representatives by a minimum gain of thirty-one seats, possibly as many as thirty-nine seats. The release stated: "Absolute victory for the President depends on the size of the vote in the five key states of New York, Illinois, Ohio, Pennsylvania and California. The President cannot lose this election. Absolute victory depends on winning one of the five major states."

In our rundown we made but two mistakes. McGrath's final listing of the Truman states claimed Maryland and conceded Wisconsin. The final results showed us losing Maryland and winning Wisconsin.

As it turned out, we would have been correct on Wisconsin if we had heeded the report of Bob Tehan, national committeeman for Wisconsin and now a federal judge, and Andrew J. Biemiller, running for Congress in the Milwaukee area. Biemiller is now director of legislative services for the AFL-CIO. Both of these men, at variance with the rest, predicted that a farmer-worker alliance would win the state for Truman. McGrath decided they were too optimistic.

In the evening we met Paul Fitzpatrick and his publicity director, George Daley. Fitzpatrick had information obtained by

291

Daley from a newsman who had attended an off-the-record conference with Dewey in Albany the night before. In this conference Dewey revealed whom he was going to choose for his Cabinet. Notable on the list was the retention of James Forrestal as Secretary of Defense.

Forrestal had been a center of controversy all through the campaign, the Jewish leaders particularly being hot against him because he advocated a policy of favoring the Arab states over Israel, reasoning simply that it was vital for the United States to have access to oil controlled by Saudi Arabia, Iran and Iraq. This may have been *"realpolitik"* but it wasn't popular in the United States.

Now I saw an opportunity to transfer some of the Forrestal dead weight to Dewey's shoulders. I called Drew Pearson and told him of the Dewey conference and of Forrestal remaining in the Republican Cabinet if Dewey should be elected. That night, on his final nationwide broadcast before the election, Pearson "revealed" this story as a scoop. That cheered me somewhat. But Pearson went on to predict ominously that Truman would be defeated.

The next day as the pace slowed—the national job was done with the exception of the wind-up broadcasts—I had a reply from the newsmen I had sicked on Dr. Gallup concerning McGrath's telegram.

Dr. Gallup's answer was: "Wait till Tuesday!"

I said I would.

CHAPTER 27

IN THE SUMMER OF 1957, fifty Democrats sat down to breakfast in the Mayflower Hotel in Washington with former President Harry S Truman. In the gathering were most of the men who furnished leadership to the party. President Truman leaned forward, looked around the room and called each man by his name. He reached Mike Kirwan, chairman of the Democratic Congressional Campaign Committee.

"Mike Kirwan," said Truman. "I'll never forget Mike. He's the only man in my experience who ever went to the White House and told a President of the United States to go to hell. You know, it took me six years to find out he was right."

Mr. Truman was referring to a matter of patronage in Mike's state, Ohio; but he was also paying tribute to a fighting jut-jawed Irishman who, as head of the Democratic Congressional Campaign Committee, had been chief engineer of one of the most unusual victories in political history.

In the preceding ten years, two elections had made political history. The first was in 1948 when Truman was elected President, after all but a very few men close to him had conceded his defeat.

The second was in 1956 when, in the face of a Republican landslide, Democrats strengthened their hold on the House of Representatives and the Senate. Electing both houses of Congress in the face of a defeat in the presidential race was unprecedented in modern politics. In 1917 Democrats had organized the House only with the aid of nine independent votes, and in 1877 Democrats elected a majority of the House of Representatives while Republicans held control of the Senate. Only these two instances have approached the 1956 feat since the present two parties became dominant in 1856—when the Republican Party appeared on the ballot for the first time.

In ten years' time the Democrats had reached the apogee of their strength, in 1948; had seen that strength whittled away by time and events until in 1952 they held neither a house of Congress nor the Administration; and had seen the fortunes of politics smiling on them once more as they reached 1957 with control of both houses of Congress and could hope to return to power in the executive branch in 1960.

In crediting the Democrats with reaching maximum power in 1948, I might get an argument. But the facts are that Dewey got all the regular Republican votes while Truman split the Democratic votes with Thurmond and Wallace. He lost four Southern states to Thurmond, and defections to Wallace cost the Democrats New Jersey and New York.

Having reached its zenith, Democratic power began to crumble almost at once. In 1949 I was asked to make a survey of Pennsylvania, where Senator Myers was up for re-election in 1950. Myers, the Democratic whip, was an Administration stalwart and an effective Senator; but the trend was toward the Republicans in Pennsylvania and it was no secret that popular Governor James Duff would be the Republican candidate for Senator.

A special election was pending in the Twenty-second District of Pennsylvania, which comprised Armstrong, Cambria and Indiana counties. The elected Congressman, a Democrat, had been killed in an airplane accident. This was July, and the election was set for September 13.

We needed first a survey of that district to determine what

294

had to be done to hold it for the Democrats, and a survey of the state to ascertain Senator Myers' position.

Sam Brightman went directly to Johnstown, the largest city in the Twenty-second District. Meanwhile I went to Philadelphia, where I posed as a beer salesman. In this role I visited all over the city. While talking beer, it was easy to ask a few questions about politics. I couldn't maintain the role of beer salesman for more than forty-eight hours without arousing suspicion, however. After two days I became a men's clothing salesman and visited both high-class and low-priced haberdasheries around town. Again I was able to get political opinions that no politician would get.

Then I took off my disguise, which consisted of wearing a hat, and went to the Democratic organization. I talked to Jim Finnegan, then Philadelphia city chairman—he ran Adlai Stevenson's presidential campaign in 1956—and to many of his aides. When I talked to Senator Myers he asked for a copy of the report as soon as it was concluded.

From Philadelphia, I drove to the Allentown-Bethlehem area where I had been fronted in as a representative of a CIO union. In this way I was able to talk political shop with labor leaders. After spending a couple of days as a union representative, I again resumed my natural role and talked to the Democratic organization leaders.

Leaving Allentown, I joined Brightman in Johnstown and concluded the congressional survey there. On the way back to Washington, Brightman and I visited county chairmen in rural Pennsylvania and discussed organization problems with them. Among these was a state senator named George Leader, a chicken farmer located near York, who later became Governor of Pennsylvania.

Back in Washington, we wrote our report. The congressional district, we said, could possibly be held. It all depended on whether or not the local Democratic organization went to work; if not, the fight was lost.

The district went Republican in the special election.

As to the state, we felt it was hopeless. We reported that the city organization in Philadelphia was not strong enough at that time to carry Myers over Duff by a substantial margin. Pittsburgh we knew would go Democratic; but the rural areas were completely unorganized. We found instances where county chairmen didn't even know that new industrial installations had gone into operation in their counties. In one case a glass factory with 3,500 workers, members of the CIO glass workers union, strongly Democratic, had been in operation for nearly two years. During that time the county chairman hadn't once visited the area, and hadn't even talked to the local union officials. He had lost the county three to one in 1948.

We concluded that Myers would be fortunate to come within 200,000 of Duff.

The report was a sensation, but not a pleasant one. Bill Boyle, then Chairman of the Democratic National Committee, ordered all copies destroyed. I was sworn to silence. Everyone was to act on the theory that if we carefully closed our eyes, the bad situation would go away.

Of course we could ignore the report. But little was done to correct the problems that existed and in 1950 Senator Myers was defeated.

The trend was slighly downward in the first two years of President Truman's term but when the Korean War hit in June 1950, the drop-off became marked. In the summer of 1950, I left the Democratic National Committee to become Assistant Postmaster General and therefore was not active in the 1950 campaign. The Democrats were defeated in many congressional races in 1950 but not enough to lose either house of Congress. Despite the politically depressing effect of the Korean War on the Democrats, by 1951 things seemed to be improving.

In 1951 and early 1952, the real problem was the coming presidential election. I deduced the President was not going to run again. He had never told me so, but I came to that conclusion from observing and listening to things in and around the White House. When the President announced formally at a Jefferson-Jackson Day Dinner in March 1952 that he would not be a candidate for re-election, I was unhappy but not surprised.

As a government official, I had little to do with the national election in 1952. I made a few speeches for Governor Stevenson in Iowa, Indiana, Illinois and Ohio but that was the extent of my participation.

The Democratic presidential campaign in 1952 was an amateurish effort with responsibility hopelessly divided between two physical headquarters: the one in Springfield, Illinois, where Governor Stevenson stayed to complete his term, and the other at the Democratic National Committee offices in Washington with Steve Mitchell in charge.

Mitchell had had some backers for the job of Democratic National Chairman in this campaign, but a stronger group favored Mike Fanning, the Postmaster of Los Angeles. Fanning was sidetracked at the very last second while he was sitting in the anteroom of Governor Stevenson's office for what was to be his final conference before his appointment. For years Fanning had held the civil service position of postmaster and was thus barred by the Hatch Act from participating in political activities. Democratic leaders realized tardily that giving the top political job in the Democratic Party to a man who was not supposed to have been politically active would suggest that he had been violating the Hatch Act. Accordingly Mitchell, a Chicago lawyer and a close personal friend of the Governor, was named instead.

Stevenson made a gallant effort; but when Eisenhower proposed to go to Korea if elected, and seek an end to the fighting, the result was foregone.

While on speaking engagements in 1952 I realized that the individual candidates for Congress on the Democratic ticket were going their own merry way, largely ignoring the national ticket. This meant defeat to me, and as early as October I privately conceded the election. However, it still looked as if the House of

297

Representatives might survive the inevitable Republican victory. And, in fact, the House was lost only by the narrow margin of 222 to 213.

Following the Democratic defeat in 1952, I resigned from the Post Office Department effective February 2, 1953. John Allen of Chicago, a Sears Roebuck executive, was appointed by Eisenhower as my successor.

A few weeks later I was elected treasurer of the National Democratic Congressional Committee of which Congressman Kirwan was chairman. Thus, almost from the start, I was active in the 1954 congressional election campaign.

Familiarizing myself with my new post I found to my astonishment that in 1952 the congressional committee had available a meager $17,000 for campaign funds. Despite this, the Democrats had missed carrying the house by only five seats. My predecessor as treasurer had been George Allen, mentioned earlier as a White House intimate of President Truman. Allen defected to Eisenhower in 1952 and did little or nothing for the congressional committee.

In the 1954 campaign the Democrats were aided by an economic recession which, of course, hurt incumbent Republicans. The election itself was fought largely on local issues with each congressional candidate making his own personal fight. In 1954 we were able to better our financial position and the reports made on expenditures in the campaign showed a total of $208,592.

The rival Republican Congressional Campaign Committee reported spending almost two million dollars.

Congressman Kirwan early in 1953 participated strongly in electing Paul Butler, of Indiana, Chairman of the Democratic National Committee, succeeding Mitchell. In one instance Kirwan had dinner with a national committeeman who lived in a seaport city. This man told Kirwan he had committed himself to vote for Mike DiSalle, Butler's chief opponent for the job.

Kirwan listened politely, then asked, "Is your appropriation for harbor improvements up in the Congress next year?"

298

The committeeman looked surprised. "Why, yes, Mike, and we're looking to you as chairman of the appropriations subcommittee to get it for us."

"So you're going to need an appropriation."

"That's right, Mike, and we're depending on you."

"Hmm," said Kirwan. "I'm for Butler."

There was a silence. Then the national committeeman ventured, "I've been thinking, Mike. Butler is the best man for the job of Chairman. I'm proud to vote for him."

Several special elections were won by the Democrats and the evidence of a swing back to the Democratic Party was pronounced. When the people went to the polls in November 1954, they returned both a Democratic House and Senate. The House margin was 232 to 203.

Shortly after the 1954 campaign, the Republicans, smarting under their defeat, organized a campaign school. Republican leaders at state and congressional district levels were brought to Washington to be briefed on how not to lose elections. The short course in political strategy lasted three days and I enjoyed it very much.

The only thing I thought of concrete value was a talk by Murray Chotiner, who had run a number of successful campaigns for the Republicans in the West. He had been a moving figure in Earl Warren's campaigns for Governor. He had been in the Knowland organization when the Senator was elected in 1946 and he masterminded Dick Nixon's campaigns for Congress, for the Senate and for Vice President.

Chotiner talked frankly. I was able to get a copy of his remarks and there was enough of interest to cause us to reproduce the paper and send it to every Democratic candidate for Congress in 1956.

Why send Republican campaigning advice to Democrats?

In the first place, much of what Chotiner had to say made sense. His outline of a model campaign organization was suc-

299

cinct. His discussion of the raising of funds and how to "sell" a candidate was classic.

His illustration of the latter was the case of Earl Warren of California. Chotiner said:

May I suggest to you that the people want to feel they are selecting the candidate rather than having the candidate tell them, "I am going to run. Hell or high water, I am the one you have got to support." It is really simple to let the people select your candidate. All you have to do is to get a number of the people saying: "Now if we can only get so and so to run for the office."

In 1941 when Culbert Olson was the Governor of California everyone seemed to have the idea that it would be impossible to defeat him because, you see, in California there are something like one million more registered Democrats than Republicans, and people wondered, at least at that time, how in the world are you going to beat Olson when you start out with a handicap of a million votes?

I remember a number of individuals started to say: "If we could only get Earl Warren to run for Governor."

Well, he was the Attorney General at that time and he did not indicate he was very interested in running. He said he was very happy where he was as the Attorney General.

Now I do not want to leave the impression with you that Chief Justice Warren had any part of the movement about helping to have the people select him to run, but Bill Knowland was the head at that time of this informal movement that started and in which we had people unofficially, all over the state, saying, "If we could only get Earl Warren to run for Governor."

Earl Warren became the candidate and he became the Governor. . . .

In addition Chotiner revealed the thinking behind the Republican use of the "smear" technique. He boasted of the effectiveness of the smear campaign by Nixon against Mrs. Helen Gahagan Douglas in the 1950 campaign for United States Senator

300

in California. He had this to say about the "smear" against Will Rogers, Jr., in Knowland's 1946 campaign:

The opposition was Will Rogers, Jr., a name much better known than Bill Knowland in 1946. Bill Knowland had given explicit instructions that under no circumstances were we ever to say a word against his opposition. Knowland said, "If I am going to be elected, I am going to be elected on what I stand for and not on any attack on my opponent."

A search was made of the record of Will Rogers, Jr. Among his many activities was a contribution to the *People's Daily World* in Los Angeles, a paper, let us say to be charitable, which has espoused a left wing philosophy of a very extreme nature.

A member of the Democrat State Central Committee made up a "white paper" in which was listed the record of Will Rogers, Jr., and it was sent out broadside throughout the State of California, obviously not from our headquarters.

Chotiner also discussed one of his successful attacks on Helen Gahagan Douglas:

Sometimes color has a lot to do with a campaign. I remember in the Douglas-Nixon campaign, we made a check of the record as to how many times Helen G. Douglas voted the same way as Vito Marcantonio [the Communist Congressman from New York] and we found she had voted with him—and we restricted our issues to national security ones—more than any other member of Congress. I remember we wanted to make up the literature; we had black and white, and blue and white, and in consulting with our printer we wanted another color. We asked to see the samples of stock that the printing company had and they showed us blue, green and black. In the stock we found a sheet of paper which had a pinkish tinge to it and for some reason or other it just seemed to appeal to us for the moment and we printed this record on pink paper.

301

It became known throughout California as "the pink sheet" and we had more requests for it than any other piece of literature.

The Chotiner talk was of interest in informing our candidates as to what to expect from the students at the Republican school who would be managing campaigns for the GOP. It was a very useful political paper.

As soon as the House of Representatives was organized after the election, officers were chosen for the Democratic Congressional Campaign Committee. By acclamation Kirwan was elected to succeed himself. Kenneth Harding, who had been filling in after the death of his father, Victor Hunt Harding, was asked formally to continue as assistant to the chairman. I was re-elected treasurer.

The loss of Cap Harding had been a blow to the party. Cap was a skilled observer of politics who had been a professor of political science at UCLA and at Leland Stanford University. Prior to that he had served as a captain of infantry in World War I, to which martial post he had gone directly from the pulpit of a community church in Pennsylvania. Cap would be sorely missed; but his son Ken was an expert.

It was extremely important to have good candidates running for Congress on the Democratic ticket. In those districts where the incumbent was a Democrat, we already had our "good" candidate. But where the incumbent had retired or for some other reason was not running again, and where we had a fighting chance to take a seat from a Republican, Kirwan went all out. Mike wanted candidates of the highest type and he was willing to work to get them.

It required diplomacy, however. One sure way not to get a candidate elected is to come in from outside and try to thrust him down the throats of the local voters. And at the same time the Democratic Congressional Campaign Committee is required to stay out of primary fights.

We took the line of encouraging state, local and district committees to seek out men of high caliber for the nomination. If we could get three or four good candidates running in each primary race, the committee couldn't lose. To further this policy, we established a headquarters at the Democratic National Convention in 1956 to which all candidates for Congress were invited to discuss the upcoming campaign.

When activities at the Capitol permitted, Kirwan made frequent trips around the country to talk to organization leaders and prospective candidates. Harding and I did the same. Often as many as four prospects from a single district would come in to see us. Through these discussions we were able to predict who would be our candidate in each district. Having a constant flow of information from the organization, we were able to match good candidates with areas where the situation was favorable. Thus we could see where our sparse funds could be used to best advantage.

At this point it might be useful to outline just how the Democratic Congressional Campaign Committee, which was organized in 1885, functions. Acting as a unit, Speaker Sam Rayburn, House Majority Leader John McCormack and Mike Kirwan as committee chairman are in charge of alloting funds—when there are any. The first rule laid down by Rayburn and Kirwan is: "All incumbent Democrats who are in trouble get maximum assistance first. If anything is left over it will then be parceled out to the best advantage."

There are possibly 175 congressional seats, mostly in the North and West, which constitute the battleground between the parties. Approximately one hundred of these are decided one way or another by five per cent of the vote or less. That is the statistical approach. However, other seats may be marginal even though the statistical margin was larger than five per cent in the preceding election. For instance, in 1954, James J. Delaney, Congressman from New York, won in his district by nearly twenty thousand votes. This, under a statistical approach, would take

303

the district out of the danger group. Yet in 1956 Delaney won by only a few hundred.

Thus the critical seats are more often determined by knowledge of the issues and of the district and by analysis of the candidates for both parties, and other factors.

Usually an initial list of possibly 150 "fighting" seats is made by Ken Harding on the basis of the information coming to him from the organization and his own appreciation of the election issues. This list is submitted to Kirwan for analysis. He may cut or expand it on the basis of his knowledge of the problems involved. Then he takes it to Rayburn and McCormack and they go through it again.

At the end, the list of districts in which the issue is doubtful either way may include possibly seventy-five to a hundred districts, generally less. Even this final list is then carded by priorities. An effort to sustain a Democratic incumbent would take priority over an effort to defeat a Republican incumbent.

Finally the money raised for the campaign is allotted for use in the districts decided upon. After all this is done, the committee must report how much money it raised and from whom, to the Clerk of the House of Representatives. It must also report to whom contributions were made.

Congressmen, or candidates for Congress, victorious or defeated, must report what moneys were raised and how they were spent and from whom the money came. All of these reports are sifted by the Committee on Elections for any evidence of wrongdoing or fraud.

Each of the 435 congressional districts is viewed as an entity and is treated individually. In districts where there is a contest, the congressional committee gives service. Where possible, pictorial aid is given. This is mostly a matter of help to incumbents who are in Washington, where the committee maintains its photo staff. However, if candidates come to Washington, they are given photo help when possible. Voting records on Republicans are maintained and these are distributed.

Thus in the 1954-56 elections Kirwan and his staff made an all-out effort to make it possible to win the Congress from the Republicans in 1954 and retain and strengthen control in 1956 in the face of a Republican presidential victory.

The single factor of good candidates was credited by many political observers as being the most important in the successful 1956 campaign to maintain control of Congress. Despite the overwhelming victory of Eisenhower in the presidential race, enough Democratic congressional candidates were able to come through successfully to bring about a final result of 234 Democrats to 201 Republicans.

In 1956 the committee spent $188,000, the largest amount ever spent by the Democratic Congressional Committee in a presidential election year. But this was not much. In the first quarter of 1956 alone, the Republican Congressional Campaign Committee reported officially contributions of $1,250,000 while the Democrats were able to report a paltry $30,000.

But the congressional victory was no upset. For weeks before the election, the reports received by Kirwan from throughout the country showed a Democratic victory at the congressional level. These reports gave some credence to our hopes for a victory for Stevenson over Ike.

Although President Truman had probably done more than any other one man to bring about Stevenson's nomination in 1952 over the fears and doubts of Stevenson himself, Truman did not throw his support to Stevenson as the 1956 campaign drew near.

True, Stevenson had been able to generate almost fanatical support from many voters in 1952 because he "talked sense to the American people." His high-minded approach to the campaign, his excellent speeches and, above all, his integrity had made a splendid impression across the nation.

But he had been soundly beaten, and Truman felt that he would not make a strong political candidate in 1956. Mixed with Stevenson's high-minded approach was a political naïveté which lessened his chances for victory. Also, he had demonstrated a seeming inability to delegate responsibility in the fierce political fighting.

Not the least important of Truman's reasons for his unwillingness to support Stevenson was the fact that in 1952 Stevenson and his intimates "ran" from Truman. Truman realized that they probably did this not with any intention of hurting him personally but because they felt that a political change of climate was necessary even within the Democratic Party.

Early in 1956 Frank McKinney of Indianapolis, former National Democratic Chairman—he had masterminded the 1952 convention and been dismissed as Chairman for his pains—made a tour of the northern and western states. He reported to Truman that Stevenson was in the lead for nomination among party leaders in the states but there were doubts as to whether he could become a good enough candidate to win.

According to McKinney, if Stevenson was slowed or stopped for the nomination, the man most party leaders outside the South would support was Averell Harriman, Governor of New York.

Truman felt that Harriman was the spiritual heir of the New Deal and the Fair Deal. His record during the twenty years of Democratic Administration under Roosevelt and Truman had been a distinguished one. Many thinking men agreed that he had more to offer as a President than anyone else in the field, but his ability as a campaigner was questioned repeatedly. However, his success in a bitter New York gubernatorial race seemed to answer this objection.

Although Truman thought Harriman would be a better candidate than Stevenson, he never lost a particle of his personal regard for Stevenson. He did not announce his support of Harriman prior to the convention, preferring to let all of the candidates make their own appeal to the people. Truman did say he would have a statement to make at the convention.

By the time the convention opened in Chicago, Stevenson, in his new personification of a political candidate, had trounced the field generally. After losing the Minnesota primary to Kefauver, he rallied—shaking hands on every street corner—and swept the field.

As Harriman had stayed out of the hurly-burly of the primary fights, there had been no test of strength between him and Stevenson before the convention. This turned out to be a mistake. In Chicago, Stevenson had too much of a head start. There was no hope of stopping him, or of even slowing him down.

Keen politician that he is, Truman knew for a week before he made his promised statement to the convention, that the New York Governor's cause was hopeless. But he had encouraged Harriman, and he felt personally bound to express his sentiments to the convention. He therefore took the course that was by that time highly unpopular: he declared for Harriman because, he said, Stevenson couldn't win.

The morning following Truman's declaration for Harriman, the Chicago *Sun-Times* attacked him editorially in the most bitter fashion. One of the items in this attack was a biting cartoon.

That same day, Mr. Truman was a guest at luncheon in the editorial offices of the *Sun-Times*. The engagement had been made some days previously by Russ Stewart, general manager of the paper and an old friend of Mr. Truman. In fact, Stewart had co-operated with Truman in 1952 in winning over Governor Stevenson to accept the nomination.

The luncheon was attended by most of the brass of the newspaper. All went well until Marshall Field, owner of the paper, offered Mr. Truman the original of the cartoon the paper was carrying that very day.

The President seemed pleased. He would put it in the Truman Library in Independence, he said.

Stewart took a deep breath. It was touchy ground. "Would you also like the original on the editorial, Mr. President?"

The former President accepted this pleasantly, too.

Still trying to wriggle out of the spot, Stewart made a remark disclaiming any personal part in the attack.

"It's perfectly all right, Russ," Truman reassured him. "I understand what happened. I must say I've learned over the years not to trust either newspapers or bankers."

Just as in 1952, there was again in 1956 a contretemps at the last minute over the selection of a Chairman of the National Democratic Committee.

Following his nomination, Stevenson served notice on Paul Butler that he was to be supplanted as Chairman by Stevenson's campaign manager, Jim Finnegan of Philadelphia.

Kirwan heard of it and took the matter up with Speaker Sam Rayburn.

"This shouldn't be," Kirwan told Rayburn. "What would the general public think? Only this afternoon Butler was shown on TV holding Stevenson's hand in the air as a sign of victory. It seems to me that a change of this sort now would show a split."

Rayburn agreed to talk to Stevenson. The Governor took a strong stand, indicating that he would follow through on his decision to replace Butler with Finnegan.

But the next day, when the National Committee convened to organize for the campaign, Governor Stevenson surprised everyone, Butler most of all, by calling for him to serve again as national chairman.

It was a nice gesture but it didn't change the facts much. Finnegan was the chairman in all but name and Butler was given little opportunity to influence the campaign.

Politics, by definition, is the art of government. Too often this definition is lost sight of and the word used in an opprobrious sense. Harry S Truman was a politician but he never played "politics."

Perhaps a better word for politics is leadership, for the best politicians are leaders. But to be successful, these leaders or politicians must have faith in people, faith that the people, when they know the facts, will take the proper course of action.

308

A politician must believe in his aims—not halfway or cynically; the belief must be total and passionate. At the same time, there must be a leavening of tolerance; for no matter how strongly he believes, he must be willing to concede his opponents' rights to their own beliefs.

A practicing politician must have a thick skin to withstand the barbs that will come his way. And the goal must be worthy in itself, for he usually gets little appreciation. Most people will not recognize the job he has performed so the recognition will probably not be his. But the role of a politician is a rewarding one in the less material sense.

The politician must remember that, in the words of Theodore Roosevelt, "The law of life is the fundamental law of strife; and it is only through painful effort, grim energy and resolute courage that we move on to better things."

INDEX

Abernethy, Thomas G., 133
Aiken, George D., 123
Akron, Ohio, 274
Alabama, 20, 81, 83, 138, 291
Allen, George, 166, 298
Allen, John, 298
Allentown, Pennsylvania, 295
American Broadcasting Company, 82, 228, 230, 231, 235, 239, 241
American Labor Party, 255
Anderson, Clinton P., 89, 102
Andrews, Bert, 146, 233, 234
Arizona, 22
Arkansas, 141
Arvey, Jack, 14, 21, 147-149, 277, 278
Ator, Malcolm, 229, 237

Baltimore *Sun*, 83
Bankhead, Tallulah, 281
Barkley, Alben W., keynote speech at convention, 185-189; nominated for Vice President, 197; mentioned, 19, 38, 39, 44, 77, 103, 165, 185-189, 194, 197, 201, 203, 221, 229, 230, 232, 278
Baron, Charles, 185, 186
Bartlett, Sy, 114, 161
Bartsch, Ed, 252, 254
Beck, Dave, 155, 156
Bell, Jack, 236, 277
Berger, Joe, 37, 44
Berkeley, California, 179
Bevin, Sir Ernest, 123
Biddle, Anthony Drexel, 204
Biemiller, Andrew J., 291
Biffle, Leslie, 94, 189, 248
Big Spring, Texas, 271

Biow, Milton H., 171, 172, 212, 213, 215
Black, Eugene F., 264
Blaustein, Jacob B., 168
Bloom, Sol, 224
Blumenthal, Fred, 120
Blythe, Joe L., 168, 234
Boggs, Thomas Hale, 128
Bonham, Texas, 273
Boston, Massachusetts, 262, 285
Boston *Herald*, 13
Bowles, Chester, 57, 120
Bowron, Fletcher, 180
Boyle, Harold V. (Hal), 21
Boyle, William Marshall (Bill), Jr., 89, 268, 269
Bradley, Gen. Omar N., 44, 144
Brazil, 74
Brewster, Owen, 105, 106
Brewster-Ferguson Committee, 105
Brightman, Samuel Charles (Sam), 15, 16, 18, 20, 22, 44, 47, 62, 82, 103, 119, 121, 122, 125, 155, 163, 182, 183, 231, 237, 242, 246, 253, 295
Brotherhood of Railroad Trainmen, 94, 95, 98, 183
Brown, Edgar, 44
Brown, Edmund G. (Pat), 160
Brown, Ned, 14
Brownell, Herbert, Jr., 141
Bruce, James, 167
Buchly, Marylee, 109
Buffalo, New York, 262
Burch, A. T., 100
Burke, Harold J., 283
Butler, Paul, 122, 298, 308

311

313